REACHING OUT

REACHING OUT:
BEST PRACTICES FOR EDUCATING
MEXICAN-ORIGIN CHILDREN AND YOUTH

by
Harriett D. Romo

Clearinghouse on Rural Education and Small Schools
Charleston, West Virginia

Clearinghouse on Rural Education and Small Schools
AEL, Inc.
P.O. Box 1348, Charleston, WV 25325
www.ael.org/eric/

Printed by Chapman Printing Co., Huntington, WV
Cover illustration by John MacDonald, Williamstown, MA
Cover design by Richard Hendel, Chapel Hill, NC

Library of Congress Cataloging-in-Publication Data

Romo, Harriett.
  Reaching out: best practices for educating Mexican-origin children and youth / by Harriett D. Romo.
      p. cm.
  Includes bibliographical references (p.) and index.
  ISBN 1-880785-22-6 (alk. paper)
  1. Mexican-American children—Education. 2. Mexican-American youth—Education. I. Title.
LC2682.R66   1999
371.82968'72'073--dc21   99-22126
                                                                           CIP

The paper used in this publication meets the minimum requirements of the American National Standard for Information Sciences–Permanence of Paper for Printed Library Materials, ANSI Z39.48-1984

This publication was prepared with funding from the U.S. Department of Education, Office of Educational Research and Improvement, National Library of Education, under contract no. RR93002012. The opinions expressed herein do not necessarily reflect the positions or policies of AEL, Inc., or the Department of Education.

The ERIC Clearinghouse on Rural Education and Small Schools is operated by AEL, Inc. AEL is an Equal Opportunity/Affirmative Action Employer.

Contents

Acknowledgments vii

Chapter 1: The Mexican American Student Population: Growth and Diversity 1
More Immigrant Students Attend U.S. Public Schools 2
Data on Achievement Status of Mexican-Origin Students 8
Innovative Programs 16
A Need to Increase Positive Outcomes 18

Chapter 2: Cultural Perspectives on Learning 21
Group Culture vs. Individualism 23
Children's Awareness of Cultural Differences 25
Culture and Classroom Organization 26
Culture and Achievement 29
Cultural Differences in Child Rearing 31
Recognizing Different Cultural Perspectives 34
Pros and Cons of Parent Education Programs 37
Successful Programs Incorporating Parents' Cultural Values .. 38

Chapter 3: Language, Literacy, and Creating Bridges to Success 45
The Bilingual Education Controversy 46
Learning English 48
Maintaining Spanish 52
Language and Literacy 57
Organizing Schools for Mexican-Immigrant Student Success . 64
Migrant Students: A Special Group with Special Needs 70

Chapter 4: Gender Issues in Mexican American Schooling 75
Gender Role Attitudes 75
Teen Pregnancies 78
School Factors 81
Peers 85
Some Practical Approaches 94

Chapter 5: Creating Family-School Partnerships 105
Family Poverty and Children's Educational Outcomes 106
Parent-School Relationships 108
Parental Involvement in School Programs 109
Community Support for Parent-School Partnerships 121

Reaching a Larger Pool of Hispanic Youth 122
Opportunities at the High School Level 123
Characteristics That Make Programs Attractive 124
Positive Programs of Parental Involvement 125
Defining Success 139

Chapter 6: Political, Social, and Pedagogical Issues Impacting Early Childhood Education and Public Schools 141
Immigration and Education Policy 142
Increased Immigration and Demands on U.S. Schools 148
The Politics of Early Childhood Education 151
Training Teachers for Diversity 157
Characteristics of Good Teachers 159
Intergroup Relations 163
Some Final Thoughts about Issues 170

Chapter 7: Resources 179
Academic References That Provide Overviews of Research ... 189

Notes 191

Bibliography 207

Tables

Table 1. Level of Education Achieved by Hispanic, Non-
   Hispanic White, and African American Youth Before
   Dropping Out of School 10

Figures

Figure 1. Origins of Hispanic Youth in the United States 1990 8

Figure 2. Percent Total College-Age Population Compared
   with Percent of Students Who Received Bachelor's Degrees
   within Five Years at Public Institutions: Hispanic and
   Non-Hispanic Rates 13

Acknowledgments

I would like to acknowledge the research assistance provided by Maria Teresa de la Piedra, a graduate student at The University of Texas at Austin. She was of great help in tracking down research articles and proofreading the manuscript. I want to acknowledge the projects mentioned in this book. Staff persons and program directors shared articles and materials about their projects and provided information about their programs' successes. I hope this book brings recognition to the many programs that do outstanding work in helping Mexican-origin students be successful.

Additionally, I would like to recognize the excellent editorial assistance provided by Pat Hammer and Tim Collins. I also thank the reviewers for very helpful suggestions for revisions.

CHAPTER 1

The Mexican American Student Population: Growth and Diversity

Our school systems are not serving Latino[1] students well, especially those from low-income families. This simple statement can be documented by looking at a number of indicators of school success, such as drop-out and school completion rates and enrollment in postsecondary education.

The research studies and data summarized in this chapter are organized to highlight key areas where schools fail immigrant children and describe ways we might prevent such failures as these children move through the various stages of education from preschool through elementary school, to middle and high schools, to college, and on to graduate or professional schools or the workforce. All along the way, U.S. schools lose talented students who could have achieved more if the right supports and programs had been in place when the children needed them.

School failures of immigrant and second-generation children are not the result of low student motivation or a devaluing of education by their families—at least initially. These children arrive in our classrooms eager to learn. They and their parents believe education is the key to their futures and a way to improve their lives and the lives of their families. But at some time in their school careers, many lose that eagerness and respect for schooling. One Mexican-immigrant teenager, when asked why so many of the students who had entered school at the same time he did were no longer attending classes, explained, "They gave up on school."[2]

Students must overcome many barriers along the way to graduating from high school and college and establishing a strong foundation for their own families. As a former fifth-grade teacher of immigrant students in Los Angeles, I know firsthand the problems and frustrations that exist in U.S. public schools. But adults—administrators, teachers, parents, concerned citizens—who care about these students also know that we can do better. On a more hopeful note, a number of educators *have* found ways to improve outcomes for Mexican-origin students, and, in the following chapters, I identify and describe their successful programs or interventions. I also include information about helpful resources and organizations. My focus throughout this book is on positive changes school staff, families, community, and students can make.

Each of the chapters uses a different lens—culture, language, gender, family/community, and social and political context—to examine issues and challenges affecting first- and second-generation Mexican-origin children. Using these lenses, I have sought out the best research literature to see what it tells us about the educational experiences of first- and second-generation immigrant students. Each chapter ends with guidance to educators about what this lens reveals about this population of students and best practices to use in meeting particular challenges they face. This book brings together information that can help readers understand why these challenges are important and the impact each set of issues and challenges can have on the ability of students to benefit fully from schooling. But my main objective is to provide practical and realistic leads about what to do.

Let us begin by looking at some characteristics of the first- and second-generation Mexican immigrant school-age population that impress upon us an urgency to improve educational practices.

More Immigrant Students Attend U.S. Public Schools

The College Board and the Western Interstate Commission for Higher Education completed one of the first studies to examine school children by racial and ethnic identification, grade by grade in each state. This study predicted that non-White and Hispanic elementary and secondary school students would increase to 13.7 million by 1994-95, representing 34 percent of the total public school enrollment. The study also predicted that White enrollment would drop to 66 percent. The researchers commented on how dramatic the changes were and how rapidly they were occurring. The College Board study predicted Asian and Pacific islander enrollment would increase by 70 percent and Hispanic enrollment would increase by 54 percent. Black students would remain the second largest racial or ethnic group behind Whites, but they would increase by only 13 percent. Predictions were that American Indians would increase by 29 percent but would remain the smallest group. The president of the College Board acknowledged that a large proportion of these students were not being adequately prepared for college because of less rigorous coursework. The researchers concluded that equal educational opportunities for all students must be a number one priority in the United States.[3]

Many of those population predictions have come true. Immigrant children and U.S.-born children of immigrants are the fastest growing segments of the U.S. child population. In 1997, immigrant children accounted for 20 percent of all American children and about 60 percent of all Hispanic children. In some states, such as California, Texas, and Florida, Hispanics already constitute a majority of the public school students in large urban areas. The U.S. National Center for Health Statistics recently reported that Hispanic children now outnumber Black children nationally.[4]

Language differences. English is not the primary language of many immigrant children entering U.S. classrooms. Thus, language is an important factor in school achievement because most instruction is conducted in English. A National Center for Education Statistics report noted that 80 percent of all Hispanic 16- to 24-year-olds in the United States speak Spanish at home. Two-thirds of Hispanic young adults who reported limited English proficiency (LEP) did not have a high school credential and were not enrolled in school in 1995. The number of LEP children enrolled in school grew nearly 50 percent from 1990-91 to 1994-95. By 1995 LEP students accounted for approximately one in four public school students in California, Alaska, and New Mexico, and about one in eight students in Texas and Arizona.[5]

3

A large percentage of immigrant youth who speak Spanish at home never enter U.S. schools and are officially counted as dropouts. If enrolled in school, however, Hispanic students who speak Spanish at home are just as likely to graduate as their peers who speak only English at home. But English speaking ability continues to be related to school success and often is a factor in the level of instruction the children receive in school.[6]

A recent California Department of Education study showed that the number of LEP students in state schools increased by almost five percent in one year (spring 1995-spring 1996). Most of that increase was at the elementary school level, particularly in grades K-6, although there was a similar increase at the secondary level. Spanish was spoken by almost 80 percent of LEP students in California.[7] The increasing number of LEP students in U.S. classrooms raises many questions about which languages should be taught in the classroom and how to best address the academic needs of these students. Opinions about the best options are sharply divided among educators, as well as among legislators and parents.

Natural population increases. Higher birthrates and the young age of the U.S. Mexican-origin population also increase the number of first- and second-generation Mexican-origin students in our schools. The number of babies born to Hispanic women in the United States has reached a record high, increasing to 18 percent of the total number of U.S. births. Much of the increase in Hispanic-origin births is the result of high birthrates among Mexican-origin women, particularly recent immigrants. Researchers estimate that Mexican American women average 3.32 births over their lifetimes, compared with 1.7 for Cuban Americans and 2.2 for Puerto Ricans.[8] As a result of high levels of immigration *and* a high birthrate, people of Mexican heritage will play major economic, political, and cultural roles in the coming decades. Their birthrates are increasing, while those of other groups are declining or remaining stable. These overall trends suggest there will be growing numbers of first- and second-generation Mexican-origin children in our public schools.

Variations in subgroup cultures. To understand the experiences of Mexican-immigrant schoolchildren, it is important to know something about the history of this particular group and how it has been incorporated into the United States. A migrant child who frequently goes back and forth across the U.S.-Mexican border will have different experiences and perceptions about schooling than a Cuban refugee child who must adjust to a new homeland in the United States and has no opportunity to return to Cuba. Central American children who were sent to the United States as unaccompanied minors fleeing military conflicts in their homelands will have yet another set of experiences. These children may have experienced the deaths of friends and relatives, abuse, and severe hardship. They may have had to leave the majority of their family members behind in their home communities. Latino children whose parents are undocumented immigrants face discrimination and hostility in some states and along the U.S.-Mexican border, where undocumented immigration has had a major impact on the public schools. Some states are far more affected by immigration than others. In 1990 five states—California, Florida, New York, New Jersey, and Texas—accounted for 68 percent of the total foreign-born population living in the United States. By a large majority, most new second-generation immigrants were under age 18 and concentrated in the same areas where foreign-born population had grown most dramatically.[9] Despite efforts to increase enforcement of immigration laws and pass more restrictive immigration legislation, immigrants continue to come to this country, and they bring their children. Many immigrants are young and will have U.S.-born children who will be citizens here.

The ongoingness and diversity of this migration are important to keep in mind when discussing strategies for how to improve the school achievement of first- and second-generation Mexican-origin students. As of 1997 about 11 percent of the total U.S. population (nearly 29.7 million residents) was of Hispanic origin.[10] Hispanic population continues to grow rapidly because of immigration from a number of different regions, including Mexico, Central America, and South America. These patterns have dramatically changed the ethnicity of student bodies across the United States, but particularly in states and regions that already have high concentrations of U.S.-born Latinos, such as California, Texas, New York, Illinois, and Florida. In 1990 more than half of the children in immigrant families were from Latin America. This represents a dramatic change from 1910, when 87 percent of the children in immigrant families were of European origin.[11]

In 1996 persons of Mexican origin were the largest Hispanic group comprising 63 percent (17.9 million).[12] Not all of these people were immigrants, though. Many persons of Mexican origin have lived in the United States since 1848, when in the Treaty of Guadalupe Hidalgo, the U.S. government acquired from Mexico land that today makes up the U.S. Southwest. The treaty provided that the Mexican citizens who remained in the transferred land could maintain their cultural and religious beliefs and participate fully in the U.S. democracy. Thus, there are many Latino children in our schools whose ancestors were here before the British established colonies at Jamestown or Plymouth. Yet, other Latinos are recent immigrants from Mexico or children whose parents go back and forth between Mexico and the United States seeking work. The number of Mexican-born U.S. residents has increased tenfold from the 1960s to the 1990s. The children of these recently immigrated residents are likely to have strong orientations toward their home country, probably speak Spanish in their homes, and may have parents who plan to return to their country of origin. Many never return, and the children grow up learning English and becoming more and more Americanized. Children of the original Mexican citizens of the Southwest are likely to know little about their Mexican homeland, and most speak English in their homes. They may remain strongly identified with their Mexican culture and heritage, or they may simply consider themselves to be Americans.

Another group of Latinos, Puerto Ricans, may also migrate back and forth from their homeland to the U.S. mainland, but their situation is quite different from that of the Mexican migrant. Puerto Ricans, whether they live on the island of Puerto Rico or on the U.S. mainland, are U.S. citizens because Puerto Rico is a U.S. territory. Puerto Rican students, concentrated primarily in the Northeast but also found in many Southwestern cities, have an entirely different history than students from Mexico. For many years, Puerto Rico was a U.S. colony. The U.S. government demanded that English be taught in the Puerto Rican schools for many years, even though the majority of students came from Spanish-speaking homes. When Puerto Rico became a territory, its legislative body voted to reinstate Spanish as the language of instruction in Puerto Rican schools. Currently, Puerto Rican residents are deeply divided over the question of becoming a state. Many want equal status with the other states, while others want the island to maintain its unique sense of Puerto Rican identity and its autonomy to govern, make policies about schools, and organize its own affairs. Spanish continues to be the dominant language spoken and taught in Puerto Rican schools. The result of this complex status for Puerto Rico is that Puerto Ricans are not immigrants, although they may arrive in New York or Chicago with school-aged children who speak little English. They may also go back and forth between the U.S. mainland and the Puerto Rican island during the school year, affecting the education of children in both places.

Cuban schoolchildren represent still different experiences. The majority of Cuban families living in the United States arrived shortly after Fidel Castro took control in 1958. Many middle- and upper-class families, fearing Communism and a socialist government, fled to the United States as refugees. Later waves of Cuban refugees included families from working-class backgrounds. The U.S. government provided special assistance to help the refugees adjust in the United States. Schools in Coral Gables, Florida, where a large number of the Cuban refugees settled, piloted the first federally funded bilingual programs in English and Spanish. Among the refugees were a number of Cuban teachers, school directors, and university professors who could transfer their skills, and sometimes even their schools, to the United States. As refugees, these Cuban schoolchildren could not think about returning home. The Cuban community was able to focus its attention on adjusting to life in the United States, learning English, and doing well in the education and occupational systems of their new resident country.

Poverty and educational levels. The education level of immigrant parents has an impact on the educational experiences of their children in the United States. The majority of Mexican and Central American immigrants are from less developed countries and tend to have relatively little formal education. Fewer than 25 percent of Mexican immigrants and only 46 percent of Central American immigrants have the equivalent of at least a high school diploma. In contrast, 77 percent of U.S.-born adults and almost 60 percent of non-Latino immigrants have at least high school diplomas.[14] With lower levels of education, these immigrant families earn lower wages, are less likely to have health benefits, and experience longer periods of unemployment. While the percentage of immigrant children in

7

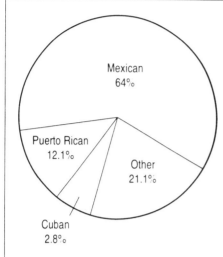

In 1990, 64 percent of Hispanic 15- to 19-year-olds were of Mexican-origin, 12.1 percent were Puerto Rican, 2.8 percent were Cuban, and 21.1 percent had origins in other Central and South American countries. The percentages of Hispanic 18- to 24-year-olds who had not completed high school corresponded almost exactly with the cultural subgroup distributions. Cubans have the lowest and Mexican-origin Hispanics have the highest percentages of youths without a high school education.[13]

Figure 1. Origins of Hispanic Youth in the United States 1990

the United States living in families with incomes below the official poverty level has decreased over the generations, in 1990, 17 percent of the third- and later-generation immigrant children still lived in poverty. Poverty level incomes make it more difficult for families to help their children with schoolwork or to become actively involved in the schools. First-generation immigrant children experience other poverty-related factors that affect educational achievement: they are more likely to live in families with five or more siblings, more likely to live in overcrowded housing, and less likely to have fathers in the labor force than second- and later-generation children.[15]

Data on Achievement Status of Mexican-Origin Students

It is impossible to make straightforward statements about the achievement status of Mexican-origin students. In many census reports, data from all subgroups are combined and reported as data on Hispanics. Additionally, ways of defining achievement status are inconsistent. Some reports use SAT scores, some use dropout rates, and some look at school completion rates. For example, a U.S. Department of Education report, *Improving Opportunities* (1998), showed considerable differences among states in terms of reporting the number of minorities in public schools and their academic outcomes. The researchers explained it was difficult to analyze changes in minority students' achievement nationally because historically many states have not kept track of students by race and ethnicity. The research associate who compiled the data for the report explains that California, Florida, New York, and Texas are experienced at dealing with multiethnic populations, but many other states are not. Many agencies that collect data on education outcomes group all Spanish-speaking students together under the general category of *Hispanic*. This is disturbing. As pointed out earlier, there are many cultural, socioeconomic, and national origin differences among the various subgroups.

There are also variations in the definitions of outcome indicators in existing data sources.[16] One major concern in trying to calculate outcome measures, such as national drop-out statistics, stems from inconsistent definitions used in school districts and state departments of education. Currently, there is considerable variation across the different agencies and institutions concerning whether those who are below the legal school-leaving age are identified as dropouts, whether those in General Equivalency Diploma (GED) programs are considered graduates or dropouts, whether students in correctional institutions are considered dropouts, and other technicalities that affect data collection. Additionally, the age or grade span included in the statistics and the type of drop-out rate varies across the data sources. National statistics do, however, allow us to compare Hispanics in general with other groups, such as Blacks and non-Hispanic Whites. The other groups are by no means homogeneous either, but the broad group comparisons give us some indication of education patterns. Broad categories are used in the majority of the national data sets on school success indicators, so we have to contrast and compare the larger groups to get some sense of the issues surrounding the school experiences of first- and second-generation Mexican-origin students.

Leaving school early. The National Center for Education Statistics reported to Congress about the high school drop-out and completion rates from 1972 through 1996. Data were collected on Hispanic, non-Hispanic White, and Black students. Hispanic students were more likely than non-Hispanic White students or Black students to drop out of school without successfully completing a high school program. They also dropped out at an earlier grade level. In 1996 more than half of the Hispanic dropouts (55.4 percent) reported less than a tenth-grade education, compared with 29.1 percent of the White dropouts and 25.4 percent of the Black dropouts who completed tenth grade. Hispanics also had the highest percentage of dropouts with less than a ninth-grade education (34.7 percent), and almost 16 percent of the Hispanic dropouts had less than a fifth- or sixth-grade education. Table 1 demonstrates the high percentage of Hispanic dropouts (over one-third) who leave school before beginning high school in ninth grade.[17]

Table 1. Level of Education Achieved by Hispanic, Non-Hispanic White, and African American Youth Before Dropping Out of School.

Ages 16-24. October 1996

Level of Schooling Attained by Dropouts	% Distribution of Dropouts, 1996		
	Hispanic	NonHisp White	Blacks
Less than 1st grade	2.1	0.9	0.3
1st, 2nd, 3rd, or 4th grade	5.2	0.7	0.6
5th or 6th grade	15.5	0.1	1.1
7th or 8th grade	11.9	11.2	8.0
Less than 9th grade	34.7	12.9	10.0
9th grade	20.7	16.2	15.4
10th grade	14.1	27.1	28.5
11th grade	20.4	35.1	34.8
12th grade, without diploma	10.3	8.4	11.4
9th - 12th grade without diploma	65.5	86.8	90.1

(Adapted from McMillen and Kaufman, Table 6 *Dropout Rates in the United States: 1996*, Office of Educational Research and Improvement. NCES 98-250, p. 16.) Percentages may not exactly total 100 percent because of rounding error.

School completion and the GED route. Looking at school outcomes in a slightly different way, researchers calculated the rate of high school completion of 18- to 24-year-olds in 1996, including both high school diplomas or an equivalent credential: Whites were most likely to complete high school with 91.5 percent reporting some type of high school credential, compared with 84 percent of African Americans and only 62 percent of Hispanics. Overall, school drop-out rates for Hispanic youths have remained consistently higher than drop-out rates of their White and Black peers since the early 1970s, with only slight gains in the high school completion rates for Hispanics since the mid-1970s.[18]

Hispanics were less likely than Whites or Blacks to complete an alternative high school program, such as the GED. In 1996 about 7 percent of Hispanics who finished high school completed an alternative program, compared with 10 percent of Blacks and 10.5 percent of Whites. Attending a regular high school, with graduation following a four-year course of study, is still considered the norm in this country, but an increasing number of young adults opt to complete their high school education through an alternative route, such as the GED. The rising number of youths choosing the GED route may have prevented increases in high school drop-out rates. In 1993, for example, about 5 percent of those finishing high school had completed high school by taking the GED test. By 1996 the percentage of 18- to 24-year-olds getting GEDs had increased to 9.8 percent. The GED exam was originally established to provide a high school credential to World War II veterans who may have interrupted their schooling to go to war. More recently, data have shown that about one-third of GED test-takers have been young people between the ages of 16 and 19. The research literature shows conflicting outcomes regarding the effects of the GED compared with the regular high school diploma in areas of employment, earnings, postsecondary program participation, and success at the postsecondary level. Although those completing the GED would have been counted as dropouts if they had not taken the alternative route to graduation, conflicting findings have led some to question the value of promoting GED programs for students still young enough to participate in regular high school programs.[19]

Gender differences in outcome. Gender differences in school outcome data for first- and second-generation Mexican-origin youth are difficult to determine because most data are not broken down by gender and ethnicity. According to one recent report, African American, Hispanic, and White females had high school completion rates higher than their male counterparts in 1995, which reflected a continuing trend of higher female completion rates. But Hispanic males in the 18- to 24-year-old group did record a 4 percent gain in high school completion for 1995 for a rate of 58 percent. The rate for Hispanic women was largely unchanged at 59.6 percent. Females seem to be doing slightly better than males, but the high school completion rate for both males and females is still below rates in the mid-1980s.[20]

College enrollment. Unfortunately, not completing high school means fewer Latinos enter and complete studies at four-year colleges. Lacking a high school diploma also makes it more difficult for them to get higher-paying jobs or help their own children with school work.

While all groups have achieved a gradual rise in SAT scores from 1987 to 1997, a large gap in test scores continues to exist between Hispanic students and majority students. The increase in SAT test scores from 1987 to 1997 for Whites and Blacks was double the increase for Hispanics.[21] Relatively low test scores and the important role such scores play in college and university decisions often contribute to Latinos' disillusionment with school.

The lower the educational level of our youths, the more likely the chances for underemployment and unemployment. According to an Ohio study, Hispanic teenagers in the 1990s who dropped out of high school were more than twice as likely to be underemployed than non-Hispanic White teenagers.[22] If the U.S. education system is perceived as a transportation system that leads from preschool through high school and on to postsecondary enrollment and good jobs, clearly this system is not working well for Hispanic youth.

While the overall Hispanic college-age population has grown by 62 percent during the past ten years, the college participation rate of Hispanic youth in the 18- to 24-year-old age group had increased only to 35.3 percent in 1995. Meanwhile, Whites recorded their highest rate of college participation at 43.1 percent. Both Hispanic males and females contributed to the increase in the Hispanic college participation rate for 1995, but women attended college at higher rates than men. A significant gap remains between Hispanic male (32 percent) and Hispanic female high school graduates (38 percent) who go on to college. The majority (55 percent) of Hispanic youths enrolling in college went to two-year colleges. The Kellogg Commission on the Future of State and Land-Grant Universities has compiled statistics about success at four-year institutions of higher education. Figure 2 looks at the total 18- to 24-year-old population in 1994, broken down into four subgroups: Hispanic males and females and non-Hispanic White males and females. It compares the college-age population to the percentage of students who obtained bachelor's degrees within five years. Hispanic males fared the worst, Hispanic females the second worst, and non-Hispanic White females the best by a large margin.

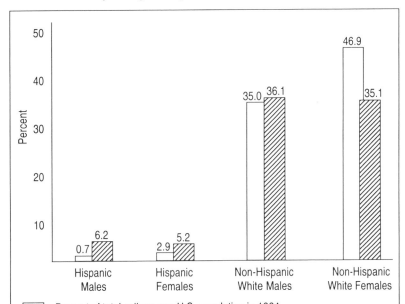

Percent of total college-age U.S. population in 1994

Percent of students who received bachelor's degress within five years at four-year, Ph.D.-granting public institutions in 1994

Adapted from Kellogg Commission on the Future of State and Land-Grant Universities. *Returning to Our Roots: Student Access.* Washington, DC: National Association of State Universities and Land-Grant Colleges, 1998.

Figure 2. Percent Total College-Age Population Compared with Percent of Students Who Received Bachelor's Degrees within Five Years at Public Institutions: Hispanic and Non-Hispanic Rates

A number of social factors help explain these devastating statistics about Hispanics. In 1997 the U.S. Department of Education published a statistical analysis of factors contributing to students' successful completion of high school and enrollment in college. The researchers looked at students with characteristics that increase their risk of dropping out of high school. These factors include being from a single-parent household; having an older brother or sister who dropped out of high school; changing schools two or more times other than the normal transition from elementary to middle school, etc.; having low grades; repeating a grade; and being from a low socioeconomic status (SES) family. They did not look at differences among racial and ethnic groups or differences in gender. They found that more than half (58 percent) of 1992 high school graduates had one or more risk factors. They also considered aspiration for a college degree, academic preparation for college, taking entrance exams needed to enroll in college, and enrolling at a postsecondary college. One of the biggest differences between students with one or more of the risk characteristics and students who did not experience those risk characteristics was educational aspirations. More than half (56 percent) of those tenth-grade students with risk characteristics aspired to have college degrees while four out of five (81 percent) of those not at risk aspired to have college degrees. Their findings suggest that students who encounter problems associated with risk factors tend to lower their aspirations for college.[23]

Another recent federal study found several patterns among students who actually enrolled in college: (1) they were academically prepared (had completed at least one advanced math course); (2) they were more likely to report receiving help in completing the college application process; (3) they were more likely to have participated in two or more extracurricular activities in high school; (4) they had discussed school-related matters with their parents; and (5) they were more likely to report that all or most of their friends planned to attend college. It is encouraging to note that many students with family backgrounds or early educational experiences that increased their risk of dropping out of high school exhibited considerable resiliency and successfully enrolled in college. Students with high aspirations and family members and peers who discussed school-related matters and supported doing well in school were more likely to enroll in college. But the researchers also found many competent students who did not take classes that adequately prepared them for college and did not receive help in the college application process, and, as a consequence, these students were less likely to enroll in a four-year college.[24]

Tracking. Since the 1920s most high schools have offered a *tracked* curriculum: sequences of academic classes varying from remedial to rigorous in content. The practice is widespread of dividing students with presumably similar abilities into groups. Tracking has persisted despite a number of studies comparing tracked versus untracked schools. These studies have not shown any consistent support for the idea that tracking benefits students academically. In fact, tracking is believed to undermine the achievement and motivation of students in the lower tracks and exacerbate existing achievement discrepancies by limiting curricular opportunities. Students are identified in a public way as to their intellectual capacities by the hierarchical system of groups, which are labeled openly as high ability/low ability. Better qualified and more experienced teachers are assigned to the high tracks, while students in the low tracks experience less time involved with learning tasks. The groups are not equally valued in schools. Individuals are then defined in terms of these group types and are labeled as *brains* or *dummies*; or as high-achieving, remedial, honors, or ESL students. Tracking persists despite growing evidence that it does not substantially benefit high achievers and that it tends to put low achievers at a serious disadvantage.[25]

Minority students are disproportionately enrolled in special-education programs, vocational courses, and low-track classes. Hispanics and African Americans are underrepresented in high-track college preparatory programs, gifted and talented programs, and advanced placement classes.[26] In 1990 only 23 percent of Hispanic tenth graders, compared with 34 percent of Whites, enrolled in college preparatory or academic programs. The patterns have persisted. More recent figures show a smaller proportion of Hispanic students (35.4 percent) enrolled in academic or college preparatory programs of study than Whites (49.9 percent) or Blacks (42.8 percent). Hispanics were also less likely than non-Hispanic White students to have completed the "New Standards" curriculum, which includes four years of English and three years of science, social studies, and mathematics (44 percent of Hispanics compared with

54 percent of Whites in 1994). Hispanics were less likely to have taken geometry, algebra II, trigonometry, chemistry, physics, or a combination of biology, chemistry, and physics. They were more likely to have taken remedial mathematics.[27]

Innovative Programs

AVID. A number of schools have tried to "untrack" classes and have been quite successful. One such program, Advancement Via Individual Determination (AVID) in San Diego, increased enrollments in four- and two-year colleges. The project placed students from low-income, ethnic/linguistic minority backgrounds in college preparation classes along with their high-achieving peers. Students took a special elective class that emphasized collaborative instruction, writing, and problem solving. The project resulted in higher college enrollment of the graduates, compared with school district and national averages. The ethnic and language minority students developed an *academic identity*, formed academically oriented peer groups, and recognized the necessity of academic achievement for occupational success. The program identified these students as members of a special academic group and provided social and academic supports to help them be successful in the college-oriented classes. Students developed a critical consciousness of the inequities in the education system but were able to acclimate to the system without assimilating. They took positive steps to achieve the socially accepted goals of graduation from high school and going to college while maintaining their ethnic/racial identity and recognizing the constraints they had to confront. The AVID program suggests that untracking can be successful but that simply putting students into college preparatory, high-level courses may not be sufficient. The students needed a support system to help overcome past inequities.[28]

Project GRAD. An innovative Houston program demonstrates another approach to reforming inner-city public schools serving large numbers of Mexican-immigrant students. Project GRAD (Graduation Really Achieves Dreams) targets high schools where in previous years 40 percent of the students dropped out before earning a diploma. The program provides far-reaching support and $1,000 scholarships for students who meet certain academic requirements and attend summer sessions on college campuses. It begins preparing children for college in kindergarten. The Ford Foundation, Tenneco, Inc., and other contributors have provided financial support, and a retired Tenneco executive took responsibility for searching out successful school improvement programs. The project has been in place since 1992 and, at this writing, reaches about 17,000 students in 24 schools. In 1997, at one of the participating schools, 273 students from an entering class of 450 graduated, a 57 percent increase over 1984-89 graduation rates. Of those who graduated, 173 met or exceeded the requirements for the scholarships, and 125 entered college. The project also has produced higher attendance rates, reductions in teenage pregnancies, fewer disciplinary problems, and better test scores. Project GRAD targets not only high schools but feeder elementary and junior high schools as well. Teachers receive extensive training and support, and the schools have implemented a Consistency Management and Cooperative Discipline plan to help teachers and students create and maintain orderly classrooms. Students learn strategies for working together and deciding on classroom responsibilities. The intent is to give students the skills to be self-disciplined instead of being constantly *controlled* by teachers and administrators. Disciplinary referrals to principals have fallen and teachers have gained instructional time because they do not spend as much time reprimanding unruly students.[29]

Success for All, a reading and writing project developed by Robert Slavin at Johns Hopkins University, has been implemented at elementary schools feeding into the targeted high school (see Chapter 3 for additional discussion of the program). Success for All requires teachers and assistants to spend an hour and a half teaching reading every day. The program includes oral reading, grammar instruction, phonics training, and language development. Students are grouped by ability but are reassessed and regrouped every eight weeks to allow them to move ahead at their own pace. Students who fall behind are provided individual tutoring. The intensive reading program follows students through middle school.

Another key element of Project GRAD is Move It Math, a program that teaches math concepts using manipulative objects. The program teaches algebra in early grades and emphasizes understanding math principles rather than memorization.

Communities in Schools is a component of Project GRAD that

assigns at least one social worker to every school to help link families with community resources for job training, health care, and other programs and services. Colleges collaborate with the schools to provide training for staff and reports of students' progress. The students and their parents sign contracts agreeing to meet the program's grade, attendance, and behavior requirements. Students have responded positively to the program, and test scores and grades have gone up.

This program's strengths are comprehensiveness and implementation at all levels: elementary, junior high, and high school. Four key components provide the foundation of the program: a consistency management program, academic emphasis (the Success for All intensive reading and Move It Math programs), social services provided by Communities in Schools, and end rewards of college scholarships for students who keep their commitment to achieve.

These successful programs reinforce the belief that curricular and organizational changes in schools can have important impacts on the outcomes of students. Given appropriate social and institutional supports, Mexican immigrant and first- and second-generation students can achieve to the highest levels in U.S. schools, and they can do so without sacrificing ethnic identity and pride in their home culture.

A Need to Increase Positive Outcomes

Without interventions such as those described above, the overall outcome of our education system is not positive for many Mexican immigrant students. They enter adulthood without a basic level of education. At the same time, they enter a workforce where the demands are increasing for high skill levels and for the ability to learn new skills quickly.[30]

Substantial empirical evidence raises the prospect that U.S. schools, as they are structured today, may be unable to provide equal educational opportunities for children from culturally diverse backgrounds. Many people, including administrators, teachers, and parents, view diversity in our classrooms as a challenge or obstacle to effective instruction. An alternative view—the one I urge in these pages—sees diversity as a resource for engaging students' interest in school and an opportunity to practice the democratic principles at the foundation of our public education system.

The majority of the new teachers being trained in our universities and colleges has little experience with diverse populations. Few teachers speak Spanish fluently enough to be able to teach in Spanish and English or communicate at all with their recent immigrant students. Some may harbor negative attitudes or biases toward Mexican-immigrant children and their families. Yet, as Jon Wagner reminds us, teachers and administrators learn from their work in schools through independent and reflective inquiry, as do parents and students. These learnings can be a form of school reform, along with policy and program implementation. Thus, the concern is to stimulate, support, and encourage learning by identifying positive efforts to reach Hispanic students and increase their success in school.[31]

Concern about the preparedness of teachers and administrators grows stronger looking ahead. In the next few decades, it will be nearly impossible for an educator to teach in a public or even a private school in which students are not racially, culturally, or linguistically diverse. In 1992 more than one million teachers had at least one student in class with limited-English-language skills. Based on state education agency data, the nationwide population of LEP students grew by nearly 50 percent from 1990-91 to 1994-95. Some states experienced dramatic increases. In Arkansas, the LEP student population grew by 120 percent, in Kansas by 118 percent, and in Oklahoma by 99 percent.[32]

Many schools are unprepared to meet the needs of Mexican-immigrant students in part because the states cannot hire enough qualified teachers to serve them. California, which has the highest number of immigrant students in the United States, has estimated a shortage of nearly 21,000 bilingual or ESL teachers. Texas newspaper accounts during the summer of 1998 reported that Houston needed about 600 more teachers, even after 300 new teachers had been offered contracts. The Dallas school district offered a $1,500 signing bonus to woo teachers. The Austin Independent School District began the 1998-99 school year needing 116 teachers, with 98 of the 116 vacancies in high-demand areas such as math, science, and certified bilingual education. The remainder of the vacant positions in the Austin District were for counselors, librarians, and elementary and secondary classroom teachers.[33]

To help parents, communities, teachers, and administrators do a better job with first- and second-generation Mexican-origin immigrant students, the remainder of this book focuses on practices that promote school achievement. The general philosophy of my approach is to affirm high academic standards and success for all students. Students face far more complex cultural, moral, and political challenges than we adults encountered in our own childhood and adolescence. There is much to be gained in learning with and from these students about how to meet these challenges constructively and in engaging communities more fully in efforts to support families. Chapter 2 uses the lens of culture to discuss how values and practices can affect achievement and students' abilities. Chapter 3 looks at language as a way to focus on the incorporation of immigrant children, their changing sense of identity, and English-language learning. Chapter 4 adjusts the lens to gender to explore differences in achievement between boys and girls and to discover how gender expectations might affect Mexican-origin students' school success. The chapter focuses on the roles of families in encouraging academic success, classroom practices that reflect gender bias, and peer group relations. Some research suggests that peers can have greater influence on student achievement than schools or families. Chapter 5 discusses how to involve Mexican-immigrant families effectively in the formal education of their children. The chapter discusses the importance of parental involvement in schools and education programs, barriers to their involvement, and some good approaches for including Mexican-immigrant parents. Chapter 6 looks specifically at policies and legislation directed at immigrant children and at efforts to train teachers to meet the needs of these students. Throughout these pages, I emphasize the need for multiple approaches to improving school success for Mexican-immigrant students and suggest some positive changes schools can make. I have included a summary of characteristics of successful schools and successful teachers.

The emphasis in this work is on Mexican-origin students because this is the largest group of Latino children. Many topics discussed here are relevant for other Latino children and for non-Hispanic children as well. I hope that the issues raised will help educators serve all children better.

CHAPTER 2

Cultural Perspectives on Learning

Sociologists and anthropologists usually define culture as the values, attitudes, and beliefs so familiar to us they are hard to discern. Individuals in a society take them for granted as common sense and the rules of everyday life. Culture is embedded in everything we do, the ways we behave with others, the kinds of relationships we establish, and the norms we follow in our day-to-day interactions. According to this definition of culture, cultural behavior can be demonstrated by a single individual or by groups of individuals. The United States is a society made up of many cultural groups. Often, each group desires to maintain its special heritage and identity as reflected in the different languages, races, ethnic backgrounds, religions, and cultural traditions we see in the towns and communities throughout the country. Much of what we do with our families and in our schools transmits culture and socializes our children to think, behave, and talk in ways that others in our cultural group believe is appropriate. Each culture may vary in its outlook on life, the content of its beliefs, the kind of adult personalities preferred, and the ways in which children are raised.[1]

At many points in life, a child is likely to experience abrupt transitions from one way of being and behaving to another—such as the transitions that occur when a baby is weaned, the first time a child leaves home and enrolls in public school, or when a child enters adolescence. These cultural discontinuities may produce negative disruptions in life patterns and interpersonal relations, or they may result in positive change. In this chapter, we use the lens of culture to look at the child-rearing practices of Mexican-immigrant families and the school experiences of Mexican-immigrant and second-generation children.

Actually, we must use the lenses of several cultures. There are group variations of culture within a large cultural group. For example, within the Mexican American cultural group, there are variations across generations as young families adapt the values and norms they learned from their parents in rearing their own children. Immigrant families may have cultural systems that result in patterns of child rearing that are distinct from second- and third-generation Mexican-origin families. The immigration process itself forces families to adjust cultural ways of doing things, traditional gender roles, and ideas about parent-child relationships. Families that have lived in the United States for a number of years may have acculturated to many behaviors expected in U.S. society. Immigrant children may experience cultural discontinuities when they leave their homes and enroll in U.S. schools. At many transitions—from elementary school to middle school or from secondary school to work or parenthood—various cultural groups may have very different expectations of behavior. Educators can learn about the cultural values in the homes of students and use that knowledge to make teaching more effective.[2]

When people in positions of power and authority—such as administrators, teachers, community leaders, or organizations of parents—make decisions based on their own cultural values, they may unconsciously discriminate against persons acting on different values and cultures. When we apply broad cultural understandings in general ways without considering individuals, we may stereotype students and families. In this chapter, we explore how cultural differences may lead us to act in ways that might harm certain groups of children and individual children. We look specifically at the child-rearing patterns of different cultural groups and the implications of those practices in education settings. I describe successful approaches to using cultural differences as resources in AVANCE, a two-generation parenting program that builds on the cultures of Mexican-immigrant and second-generation families. I also describe Funds of

Knowledge, a program based on home visits and based on teachers as researchers. Educational approaches that view the culture of families and children as rich resources to be incorporated into the activities, curricula, and goals of education programs are more effective with recent Mexican-immigrant children than those that ignore the children's culture or expect them to substitute mainstream cultural patterns for their own.

Group Culture vs. Individualism

Eugene E. Garcia and Barry McLaughlin help us understand how culture relates to successful learning and appropriate teaching practices for first- and second-generation Mexican-origin children. These scholars focus on meeting the challenges of linguistic and cultural diversity in early childhood education. The issues they discuss, however, are relevant to children of all ages. For example, they make distinctions between group culture and individual culture. They define group culture as the complex knowledge, beliefs, art, law, morals, customs, capabilities, and habits that help to identify an individual as a member of a particular society. An individual view of culture sees each child as an individual who may vary within that group culture. The individual perspective of culture also views individuals as actively constructing their social heritage by manipulating, recombining, and transforming their inherited social culture. For those using an individual-oriented concept of culture, each person's private system of ideas is a culture. This notion helps explain freedom of individual action within the larger group culture.[3]

According to Garcia and McLaughlin, the group culture concept acknowledges that members of different societies display different behaviors and ways of thinking and valuing. Those seeing the world from the lens of a group culture, for example, would recognize that Mexico, Japan, and the United States may organize their education systems differently to reflect the group cultures of each of these countries. A group cultural perspective would tell us that Mexican-immigrant parents may raise their children differently from third- and fourth-generation Mexican American parents or Anglo American parents or African American parents. Each group may value different kinds of behaviors in children. Other differences could include ways of disciplining children, communicating verbally, and playing with children. The discussions of group culture most often remain at the level of the group. Individual variations within those group cultures are kept out of focus in an effort to find the essential sameness within each of the different societies. The areas of similarity in ideas, emotional responses, and habitual behaviors are believed by researchers to have been learned through instruction or imitation by members of that society to a greater or lesser degree.

Garcia and McLaughlin point out that a group-oriented cultural perspective may distract the teacher from recognizing each student's individuality within the group culture. Teachers may not recognize ways that families, students, and teachers generate culture in their everyday activities. Focusing only on group cultures and group cultural differences may stereotype students and interfere with effective instruction. For example, a teacher might interpret a child's behavior in terms of a stereotyped characteristic attributed to that child's group culture. If a Mexican-immigrant child does not participate actively in class, the teacher might dismiss the lack of participation as an attribute of Mexican culture in which children are passive and respectful of adults' authority. The teacher may not take the time to determine whether the child has understood the assignments and class activities or to assess the child to see if a language difficulty has prevented participation. By acting on a group cultural interpretation of the behavior, the teacher might miss a learning problem that, if properly and promptly remedied, could allow the child to participate. Garcia and McLaughlin suggest teachers should have background knowledge of cultural orientations held by ethnic communities represented in their classrooms and then work with children as individuals. Teachers must be aware that each child has access to a wide variety of behaviors. A child may choose behaviors that are culturally learned within his or her family or community groups or may adapt those cultural behaviors to his or her own individual needs and temperament.

Teachers must also be aware of group stereotypes and be careful to avoid those stereotypes when working with Mexican-immigrant families and children. Ray C. Rist reminds us that when teachers act in ways that reinforce stereotypes, the results may be what has been termed the *self-fulfilling prophecy*. Rist studied teacher expectations of kindergarten and first- and second-grade children in a poor, urban school. He noticed that teachers made judgments about the academic potential of children in their classes using criteria having nothing to do with academic ability or performance. Teachers seemed to base judgments about academic abilities on the children's physical appearances, interactive behavior with one another and with the teacher, use of language (standard American English or "school language" versus a dialect), social status, and family conditions. The teachers' judgments resulted in the identification of some students as slow and subsequent placement of those children in low-ability groups. Over time, those groups became fairly rigid or institutionalized, and the children were treated as low-achieving students.[4]

The example above shows that if teachers are unaware of the cultural experiences their students bring from home and the types of behaviors expected in the home cultures, they may make incorrect judgments about an individual child's abilities. Because children learn the cultural patterns in which they are raised, it may be difficult for a child to adapt to the classroom's culture. For example, if a Mexican family values a child who does not demand adult attention, their children will learn to be quiet and stay out of the way of adults. If a family believes a child should be seen and not heard, their children will not likely speak up in the classroom and may not ask questions or be comfortable talking to adults. An understanding and acceptance of the behaviors a child brings to school, plus encouragement and reinforcement of desired behaviors in the school setting, can help children participate more successfully in the school culture. High expectations based on knowledge and understanding of each child provide the best chance for growth and development of individual children.

Children's Awareness of Cultural Differences

In preschool, very young children pay little attention to different cultural groups. They may notice that someone has a different type of hair or skin color, but those differences do not yet have the value associations of the larger society. As they grow, they begin to define themselves in the ways that the larger society defines them—usually in terms of being male or female, tall or short, chubby or skinny, and sometimes in terms of being good or bad, smart or dumb. Family characteristics—such as cultural knowledge, language, generation of migration to this country, and extent of cultural group identity—influence the extent to which parents pass along a cultural identity to their children. Through teaching, role modeling, and nonverbal communication, all children receive some cultural socialization from family members.[5]

By about four years of age, most children have begun to form cultural values and be aware that a racial-ethnic cultural hierarchy exists in society.[6] A study of young children's social construction of identity found that although racial or ethnic group was not always the most salient category of identity for young children, they often, especially minority group children, responded to commonly held stereotypes.[7] Somehow, these children had internalized some common negative attitudes held toward their group and attempted to define themselves as *not* being that. Another study found that children shape their own sense of self from images in their homes, their communities, and their schools. Children in Head Start often described themselves in terms of images of their racial/ethnic group. For example, young Latino children, when asked questions about who they were, often included in their descriptions of themselves reflections of stereotypes. Along with positive attributes, such as "I'm nice" or "I'm smart," and gender identities, such as "I'm a girl" or "I'm a boy," children often responded with comments such as "I'm not lazy, I'm a hard worker" or "I don't just speak Spanish, I speak English, too." Mexican American and African American children told of being excluded by peers when adults were not around and being called names that hurt them. White children, too, expressed concerns about being called "Whitey" by peers. As young as the preschool ages, children are likely to have developed images or assumptions about others. These assumptions come from peers, parents, where they currently live, and communities of origin. They also come from the media and from what they have been told. The absence of people of color in most historical accounts and much of the curricula taught in schools means that many stereotyped assumptions may go unchallenged for a long time.

Culture and Classroom Organization

The ways teachers organize classrooms and respond to students may be based on lack of knowledge about the cultural backgrounds of their students. Teachers may go about their work with the best of intentions, but stereotypes, omissions, and distortions can contribute to the development of prejudice and discrimination. A clear example of cultural differences and their influences in the classroom can be seen in the work of Susan U. Philips, who studied communication patterns in classrooms and in the Warm Springs Indian Reservation community. Philips found that the American Indian preschool children living on the reservation learned ways of organizing verbal messages that were different from those of Anglo American middle-class children. These differences made it more difficult for the Indian children to comprehend verbal messages conveyed through the public school's Anglo middle-class ways of organizing classrooms. In the Indian families, the adults and children did things together without verbally talking about the behaviors. They had ways of getting the speaker's attention and taking turns in speaking that were different from behaviors used in the classroom. As a result, teachers misinterpreted the Indian children's behaviors. Teachers thought the Indian children were not paying attention and did not give them sufficient time to answer questions in class. Philips concluded that American Indian and American Anglo children had already learned different systems of interaction by the time they came to school and that the Indian children were at a disadvantage because they did not know the classroom culture.[8]

Another example of different interactions occurred in my recent fieldwork in a Mexican American rural community. For about eight years, I have evaluated programs for Mexican American families and children, including Head Start, Early Head Start, Even Start, and a preschool intervention program for abused and neglected children in San Antonio, Texas. My research approach is ethnographic, based on extensive observations, interviews with participants, and documentation of what families, children, and staff think and say about their programs. In this case, the fieldwork involved visiting and observing in prekindergarten public school classrooms to describe the transitions from community-based, family-oriented early childhood programs to formal schooling.

In this classroom of predominantly Mexican American and Mexican-immigrant children, the young White teacher had implemented a behavior modification system based on rewards for good behavior over the week. The teacher kept a detailed chart of children's behaviors on the chalkboard at the front of the classroom. Children's behaviors were color coded using *green* (good behavior), *yellow* (cautions for misbehavior), and *red* (for misbehaviors). Each child's name was on the chart in big letters with a color mark for each day's behaviors. At the end of the week, children who had received all green got to take prizes from a treasure box. On the Friday of the observation, a number of four-year-olds in the class were crying because they did not get to draw treasures from the box. One child tried to defend herself by protesting to the teacher, "But I helped others." Another taunted his classmate, "I'll tell your mother" when his friend did not get a good behavior reward. The reward system implemented by this caring teacher was based on a system that made each individual child responsible for his or her own behavior. Our research in the community found that working together and helping others was a value highly rewarded in this community. Because of the hardships of immigration and poverty, families in this community were tightly interrelated.

Our research suggests that the teacher's disciplinary system would have been much more effective if she had worked within the community culture and based her system of reward on group solidarity, expecting children to help one another behave and encouraging the children to share responsibility for order in the classroom. In this case, the lack of understanding of cultural differences strained relations between the teacher and the children and between the school and the community. Instead of all working together toward the shared goal of student achievement, the system created negative school-family-community relations.

Both examples—the Indian reservation classroom and the classroom of Mexican-immigrant students—illustrate what sociologists call "cultural discrimination." Cultural discrimination occurs in situations where those with decision-making power use their own cultural values to impose a system on others whose cultural values are different. Because of the power differential in the classrooms—teacher policies that disadvantaged the students—the classroom organizational systems discriminated against the children's cultures. The unintended result was negative feelings toward the school on the part of the children and their parents. The systems the teachers imposed did not accomplish their purposes: to engage the Indian children in classroom dialogue or eliminate discipline problems in the Mexican-immigrant classroom.

Culture and Achievement

The above examples illustrate some problems schools face in adjusting to increasing numbers of immigrant and culturally diverse students. In Chapter 1, I noted one factor that contributes to Latino students leaving school at high rates: Immigrant youths who may never have entered U.S. schools are counted among those who have dropped out. In fact, educators have noted that many schools in regions with high percentages of immigrants and large populations of low-income Latinos report 35 to 50 percent of their students have dropped out of school.[9]

The research literature on the influence of immigration status on school outcomes is mixed, however. Some studies suggest certain groups of immigrants have not brought with them life experiences and cultural values that allow or encourage them to take advantage of educational opportunities in the United States. Other observers take a different perspective and argue that group cultural explanations of differences in educational attainment are based on beliefs that some cultures are superior to others. Stephen Steinberg argues that group cultural perspectives fail to take into account the structural situations in which first-generation immigrants frequently find themselves in their new communities. Among many groups, the first generation of immigrant parents had opportunities to achieve economic success that led to the educational success of the second and later generations.[10]

John U. Ogbu makes the distinction between immigrant minorities (those who came voluntarily to the United States), such as recent Mexican-immigrant families, and caste minorities (those involuntarily included in the United States), such as African Americans, American Indians, and Mexican Americans in early generations. Ogbu argues that immigrant minorities frequently achieve success in ways caste minorities do not because new immigrants are unconscious of the cultural limits the majority places on them. He claims that immigrants do not experience the same discrimination as those born and reared in the United States. According to Ogbu, immigrants compare themselves to their conationals who remained at home as a measure of success. According to Ogbu's theory, Mexican American youths from families who have lived in the United States for several generations are acutely aware of their location within the class structure of U.S. society, the jobs they will not get because of discrimination, and the lack of success they will experience. As a result, their cultural orientations are quite different from those of more recent Mexican-immigrant youths. Ogbu argues that because U.S.-born minority students perceive performing well in school as "acting White" or "selling out," they have rejected schoolwork, spent little time on homework, and have been disruptive in their classrooms.[11]

Recent research challenges Ogbu's interpretation. James Ainsworth-Darnell and Douglas B. Downey criticize Ogbu for applying this oppositional culture model to all "colonized" groups of students. Ainsworth-Darnell and Downey use data from the National Education Longitudinal Survey (NELS) to find that many caste minority students have more positive attitudes toward school than Whites and do not perceive fewer returns to education or limited opportunities. In fact, the minority students doing well in school reported more proschool attitudes than White students and considered themselves to be popular with their peers. Ainsworth-Darnell and Downey do find that dropouts between the eighth and tenth grades tend to be like the students Ogbu describes—frustrated with occupational chances, pessimistic about their futures, and resistant to school goals. When a full range of students is considered, however, the patterns of oppositional culture do not persist. Thus, the school problems of the most disadvantaged immigrant and second- and third-generation Mexican-origin students are not necessarily characteristic of the experiences of all Mexican-origin students.[12]

Lingxin Hao and Melissa Bonstead-Bruns note that social capital—resources generated from social relations, such as the parent-child relationship and the family's relationship with the community—plays an important role in immigrant student achievement. They argue that the amount of social capital generated from the parent-child relationship among immigrants depends on their process of *acculturation* (i.e., language and culture learning). When Mexican-immigrant parents do not actively learn English and U.S. cultural norms, the children take cues from their native-born peers not to learn in school. These researchers conclude that immigrant children need strong family and community support to encourage achievement. When both the parents and the student have high expectations for achievement, the student does better in school. The researchers also note that when students attend public schools of lower quality with large numbers of students who achieve poorly, Mexican-immigrant students and their parents have lower achievement expectations. Parent-child interactions in learning raise both parents' and children's expectations of achievement. Hao and Bonstead-Bruns recommend providing opportunities for parents and children to participate together in learning activities to improve student achievement.[13]

Cultural Differences in Child Rearing

With the increasing number of group cultures among U.S. children, most school programs do not have staff who are prepared to deal with the linguistic and cultural diversity that first- and second-generation immigrant children bring to their classrooms. Understandably, parents are reluctant to leave their children with caretakers who cannot speak their home language and who may not be able to understand their children.

A number of studies have found that cultural differences may have profound implications for the ways parents interact with their children.[14] Certainly, other variables also affect how mothers interact with their children, such as the education level and economic resources available to the family. Mexican-origin mothers, for example, have a wide range of educational attainment, even if they have culturally similar backgrounds and live under similar economic conditions. Some Mexican mothers have migrated from rural villages with limited or no schooling, while others come from urban areas with expanded opportunities to attend school.

Sarah LeVine notes that mothers' education levels strongly influence maternal beliefs about infants' communication abilities. These variations in beliefs, in turn, influence how mothers interact with their infants. LeVine and other researchers are concerned about how mothers' school experiences influence early interactions with children. They are also interested in the influence of parents' interactions with their children on subsequent child development, particularly within the context of Mexican culture. A central hypothesis of LeVine's work is that the number of years a mother spends in school increases her tendency to think of infants as capable of communicating with adults. Mothers with higher education levels are thus more likely to engage in verbal interactions with their infants, which influences child development.

A number of studies indicate a direct link between parents' beliefs about an infant's ability to communicate and the ways mothers interact with their babies. And these beliefs vary from one culture to another. For example, Barubi B. Schieffelin and Elinor Ochs have found that mother-infant styles of communication, what they call *communicative accommodation*, vary because of different culture-specific norms for interacting with infants. In some cultures, mothers sing lullabies to restless or fussy children. This is a form of communication, but the lullabies do not initiate communicative exchanges with the child, that is, the mothers do not expect the child to "talk" back on hearing the lullabies. In other cultures, mothers initiate communication with their infant and expect the infant to coo or smile in response. In some cultures, mothers respond to crying but ignore babbling. In still other cultures, parents respond to babbling as if the infant were attempting to talk, and they carry on a conversation with the babbling child. The researchers conclude that there is cultural variation in the ideas and practices concerning infant abilities to participate in verbal interaction and that those variations might be related to cultural differences in general interactions of mothers with infants and young children.[15]

These cultural variations also have an impact on the language and literacy development of children. For example, many research studies on child development have found that when mothers interact verbally with their children, the children develop greater verbal and social competence. Play and verbal interactions with adults enhance infants' vocabulary and social development. Mothers usually model the kinds of interactions they observe among other mothers with infants in their communities. They incorporate these ways of interacting with infants through socialization, family interactions, and other social activities during childhood and adolescence. Mothers who have attended school are more likely to be open to other ways of interacting with their children as they learn more about child development.[16]

According to Robert A. LeVine and colleagues, babies in the rural Mexican community they studied were breast-fed intensively and slept with their mothers. Good health and a docile baby were the mothers' goals, with the ideal infant sleeping quietly, lying in bed and making few demands for interaction. There was a great deal of holding, hugging, and kissing babies and infants, but these demonstrations of affection did not involve conversation-like interactions. Mothers and fathers were expected to punish toddlers physically with light spankings, *nalgadas*, on the buttocks or with a switch at two to three years old. A belt was appropriate for punishment by age four. Communication between parents and children in this Mexican community tended to be formal in order for parents to maintain authority in the household. Many cultural patterns of interactions changed among families who moved to urban areas and became involved in schools.[17]

In a case study of Mayan parental belief systems, Suzanne Gaskins found that Mayan parents interacted with their babies and played with their children in ways distinctly different from the ways U.S. parents interacted with their infants. Mothers in the United States spent more time than Mayan mothers giving the baby objects, taking them away, and playing verbally with the baby with the object. Mayan infants spent less time oriented toward the mother than U.S. infants. Mayan infant play was quite different from the play of U.S. infants. Gaskin explored the parents' definitions of play, the parents' concern or lack of concern about children's stages of development, how parents asserted authority, what parents regarded as good parenting, the amount of time parents spent in play with children, what was appropriate play, and how much face-to-face interaction parents had with children of different ages. She found that parents' culturally determined ideas about play can lead to the structuring of children's environments in ways that encourage a style of play very different from the style taken for granted in mainstream U.S. culture.[18]

Another example of cultural differences in child rearing is presented in Ann R. Eisenberg's research on teasing. In the Mexican-immigrant homes she observed, teasing was primarily a means of playing with a child. Adults would tease children to establish or maintain interactions with them. Interpersonal relationships with intimates were considered extremely important in the families Eisenberg observed, and an important component of those relationships was verbal contact. Teasing was a way to interact and to have fun with interaction. Teasing also reinforced relationships in the alignments it created among individuals. For example, when an uncle teased a child and another adult helped the child respond to the teasing, they created close and special bonds between themselves and the child. Teasing was also used for social control. Although many of the adults' threats were not intended seriously (such as telling a child that the adult no longer loved him), children might fear it was true. Because adults in the Mexican-immigrant community admired teasing and joking, these were skills Mexican children had to learn in order to speak like adult members of their cultural group. Learning to participate in teasing, learning the boundaries of who could appropriately be teased, and learning what subjects were acceptable in teasing sequences required learning complex social rules. Since cultural and social values are continually expressed through social interactions, learning about those interactions in parent-child relationships can help teachers to understand immigrant students' cultures.[19]

These studies demonstrate the considerable extent to which behavior of even very young children can be culturally mediated in important ways. These cultural variations have been found in behaviors that have usually been considered both universal to all cultures and biologically based, such as how children learn to talk and the stages they go through in development. The implications of this kind of research are especially important for education programs serving first- and second-generation Mexican-immigrant children. Unless we understand culturally specific parental theories of child raising in the context of parents' general cultural theories of child development and socialization, we cannot understand children's behaviors. These cultural misunderstandings often cause conflicts between Mexican-origin parents and schools. Parents do not become involved and are reluctant to have their children participate in school programs that do not reflect their beliefs and values about raising children.

Recognizing Different Cultural Perspectives

A lack of attention to cultural differences may invalidate well-planned education programs. Guadalupe Valdés, who studied a Mexican-immigrant community in California, questions the efficacy of family intervention programs in general and is even more critical of the utility of such programs for Mexican-origin families. She acknowledges that the families she studied were not producing successful schoolchildren and that there were many things the families did not know about American schools and teachers. They were, however, good parents. The mothers loved their children and cared for them. The fathers worked hard to provide for their families. They were intensely concerned about raising their children and wanted them to have better lives than they, as parents, had experienced. In the eyes of the teachers who did not understand the cultural values of the families that Valdés studied, these families were failing their children. These parents did not respond to school notices promptly, help their children with schoolwork at home, or become actively involved in school activities. They did include children in many adult and community activities, they cared for their children, and they provided guidance to help them grow to be successful adults. Valdés points out that the families she interviewed had different views and ideas about achievement. They were guided by beliefs and behaviors of child rearing that emphasize respect and obedience. They did not understand the mother's role to include teaching school lessons to their children. Valdés expresses deep concerns about school and parenting programs designed to change the patterns and practices of these families. She argues that school and parental programs must be based on an understanding and an appreciation and respect for the internal dynamics of the families and their cultural values and beliefs. Effective programs must view parent-child relationships as embedded in family relationships and family cultures. These relationships are also embedded in a cultural community, which, in turn, is part of the wider American culture.[20]

In a project exploring perceptions of fatherhood among working-class Mexican-origin families in a rural community in Texas, my colleagues and I found that cultural differences affected the ways families defined involvement in their children's education. The project was part of an evaluation of an Early Head Start program in the community. Definitions of fatherhood varied, depending on the father's age and origin; but a dominant perception among the Mexican-immigrant fathers interviewed was that the father is the one who works to provide for the family's basic needs. The fathers also saw themselves as heads of the household, responsible for raising the children and educating them properly. This meant making sure the children could go to school, teaching them how to support themselves, being a guide and example for them, teaching them respect for the family, spending time with them, playing with them, and showing them they were loved. The fathers saw themselves involved in the moral education of their children.[21]

The fathers were puzzled when asked how they wanted to participate in the Early Head Start program. They did not feel capable of helping with classroom activities or tutoring because they themselves had little formal schooling. Program staff had planned opportunities for parents to work in the classrooms, participate in policy council meetings, attend monthly meetings about Head Start, and read to their children at home. These activities were not how the fathers had envisioned themselves as being involved. Even with a Mexican American male staff person hired as a family advocate, the program had a difficult time organizing fathers around these goals. The fathers did participate actively in discussions about fatherhood and enjoyed talking about ways to help their children. They also participated in family events planned by the Early Head Start program but usually more as observers than active participants. The Mexican working-class fathers preferred their versions of parenting styles and did not want to replace them with the parenting styles based on middle-class values and beliefs suggested by the schools and the Early Head Start program.

One father reported that when he spent time with his children and took them to events, his male relatives teased him about being a *mandilón*, a Spanish term derived from *mandil*, an apron. The term implies that the man is dominated by his wife. The Mexican parents did incorporate some suggested parenting strategies, those they agreed with and felt would be helpful for their families. But they wanted to maintain their views of disciplining and interacting with their children. Many of the ways the Mexican-immigrant fathers perceived as being involved in their children's education were not recognized by the schools or the Early Head Start program. But, these families enrolled their children in Early Head Start, and the mothers participated in many of the organized activities. This experience suggests that they valued the program and were involved in their children's formal education; they simply held differing perceptions of parent involvement.

Over time, the Early Head Start program incorporated more activities that the Mexican parents preferred. Staff spent more time on home visits and helped families avail themselves of the resources for children in the community. They provided more time for English language classes for parents. They provided computer and driver's license classes so parents could upgrade their work skills. They helped children get immunizations, medical examinations, and dental care. They provided discussion sessions on topics the parents wanted to know more about, such as special education placement and how it might affect their children, what to do if their children are in fourth grade and cannot read, and how to deal with teens who do not respect traditional Mexican family values.

Pros and Cons of Parent Education Programs

Valdés is critical of parenting programs, particularly programs aimed at making parents "first teachers," "involving" them in classrooms, or "empowering" them.[22] She believes an underlying principle in all of these programs is the belief that Mexican-immigrant parents have to be taught to be better parents, and to do that, they must give up their cultural values and buy into the American value system of viewing achievement as success. She argues that by adapting to the ways middle-class families get involved in education, their children will no longer value family relationships or work to help support a communal family effort. She claims advocates of these programs subscribe to the myth that the school can right all social wrongs, and they ignore other influences on educational outcomes.

While I find myself agreeing that the values many Mexican-immigrant families embrace are important ones, I also believe that strong families can keep their values while participating in parenting programs. Many immigrant families we interviewed were selective. They took from the programs the aspects they believed could help their families, and they maintained a firm commitment to the family and many other Mexican cultural values. For example, the father whose friends and relatives teased him for spending time with his children told us he enjoyed being with his wife and family and planned to ignore the remarks and continue to discuss school with his children, take them places, and help his wife in the home. He also planned to continue disciplining his children by spanking and asserting his authority as a parent; however, he understood how hitting his children could have negative consequences and said he would consider those consequences when making disciplinary decisions.

Immigrant families are survivors. Their families will be pressured by outside forces, particularly U.S. peer cultures, whether or not they participate in parenting programs. Parents will be at a disadvantage if they do not know how the organization of schools and how American cultural values will affect their children's life chances and their families.

Certainly, intervention programs organized to view immigrant families as having deficits that need fixing are inappropriate and can be paternalistic and damaging. But there are programs that offer positive resources to families and programs where the parents participating do take active roles in shaping the programs to meet their needs and values. Learning to build positive relationships within families through positive parenting strategies can enhance Mexican-immigrant values and family orientations. Plus, many programs reach out to families that do not have the strong, cohesive family bonds and positive parent-child relationships Valdés describes. Some families *do* need "fixing." If programs are well run, they will value existing strengths of the families, and the staff will work in partnership with the families to fulfill the families' goals.

Successful Programs Incorporating Parents' Cultural Values

AVANCE. One program that has incorporated family culture to achieve significant successes with recent and second-generation Mexican-immigrant families is AVANCE, a preschool parenting program in San Antonio. AVANCE is a Spanish word meaning *to advance* or *to progress*. The AVANCE curriculum is described here so readers will better understand how a program can incorporate the cultures of families and children.

AVANCE is a nonprofit community-based family support and education program that has been extremely successful and popular with first- and second-generation Mexican children and families. The program began in San Antonio in 1973 based on the idea of involving parents and helping them make toys to help their children. The program targets low-income, often single-parent mothers with young children. In the first nine months of the program, mothers attend classes one morning per week for three hours. Infants and toddlers accompany their mothers to the program and are placed in day care that provides appropriate developmental and educational activities. Trained educators visit mothers in their homes. The mothers may choose to participate a second year to develop their own educational and vocational skills. Participants are recruited through door-to-door surveys to locate Mexican-origin families with a child from birth to age two. The program has branched out to other cities and expanded services to provide adult literacy, father involvement, and other programs for about 6,000 Latino families.[23]

An evaluation found that the program has had positive effects in helping mothers provide educationally stimulating and emotionally encouraging environments for their children and in reducing isolation and depression. Mothers participating in the program were more emotionally and verbally responsive to their children, avoided restrictive and punishing behaviors, and provided more variety in their children's daily routine, compared with mothers in control and matched groups who did not participate in the program. At the end of the program, participating mothers praised their children more and encouraged their language development. Mother-child interactions were marked by enhanced mutual enjoyment, and mothers and children participated in a greater number of joint, rather than parallel, activities. Participating mothers also developed larger nonfamily networks of friends, knew more about community resources for families, and used these resources more than mothers in the control group. Mothers in the program were more likely than mothers in the control group to enroll in and complete courses for the General Equivalency Diploma (GED) or English-as-a-second-language (ESL) classes. The program leaders expect that as the mothers develop their own competencies, they will be able to assist their children over the years and help them develop to optimize their school success.[24]

The AVANCE curriculum includes eleven units that provide information and strategies for parenting. Talented people sensitive to the cultural values of the families have developed the units described in the following paragraphs.

Unit 1 introduces the role of parents in meeting a child's basic needs. It provides basic information about child development and emphasizes the importance of a child reaching his or her potential with the help of parents, family, environment, and experiences. The unit emphasizes the role of parents not only as teachers but also as sources of knowledge about what makes their children happy, healthy, and smart.

Unit 2 introduces the stages of physical growth in raising a healthy child and the importance of parents' contributions to that development. It covers lessons in growth and development of children, safety and supervision, childhood trauma and first aid, and infant and childhood cleanliness—such as tips on bathing an infant, sterilizing bottles, and cloth diapers vs. disposable diapers.

Unit 3 addresses the question of acceptable and unacceptable behavior. It helps parents confront children's behavior they view as unacceptable and helps them change this behavior through love and concern. The activities emphasize meeting a child's basic needs in a positive manner. The unit discusses how a child's temperament and the stress of life events can affect his or her behavior. Discipline and the maltreatment of children are addressed in a culturally sensitive way aimed at recognizing and preventing child abuse.

Unit 4 focuses on the cognitive needs of children and the significance of a parent's role in providing learning experiences. The unit aims to help parents become aware of children's learning processes, basic concepts that children need to learn, and the importance of providing language experiences for children. Parents are shown how language development affects a child's learning and success in school.

Units 5-8 provide a guide for parents in recognizing infectious childhood illnesses, providing proper nutrition, understanding a child's emotional needs, and guiding the socialization process.

Unit 9 encourages parents to examine their own lives and think about how past relationships and experiences have affected their families. Families are encouraged to set goals to promote parents' continued growth and development, not only for themselves but for their children.

Units 10 and 11 discuss prenatal care and infant needs.

The AVANCE curriculum always emphasizes that the family, as well as the larger society's mores, values, attitudes, and beliefs, plays a part in the development of a young child. The program does not focus on academic success and achievement outcomes as the primary outcomes. The integrity of the family and happy, healthy children are the main goals. Ongoing program evaluations have focused on maintaining the quality of the model's implementation and continuing to assess the program's impact. Program staff continue to add new curriculum and program service models in response to the needs of the parents and children.

AVANCE has been especially successful with families living in poverty for several generations and with parents who have low education levels and high degrees of stress and isolation. AVANCE is an excellent example of a two-generation program that targets mothers who want more knowledge about child growth and that builds upon a family's cultural strengths to provide knowledge and experiences to enhance children's development.[25]

Funds of Knowledge. Successful programs for recent Mexican-immigrant children have recognized the importance of culture and made special efforts to address the cultural needs of Mexican-origin families. These programs have involved parents in the planning and implementation of services, building on the strengths of families and value cultural diversity. Norma Gonzalez and her colleagues helped teachers study their students' households to discover the *funds of knowledge* within the children's families that could be incorporated into the classroom curriculum. These researchers pointed out that many times in the past, instead of focusing on knowledge Mexican-immigrant students bring to school and using it as a foundation for learning, schools have emphasized what these students lack in language and knowledge forms sanctioned by the schools. Gonzalez and a team of professors, teachers, and parents worked together as *communities of learners*. Teachers were encouraged to think, reflect, and analyze with others to transform their teaching in positive ways. There were three key domains of change: (1) the teachers became qualitative researchers and went into the homes to learn about their students, (2) the teachers established new relationships with families, and (3) the teachers and families perceived local households as containing important social and intellectual resources for teaching. The team began by studying the local community, a predominantly Mexican working-class neighborhood in Tucson, Arizona. The teachers learned about the origins and development of the community; the labor and educational histories of the families; and the skills, abilities, ideas, practices, and knowledge were essential for each household to function. They learned information about building trades, agricultural practices, and trade and business on the U.S.-Mexican border. They learned about the social networks within the community and within the families. The teacher-researchers were careful to make no attempts to teach the parents or complain about the students.

After the home visits, the teachers met with university researchers in education and anthropology in after-school study groups to discuss what they were finding in the fieldwork and to plan, develop, and support innovations in instruction. Teachers used specific techniques in participant observation, writing field notes, interviewing, and eliciting life stories, but the emphasis was on joint construction of knowledge. Teachers talked about how they were teaching and why they were teaching that way. Some kept journals about their feelings as they worked on the project. The teachers developed questionnaires to help them gather information about family histories, family networks, daily activities, educational history, language use, and child-rearing ideologies. They reported that this experience was different from other in-service training or teacher meetings, where they were "talked at" and "fed information."

The teachers found that once they were involved in learning about the households, they were in a much better position to plan for the students' learning activities. They viewed culture differently. The prevailing notion of culture in the schools was centered around dances, foods, folklore, and celebrations. Teachers began to see culture as a way of living, the practices of their students and their families, and relationships. The idea of culture was expanded to include the ways children and families organized and made sense of experiences. The most important outcome was that the teachers saw that families had much worthwhile knowledge and many experiences teachers could draw upon to make their teaching more meaningful. They understood the sacrifices the families had made for their children and the responsibilities of various family members. They were able to connect in their classroom discussions to things the students understood. As the teachers learned more about their students and their students' families and experiences in Mexico and the United States, they came to view the students as competent participants in households with many rich resources. The teachers also raised their expectations of their students' academic abilities.

Parents also benefitted from the process. They felt increased access to the school, a mutual trust with the teachers, and more confidence in themselves as partners in the learning process. The relationships between teachers and families became more positive and supportive. Gonzalez and colleagues noted that the teachers faced many constraints in becoming teacher-researchers. Conducting home visits, writing field notes, and meeting in groups demanded considerable time on top of already busy teaching schedules. Teachers also needed assistance and support in incorporating the knowledge they learned from their students' homes into classroom practices and curriculum units. Key to the success of the Funds of Knowledge project was that teachers entered the homes as *learners* and interacted with parents as partners in the learning process.[26]

In Chapter 5 we explore family-school partnerships in greater detail. But first, in Chapter 3, we look at language and the many ways that language interacts with achievement.

CHAPTER 3

Language, Literacy, and Creating Bridges to Success

M any countries around the world struggle with issues related to language and educating immigrant children. All nations with immigrant guest workers, undocumented immigrants, refugees, or native-born minority-language groups have children living within their borders who do not speak the national language or who are bilingual and use the national language in public and another language in their homes. The United Nations Educational, Scientific and Cultural Organization (UNESCO) has brought scholars and educators from many different countries together to discuss policies and practices used to educate immigrant children. In the majority of these countries, children who do not speak the national language (often the dominant language used in the schools) face many difficulties in learning and usually cannot understand the language teachers use in their classrooms.[1]

Language difference has been a common and persistent explanation for lack of educational achievement among Mexican-origin students. But contradictory evidence suggests that recent-immigrant students do extremely well in American schools despite language differences. Some observers caution that competence in spoken English may mask the inability to read and write and do high-level academic work in English. Despite significant literature on the cognitive benefits of bilingualism and the prestige associated in many other countries with speaking more than one language, many educators in the United States view bilingualism as an educational liability.[2]

Political battles in California and Texas to restrict access of undocumented immigrants and their children to various social and education services have placed schools in the middle (see discussion in chapter 6). Many of these battles target immigration. Other battles target language programs serving a large number of Latino students. The use of bilingual education in public schools has provoked bitter controversy for some time in the United States. The debates intensified in the 1990s as California legislators attempted to declare bilingual education an inappropriate educational strategy to teach immigrant students.

The Bilingual Education Controversy

In June 1998, 61 percent of California's voters passed Proposition 227, a voter initiative that virtually eliminated bilingual education from California classrooms. Article 2-305 of the proposition states, "All children in California public schools shall be taught English by being taught in English." The law also states, "Children who are English learners shall be educated through sheltered English immersion during a temporary transition period not normally intended to exceed one year." Although the law applies only to California, the initiative has profound pedagogical and political implications nationwide because it forbids the use of bilingual education.[3]

Proponents of Proposition 227 believed bilingual programs had failed, turning out students with little knowledge of English, thus condemning them to menial jobs. What may not have been taken into consideration in this debate, however, is the fact that only 30 percent of California's schoolchildren who qualified for bilingual education and needed English instruction were actually enrolled in programs. Yet, supporters of Proposition 227 pointed to bilingual education as the cause of high drop-out rates and other education ills, claiming that immigrant children were not learning English fast enough or well enough. Such critics believed immigrants had been poorly served by bilingual programs lasting five or six years yet still leaving children behind in basic skills. Some claimed that bilingual education was a political tactic of self-interested Latino leaders and that the programs "blocked the integration of minority children into mainstream society." Proposition 227 is known as the *English for the Children Initiative*, or the *Unz Initiative*, after its author and chief financial backer Ron K. Unz, a Silicon Valley businessman. Unz pointed out that generations of immigrants had learned English and entered the broader American culture without bilingual education. Many Latinos have also criticized bilingual education, arguing that bilingual programs have not been properly implemented and are not adequately supported to be successful.[4]

Critics of Proposition 227 suggested that inadequacies attributed to bilingual education may have overlapped other conditions affecting the school achievement of immigrant children. For instance, most English-language learners in the United States live in families and communities with high poverty rates and experience stressful economic and social conditions associated with being poor. Under such circumstances, it is difficult to separate effects of poverty from effects of limited English proficiency in education settings.[5]

Bilingual education supporters also remind us that the original idea behind bilingual education calls for teaching core subjects, such as history and mathematics, in students' native tongue so they do not fall behind, while gradually increasing their skills in English. After three to five years, immigrant students would make the transition into all-English classrooms. Further, bilingual education supporters want immigrant students to function well in the majority culture while maintaining the traditions and languages of their own cultures.

Research provides strong evidence that advanced bilingualism promotes academic achievement.[6] It is clear that children learn best in languages they can understand. Many observers acknowledge that many bilingual education programs are poorly implemented, but they want to "mend them, not end them." Kenji Hakuta concludes in his respected and scholarly book about the bilingual debate, *Mirror of Language*, that all students in the United States should be bilingual. Hakuta reports that research largely supports the contentions of bilingual education advocates—that well-implemented bilingual education can enhance learning and cognitive development. Patricia Gándara's study of successful Mexican Americans shows that children who can function in their native cultures and languages, as well as functioning in mainstream American culture and speaking English, can adjust and achieve well academically. More recent reviews of research and evaluation studies concerning bilingual education and second-language learners also show bilingualism's positive cognitive outcomes. Diane August and Kenji Hakuta conclude, "In an increasingly global economic and political world, proficiency in languages other than English and an understanding of different cultures are valuable in their own right and should be among the major goals for schools."[7]

Learning English

What are the program options for Mexican-immigrant children learning English? What can schools do to improve the achievement of these students? Researchers and educators have identified sociolinguistic, programmatic, and instructional factors that contribute to successful school programs.[8] Listed below are important features of effective programs for English language learners:

- high expectations for all students
- sufficient time in the program to develop bilingual skills
- rigorous academic content in the curriculum
- quality language instruction in both languages
- equal status of the two languages and a school climate that values bilingualism
- opportunities to learn the second language while continuing to develop proficiency and literacy skills in the first language
- positive opportunities to interact socially with speakers of the second language
- use of effective language-teaching strategies and opportunities for group/cooperative learning
- incorporation of effective school characteristics into programs (e.g., strong administrative leadership to encourage positive attitudes toward diversity and to implement strong programs, well-qualified and highly motivated staff, adequate materials, support for staff development, and home-school collaboration)

- adequate initial and ongoing assessments with instruction designed to address a range of abilities and challenge all learners

Bilingual programs are still available at the elementary level in many states with large numbers of immigrant students; in some states, such as Texas, such programs are mandatory. Once immigrant students reach middle school or high school, however, program offerings frequently do not meet their needs. Some secondary schools offer no special programs for immigrant or migrant students. A high percentage of Mexican-origin students never reach middle school because of inadequate instructional programs and support services. According to a U.S. Department of Education report, students from low-income families, those with older siblings who have dropped out of school, and those who changed schools two or more times are at risk of dropping out of school. All of these risk factors are commonly associated with Mexican-immigrant students.[9]

Secondary schools that have established programs for recent Mexican-immigrant students tend to be either (1) intensive English or English-as-a-second language (ESL) classes, (2) bilingual programs that teach subject courses in students' native language as they learn English, or (3) newcomers' schools, which try to address the cultural and academic adjustments of immigrant students. Instructional quality suffers in each of these programs because of students' varying levels of academic skills and English proficiency and a curriculum that usually does not parallel that provided to English-speaking students. But many program approaches also have strengths.

ESL classes are typically found in schools that enroll students with several different native languages. English-language instruction in these classes tends to focus on goals that students appreciate and find useful. Immigrant students and their parents have a strong desire to learn English for its economic utility—opening up more and better job opportunities in the United States. Immigrants are, therefore, eager to participate in English classes. However, ESL programs tend to emphasize oral language while not cultivating students' reading and writing skills, other specific academic needs (such as specialized high school courses), or critical thinking. Also, teachers in these classes, although sympathetic to the needs of Mexican-immigrant students, seldom have specialized training in teaching English as a second language. The teacher is usually someone who can speak

Spanish or has shown a special interest in immigrant students.[10]

Guadalupe Valdés followed the school careers of two immigrant students in California and observed their English classes. She noticed no effort to adjust the level of English used in instruction to the various levels of the students in the class. Students had few opportunities to speak or practice oral English and spent most of their time doing worksheets with pictures of objects they were told to identify and color. Teachers did not have enough textbooks, and few students exited the program. When students did move to regular classes or higher levels of English instruction, it was because of overcrowding, not student ability.[11]

Sheltered language content programs placed beginning English-learning students in subject matter classes (e.g., mathematics, science) in which teachers attempted to simplify their English. These classes do not appear to have been successful either. For example, Valdés notes in classes she observed that all beginning ESL learners were placed in the same mathematics class. Sixth, seventh, and eighth graders with sophisticated mathematics backgrounds mocked students who were barely learning their multiplication tables. The science class Valdés observed was little better. The teacher did not have a strong background in science and struggled to explain concepts. Sylvia Celedon describes a mathematics class for English learners in which the teacher did not have mathematics training. The students covered less material than the students in the regular class and struggled with the English mathematics terms and word problems that were culturally embedded. Students in these classes were bored and disruptive. They knew they were not making much progress in learning English or the subject content.[12]

Bilingual programs teach academic concepts in a student's strongest language while simultaneously teaching English language skills. There are a number of different program models for implementing bilingual education in the United States; some are more effective than others. The models vary in the amount of a student's home language used, the length of time the home language is maintained, approaches to staffing (e.g., the use of native language teachers, team teaching, or bilingual tracks with strands of classes identified as bilingual), and whether the goal is to transition into English quickly or to promote bilingualism and biliteracy in both the home language and English. The catch for adolescent immigrants is that bilingual programming is more comprehensive in elementary schools. Most secondary bilingual programs are limited to the core subjects of reading, writing, and basic math. The shortage of certified bilingual faculty to teach specialized high school subjects means that, no matter how great the need, providing expansive course offerings in the bilingual track is very difficult.[13]

Newcomers' programs provide transition courses that allow recent immigrants to learn about American culture and receive counseling on adjustment problems. Some school districts have organized newcomers' schools separate from regular schools. The newcomers' programs teach English language skills that help students make the transition into a regular school program. The programs facilitate adjustment, but grouping recent immigrant students with other newcomers cannot by itself give these students access to mainstream activities and social groups.

These programs commonly segregate immigrant students from their English-speaking peers and tend to track them away from academic or college-prep courses. Some observers have found that programs for immigrants promote academic marginalization and separateness while pressuring immigrant students to speak only English and drop their native languages to participate in the academic and social life of the school.[14] Also, separating immigrant students deprives them of opportunities they need to socialize with English-speaking U.S. youth in order to gain U.S. cultural knowledge.

Mexican-immigrant children may not have the opportunities to gain access to White middle-class society, no matter how acculturated they become. Recent studies have suggested that the path to full participation in mainstream society is less clear cut for Mexican-immigrant children, compared with those of earlier European-immigrant groups. The deterioration of public schools and the adversarial culture of many minority youth in inner cities contribute to an environment with fewer incentives and opportunities for second-generation immigrant children to get ahead. Without a good education and the exposure to American society that comes with attending school, immigrant children could continue to experience subordination and disadvantages, remaining segregated in their ethnic communities. If we expect young Latinos to fully participate in U.S. society, they must be given opportunities to gain strong academic skills.[15]

Maintaining Spanish

The debate over bilingual education is not a new one. American Indian children were forbidden to use their tribal languages in reservation boarding schools. Mexican children in Texas were punished for speaking Spanish on the playgrounds of their schools and forbidden to speak their language in the classrooms. On the other hand, German American children were separated into German language schools so that they could maintain their German culture and language as they learned English.

Laurie Olsen in her recent book *Made in America*, based on a study of the adjustment of middle-school immigrant students, claims that "no other aspect of adjustment to life in the United States receives as much programmatic attention or generates as much political focus and controversy as language."[16] As mentioned earlier, Proposition 227 ended most bilingual education programs in California and required students to be taught almost entirely in English. Fierce arguments about how to teach children whose native languages are not standard English have intensified as the number of immigrant children in our public schools has grown. All parents want higher academic achievement for their children in our public schools so students can complete high school, attend competitive postsecondary colleges, and get good jobs. Feelings run high in these language debates because so much is at stake.

Many who favored Proposition 227 in California feared the demise of English. Recent research suggests those fears were exaggerated. Latino children, including the children of new immigrants, possess not only widespread competence in English but also demonstrate a preference for English in everyday communication. Their parents, also, are very much aware of the importance of English and want their children to speak it well. The longer these children live in the United States, the more strongly influences of linguistic assimilation lead to a steady shift toward English. The main risk for Mexican Americans and Mexican-immigrant children, contrary to nativist fears that they are not learning English, is losing their Spanish.[17]

The majority of bilingual education programs in the United States are transitional, meant to teach children in their native languages while they gradually learn English. In these bilingual programs, limited-English-proficient (LEP) children can progress at grade level in mathematics, science, and other core subjects until they are ready to make the transition to all-English instruction. Transitioning too early into all-English programs may mean students will not be able to complete the academic work at their appropriate grade level.

In large urban school districts in the United States, many different languages are spoken, although Spanish is dominant among English language learners. It is difficult to find competent bilingual teachers who are truly fluent and literate in both languages. Teaching in bilingual settings often requires teachers to create their own bilingual materials because adequate Spanish language materials and resources are unavailable. The many wonderful materials available in Mexico, Spain, and Latin America often do not reflect variations of Spanish spoken in the United States or the cultural experiences of Spanish-speaking students of the U.S. Southwest. Non-English-speaking students speak various dialects of their native languages, while many Spanish-speaking students in the Southwest code-switch (blend their native Spanish language with English in an adaptive communicative strategy). Other Spanish-speaking immigrant children are too old for their appropriate grade level in U.S. schools and lack basic literacy skills in their native language. In addition, even the most successful programs, regardless of language of instruction, fail to eliminate the problems associated with poverty that influence student achievement.

Maintaining Spanish through bilingual education does not have to come at the cost of timely English acquisition. Very often, the maintenance of Spanish is framed as "un-American." This view has become a major issue in the socialization of immigrant children into the United States—particularly Spanish-speaking children, because they constitute the largest immigrant group. Those who promote using a child's home language extensively in U.S. schools argue (1) a child learns most readily in the language he or she knows best, (2) a child can learn a great deal academically in his or her home language while simultaneously learning English, and (3) what is learned in a first language actually helps in learning a second language because skills learned transfer from one language to another.[18] Despite research findings that confirm these arguments, programs emphasizing Spanish language maintenance—with bilingual development as a goal—generate enormous controversy. As a result, we are far from implementing education programs that maintain Spanish as a national resource.

Maintaining Spanish in the classroom. Immigrant students quickly attempt to abandon use of their Spanish on school grounds and in classrooms because English-speaking kids reject, put down, and leave out non-English speakers. Speaking English is viewed as necessary for acceptance and success among students and in the larger U.S. society. Few young children or adolescents put a premium or value on continuing to develop their Spanish. They take it for granted. Or they do not understand that not using their Spanish will lead to loss of their skills. Many students are laughed at for incorrect English, teased for heavy accents, and intimidated about asking for clarifications of English. These peer pressures to conform and other social dynamics of assimilation speed the switch to English.

Many students who learn oral English still lack the communicative competence necessary to interact in classrooms. One Mexican American student confided that she did not understand the words her teachers used in her classes. She had learned oral English and did not speak Spanish fluently. She explained that she was "not really into reading." She repeatedly failed her high school English classes and had difficulty with the word problems in geometry. She worried about her lack of writing skills in formal English. She explained, "I can write if I can write in words I understand."[19]

Other research describes the complex sociolinguistic skills students need to ask questions, participate in class discussions, clarify assignments, and interact with other students and their teachers. To participate successfully in all these classroom interactions and learn academic subject matter, immigrant students must be able to comprehend the spoken language of their teachers and the written language used in textbooks. Unless classroom environments allow students to use the strengths of their own language experiences—whether these be dialects, code-switching, or other styles of Spanish and

English—these students are at a severe disadvantage in gaining access to the content knowledge essential for successful school achievement.[20]

Language and ethnic identity. Looking at language maintenance over the generations, Spanish is on a firmer footing than other immigrant languages because the large-scale immigration of persons who speak Spanish is likely to continue, if only because of the proximity to Mexico. Spanish speaking in Southern California and in Texas has not been so widespread since the 1848 Treaty of Guadalupe Hidalgo, when Mexico ceded territory comprising today's U.S. Southwest. The ethnic community may maintain the Spanish language because of newcomers who constantly renew the language within that community, but most Spanish-speaking children become monolingual English speakers.

It is clear, however, that language use will continue to be an important symbolic issue in the struggle for ethnic rights and the struggle of power relationships among groups in the United States. California, the source of much antibilingual sentiment, has a third of the nation's Spanish speakers. The Southwest, in general, has a rich history with the Spanish language, and in many urban areas, like Los Angeles, Spanish can be heard everywhere. In southern California, in many occupations and worksites, virtually all the workers speak Spanish. Some observers of this situation feel concerned that language will become a rallying point for separateness.[21]

Yet, in a recent study, few Mexican American youth reported speaking Spanish at home, unless a family member was a recent immigrant. English monolingualism is associated with upward mobility. With no supports for continued development of their Spanish language, immigrant students not only fail to develop literacy in their native language, they begin to lose their oral skills. This research found that Latinos experience a less rapid shift toward only English compared with other immigrant groups, but it is a substantial shift nevertheless.[22]

Mexican Americans often have the option of choosing whether to identify with their Mexican ancestry or to ignore it in favor of a nonethnic or "American" identity. By the time they reach late adolescence, many Latino youth realize that the loss of their ability to communicate in Spanish means the loss of an important part of their ethnic identity. The process of relearning Spanish becomes embarrassing and painful. Mexican American students enroll in Spanish language classes in high school and are teased by peers or teachers because they cannot pronounce Spanish words or speak Spanish fluently. One student reported feeling so uncomfortable in Spanish class that he stopped taking the course. He explained: "And, Spanish, I don't like volunteering in there. I don't volunteer there. She gets mad at me. They expect me to volunteer since I'm Mexican, but I don't do it. The teacher gets mad at me. There are only, like two or three Mexicans in there. I told them, 'You know, if I knew Spanish, why would I be taking the class?'" Other students like this one are humiliated they do not know the language of their heritage, and to save face, they avoid situations in which they would have to interact in Spanish, making them even less likely to acquire new skills in the language.[23]

In the absence of policies promoting bilingualism, our children's intellectual and cultural resources in Spanish will likely be lost in two or three generations. Even highly educated parents, those who can afford extracurricular Spanish classes and tutors, do not have much chance of having their children and grandchildren maintain their Spanish language. Researchers found that while nine out of ten of the youths surveyed spoke a language other than English at home, almost the same proportion, 88 percent, preferred English by the end of high school. Another study examined patterns of language adaptation by more than 5,000 second-generation students in southern Florida and southern California. Among most immigrant students studied, knowledge of and preference for English was nearly universal, and only a minority remained fluent in their parents' languages. The authors concluded, "English is alive and well among second-generation youths, but the languages their immigrant parents brought with them are not".[24]

The researchers' findings suggest that linguistic assimilation and bilingualism are influenced by a complex process of causation. Socioeconomic status alone does not have a significant influence on maintaining the parental language, but socioeconomic status does play a role in whether a student will acquire good bilingual skills in both English and the home language. Latino students exhibit consistently higher levels of retention of their first language than Asian students, although it is not always accompanied by bilingualism. The authors note that this is likely because the use of Spanish is more strongly supported in the United States than the use of other foreign languages, and attachment to Spanish remains strong in Latin American immigrant communities. The researchers concur with other research literature on the positive intellectual effects of bilingualism, but they conclude that the passage of time will further diminish the proportion of those immigrant children who are able to speak their home language fluently.[25]

Language and Literacy

A variety of education studies have focused on the lingual and cultural diversity of families and communities as contexts for teaching reading.[26] Despite popular attention and discussion about social and cultural contexts that influence learning, most studies and research about teaching reading barely mention the complex issues of language diversity among literacy students.[27] In some cases, educators have been successful in using knowledge about children and their families to improve reading instruction and support.[28]

Second language literacy. Diane August and Kenji Hakuta directed a committee at the National Research Council charged with reviewing what is known about the linguistic, cognitive, and social processes involved in the education of English-language learners. They were asked to make recommendations regarding research priorities. According to their findings, second-language literacy is one of the key areas where research is lacking. They concluded that we know little about the nature of content learning and the ways that language learning and the structure of two languages might interact with learning in areas of second-language literacy. We do know that people successfully learn to read under a wide variety of circumstances. Many children learn to read with very little formal instruction. Yet a large group of normal children have problems learning to read and remain below reading level throughout elementary school and end up years behind their peers in secondary school. Many children who have problems learning to read come from low-income homes where the parents have little education and the children do not speak English as a first language. Both English monolingual and

Spanish-English bilingual Mexican-origin children are part of this group. Children from literate households who have been read to and whose parents are highly educated and read regularly are most likely to become successful readers. Children who learn to read quickly arrive at school understanding about letters, language, and symbolic systems. Important skills children must have at early stages of reading include abstract knowledge of the sound structure of language and the ability to rhyme, recognize particular sounds, and identify relationships among words.[29]

Acquiring these prerequisites for reading is complicated for Mexican-immigrant children learning English as a second language. Many recent Mexican immigrants come from rural Mexico, where the parents have had few opportunities to learn to read or write. Some agricultural communities provide few situations where it is necessary to use written language. Researchers have made several observations about literacy instruction. The types and uses of literacy vary among cultural groups and among the various homes within cultural groups. There is much discussion about the interplay among culture, first- and second-language learning, and learning to read. It has also been noted that lessons in reading and writing rarely extend beyond the classroom to incorporate ideas, interests, or activities of students and their families. Literacy instruction is heavily dependent on basal readers, and teachers usually decide what will be read or written. When teachers and researchers engage students in reading and writing projects initiated by students about topics of their interest, teachers gain a more sophisticated perspective on what students are capable of doing.[30]

Other research has shown that bilingual students do better on academic tasks when students have opportunities to develop academic skills in both languages. High levels of skill in Spanish first-language reading facilitate English second-language reading. Successful bilingual readers use certain strategies for comprehending both English and Spanish texts and use information from both languages to comprehend, make inferences from, and interpret unknown words. Generally, research suggests that children learn to read in a variety of different language circumstances, but literacy skills in one language usually facilitate learning in the second language.[31]

There have been ongoing controversies about the best ways to teach initial reading, with proponents of whole-language approaches on one side of the debate and proponents of phonics and direct instruction on the other. These debates shed little light on teaching Mexican-immigrant students or second-generation Mexican American students who struggle with reading. Most of the research in these debates has related to English-language speakers and not English-language learners. Some researchers now suggest that a smart approach to teaching reading might be to combine direct instruction of reading mechanics with meaningful communication and literacy activities. Often, immigrant students lack the background knowledge and familiarity with the vocabulary needed to promote successful reading in English. Nonetheless, the research demonstrates that children from low-literacy homes with a number of risk factors can learn to read in a second language if they receive sound instruction.[32]

A number of issues affect the approaches used to teach reading and writing to English-language learning students. Some sociocultural knowledge may be more valued than other knowledge. For example, experiences of a low-income, Mexican-immigrant child may not count as much in the classroom or when taking tests as experiences of a White or a Mexican child from a middle-class home. Teachers who understand the family backgrounds of students can contribute in special ways to children learning to read and becoming more comfortable in school settings. The ways schools approach literacy with families and children affect what children think of themselves as learners.[33]

An intergenerational approach. Vivian L. Gadsden recommends an intergenerational learning framework based on *family cultures*. Family cultures are defined as sources of knowledge that elaborate upon or expand the reading experiences of children within school and home. These family cultures, much like the home visits in the Funds of Knowledge project discussed in Chapter 2, are based on family histories; the practices of parents, grandparents, and great-grandparents; accepted ethnic traditions and cultural rituals; histories of the community; religious practices and beliefs; and the various roles individual family members play within particular families over time. Assumptions about race, discrimination, and cultural differences are also deeply embedded in family cultures. Parents, grandparents, and other adults in the community transmit knowledge, beliefs, and practices to children through formal teaching and informal activities. Adults also learn from the children, particularly in immigrant families. Children are exposed to more extensive uses of English and English literacy than their parents and are the first to learn the culture of their peers and the cultures of the wider U.S. society. Family cultures also influence how family members use literacy and their persistence in education programs.

In a Philadelphia Head Start program, Gadsden found that Mexican-origin parents were eager to improve their children's literacy to empower the children and adults in the communities to combat societal inequities. Parents' views about literacy, the ways they defined literacy, the literacies they valued most, and the value they assigned to literacy in general were critical. Understanding the values of these families helped teachers understand the behaviors of their preschool and school-age children. Some parents explained in interviews that teachers could encourage children to want to learn or discourage them from learning. The ways teachers organized reading instruction could make reading seem easy or hard. Parents recognized the difference between teachers who look down on and have low expectations of children who speak with accents and teachers who respect the diversity of the children in their classrooms and used books reflecting different ideas. These families' ideas, beliefs, and perceptions about literacy impacted learning and the meaning of success.[34]

Models of literacy instruction. Too often, program planners who view Mexican-immigrant children as coming from deficit home environments and deficit communities organize programs to change parents and homes. Focus on deficits rather than strengths leads to further stigmatization of children from low-income ethnic-minority backgrounds and alienates families and communities from the programs intended to serve them.[35]

A better understanding of Mexican-immigrant children's home culture, language use, and patterns of social interaction can help make education programs more effective. For example, one research team is studying a group of children from low-income homes from age three through middle school. Their goal is to identify home and classroom supports for the language and literacy development of low-income children and to trace the impact of early experiences and development of skills on later literacy. In their observations of teacher-child interactions, the researchers are recording when teacher talk is addressed to children, what the content of the talk is about, whether the teacher dominates verbal interactions or allows the child to initiate the conversations and participate, and whether the teacher talk elaborates and develops topics. The research focuses on what features of children's social and linguistic environments help them develop language and literacy skills and on factors affecting their ability to learn a second language. This kind of research can help teachers of Mexican-immigrant children analyze their behaviors in the classroom and orient their classrooms toward positive child growth and development.[36]

Incorporating family cultures. In a recent article, Gadsden describes how a second-grade teacher used family cultures success-fully in her New York City classroom to engage parents and students in reading and writing. The teacher planned the project over the summer by exploring her own family culture through interviews with family members, reading materials in her family records, and keeping a journal of ideas. She began the school year by visiting the families of each of her students. At a group meeting, 25 parents agreed to participate in weekly exchanges of information and monthly meetings to learn about family cultures and to share literacy events and experiences. Students, parents, and the teacher designed field trips, reading activities, and projects centered on family cultures of each of the students. They kept journals and read quantities of materials. The teacher and parents met to discuss family experi-ences, cultural expectations, and contributions. Parents and chil-dren participated in several literacy activities together inside and outside of school. Children developed family stories, shared them with other children, read books, and compared the books with their own stories. Over the year, the children showed an increased willing-ness to read and made modest improvements in reading fluency and comprehension.

In this project, the teacher's role changed from one of being the "source of knowledge" to one of creating opportunities for mutual exchanges of knowledge. She had to confront her own assumptions about her students and their families while the parents had to build their own literacy skills. But the students, parents, and teacher were all committed to improving the children's literacy, increasing the children's interest in learning, and constructing new curricula that responded to the multicultural histories of students. This process created a deep understanding of the nature of home and community cultures, how parents use literacy, their potential contributions to children's literacies, and recognition that learning is two directional: from home to school and from school to home.

Gadsden argues in her article that this kind of cultural engagement is necessary if we are to involve children in learning and keep them involved. Her research suggests that the cultural and social practices of children and their families tell us about the strengths of the families and the ways families prepare their children for school. A family culture approach to literacy enabled these families to access and use school and teacher resources more effectively.[37]

Success for All. As discussed earlier, recent-immigrant children are isolated in many separate newcomer programs, separated out for intensive ESL instruction, or placed in sheltered content classes in which regular subject matter is presented by a teacher sensitive to the learners' special language needs. In many programs for immigrant students, education services are provided to children through the practice of pulling them out of class for remedial instruction. The students' learning experiences lack integration, and teachers do not work together to coordinate content. Additionally, much instructional time is lost in the transitions between regular and pullout sessions. In contrast, the Success for All program was designed to ensure that all school personnel would work together to promote the success of every child.

The ESL teachers work with reading teachers to integrate the instruction in English with the requirements for success in the regular classroom program. The reading teachers know how to build on learners' skills in their first language to teach English language reading. Students proceed through a well-specified hierarchy of skills. They are tested at each level to determine readiness to move on to the next skill. Careful records are kept of each student's progress, and these data are used to make grouping, remediation, and other decisions. Students are constantly grouped and regrouped. Teachers deliver most instruction to groups of students at the same instructional level. Tutors work one-on-one with students who have difficulties keeping up with their reading groups.

Family Support Teams provide parenting education and work to involve parents in reading to their children at home, volunteering within the school, and working with teachers to help each child reach his or her highest potential. All parents are encouraged to support their children's success in school. Children who do not attend school regularly or who misbehave in class receive family support assistance. There is a concerted effort by staff and parents to help students achieve.

The Success for All program has been implemented with positive learning outcomes in a number of areas with high concentrations of Mexican-immigrant children and in schools with varying characteristics. Language of instruction has not been the most important variable in this program. Keys to the Success for All approach have been (1) high expectations for all children to be successful, (2) excellent quality of instruction, (3) appropriate levels of instruction, (4) incentives to make the program work, and (5) time in the program to make the most impact on student achievement.

Research, summarized by Robert E. Slavin and Nancy A. Madden, shows that reading performance has been low for English-language learners in high-poverty schools without any special program, whether they are taught in English or their home language. By comparison, English language learners in the Success for All schools have scored better than their control counterparts, with many students scoring at grade level or above on individually administered tests. Slavin and Madden conclude that more research is needed to understand better how reading programs, such as the Success for All project, affect English language learners. The authors suggest that in-depth qualitative investigations of instructional practices are needed to look at how practices in bilingual programs and ESL programs differ and to determine which instructional strategies best ensure the success of immigrant students.[38]

Organizing Schools for Mexican-Immigrant Student Success

A growing body of research identifies characteristics of programs that effectively meet the needs of Mexican-immigrant students.[39] Many of these characteristics describe good schools in general; others are specific to immigrant students. Successful programs for second-language learners tend to include seven key components: (1) valuing students' home languages and cultures, (2) adequate assessment of language proficiency and academic needs, (3) positive school leadership, (4) outreach and communication in the parents' home languages, (5) instruction based on previous educational experience, (6) reducing the isolation of immigrant students, and (7) transitions from school to work or college. Each of these components is discussed in this section.

1. Valuing students' home languages and cultures. Helping immigrant students maintain attachments to their cultures of origin is essential to a good education and nurtures a deep respect for U.S. society. Teachers can incorporate the home culture in class while teaching majority culture norms by including it in curriculum materials, building on the home language in instruction, and observing the values and norms present in the home culture. Trying to make sense of a whole new culture, language, and way of life can be very difficult for students who have spent a portion of their childhoods in another place. The home culture and the U.S. culture may have different expectations for student behavior, parent involvement, sex roles, and what it means to be mature and responsible.[40]

Effective programs for immigrant students recognize that individuals cannot lose their home cultures without losing their identities. Immigrant students should not be faced with a choice between rejecting their own cultures and assimilating in order to do well at school or resisting majority cultural norms, which often leads to failure in school.[41] One study found that successful students were more acculturated (that is, they had taken what they needed from American culture); had clearer senses of themselves (based in both their native culture and their ability to negotiate American culture); had higher occupational aspirations; and desired stable, responsible jobs.[42] Including references to students' cultures in the learning environment helps them make that positive transition. Teaching across the United States must take into account our increasingly complex understanding of ourselves as living within a multicultural reality. In the Southwest, for example, U.S. culture has evolved along with Mexican culture, and this multiculturalism provides an interesting and healthy base for high school curricula.

2. Adequate assessment of language proficiency and academic needs. One of the most troublesome practices for new immigrants is the use of standardized testing. Assessment of immigrant students should be embedded in teaching and learning, and it should be used to inform skillful and adaptive teaching that leads to greater student success, not to sort students into low-level classes.[43]

Language assessment can help schools identify the immigrant students in their schools and recruit them to the programs that best meet their needs. But, the availability of adequate tests for language-minority students remains a problem.[44] The most common methods schools use to determine a student's English language proficiency involve tests of oral proficiency in English, focusing on vocabulary, grammar, and ability to produce basic English sentences. Few tests assess students' reading and writing skills. Many schools also use a home language survey that asks students to report the language most often used in their homes, the language they first learned, and the students' dominant language. To meet students' needs best, schools should determine—whether through formal tests or informal teacher assessments—students' proficiency and academic achievement in their native languages as well as in English.

Standardized tests in English cannot provide an accurate assessment of the skills of immigrant students who are learning a new language, adjusting to a new culture, and dealing with traumas of immigration. These students may need more than the usual nine months associated with the grade level learning that is the basis for determining progress on standardized tests.[45]

School staff need adequate assessment tools to determine language proficiency and academic achievement levels of immigrant students to place them in appropriate classes. Problems of academic performance of new arrivals who know little English should not be confused with the achievement problems of second-generation immigrants who have mastered English but lack strong reading, writing, or mathematics skills. Mexican-immigrant students have too often been viewed as lacking intellectual ability, instead of lacking English proficiency. IQ tests, standardized tests, and, more recently, competency tests have been used too frequently to channel language-minority students into low-level classes, labeling them as mentally retarded and discouraging them from higher education. Effective programs recognize the wide range of language proficiencies and academic skills among immigrant students and address those needs accordingly. Schools need to maintain achievement data on immigrant students and compare their achievement with that of the general student population so their programs for immigrant students can be improved when necessary. Maintaining follow-up achievement data for former immigrant students could help school personnel see how these students perform over time.

3. Positive school leadership. Teachers' and counselors' negative feelings about immigrant students tend to be reflected in their expectations of the immigrant pupils. Controversies over controlling immigration, restricting immigrant students' access to schooling, and debates surrounding bilingual education spill over into the classroom and school interactions. Many factors affecting immigrant students' integration into schools, such as educational guidance they receive and teachers' attitudes toward them, relate to school atmosphere and staff behavior toward immigrant students. Successful teachers have high expectations of immigrant students and confidence in their abilities to learn. Teachers who are effective with immigrant students are able to create classroom communities that promote student learning. Making immigrant students a priority often means offering special programs to meet their distinct needs. Good programs provide strong academic skills and opportunities for caring adults to interact with immigrant youth.

Mexican-immigrant students are more likely to attend segregated schools today than in 1954 when the U.S. Supreme Court's *Brown* decision desegregated schools.[46] Whether they attend all-Latino schools or ethnically mixed schools, immigrant students are easily identifiable and often targets of racism. Their experiences with discrimination are often reflected in their general feelings of satisfaction or dissatisfaction with school. Students who have experienced racism from peers or negative attitudes from teachers are less motivated to go to school than students who have not suffered in this way. Teachers and counselors need to be aware of the effects of racism and negative attitudes and should have skills to help students mediate these situations.

The vast majority of teachers and administrators are White, a circumstance unlikely to change in the near future. Few have had personal experiences dealing with other cultures or non-English speakers. And, a large number of poor and immigrant students are taught during their entire school careers by the least-qualified teachers.[47] Strong school leadership must assure that immigrant students, as well as all other students, have experienced and well-trained teachers.

4. Outreach and communication in the parents' home languages. Limited-English-proficient and undereducated parents are often dependent upon their children to navigate the schools and learn the host country's language. A strong factor in an immigrant child's school success is the educational level of the immigrant parents, especially the mother. Studies have shown teachers and administrators expect immigrant children to have educated family members who are familiar with how schools work and who can help their children with homework in ways that complement teachers' efforts. When immigrant children's families do not fulfill these expectations, school personnel often assume parental neglect, troubled homes, or lack of interest in education. In fact, compared with parents of nonimmigrant students, a number of barriers cause immigrant families to be substantially less involved in school functions or as volunteers. Some of the most daunting barriers include lack of English language skills or knowledge about the education system in the United States, fear of deportation, demands of small children at home, and embarrassment due to limited literacy skills. Failure to understand these barriers has led some school staff to criticize Mexican families in the United States as passive, inactive, uncaring about education, and unwilling to participate in school activities.[48]

Immigrant parents tend to participate more in elementary schools than in later schooling. Persons with limited-English-literacy skills tend to have more opportunities to participate in early childhood educational activities, and children in elementary school are less likely to discourage parental involvement, unlike most adolescents, who get embarrassed when their parents come to the school. Good programs recognize the family's vital role in a child's education and find ways to encourage parents to participate. Parents who have high educational expectations for their children and engage them in extensive school-related discussions can help their children overcome other risk factors.[49] Enabling parents to have these discussions often requires providing information in a language they understand and working with a wide range of education levels, including parents who cannot read or write or even sign their names in their native languages.

Schools also need to recognize that some immigrant youth do not have parents who can become involved in their schooling. Decisions that youth usually make with help from their parents become the sole responsibility of the adolescents themselves when they live with siblings or unrelated adults instead of their biological parents, or when their parents do not read or speak English. Parents may have remained in the sending country or may have followed the migrant stream, leaving older children behind to attend school. In focus group meetings I conducted with immigrant students, one high school student explained that her parents attended activities at the primary school with her younger brothers and sisters, but at the high school, her parents were uncomfortable about participating in activities because of their poor English skills. She was the oldest child and knew some English, so she was expected to resolve her own school problems and help her parents resolve those of her younger siblings. Other adolescents reported living with older brothers, sisters, or other relatives and not having parents to become involved in their education. Even in families with parents in the home, older siblings oriented younger siblings to the ways of the school, helped with homework, and modeled positive school behaviors.[50] These roles of siblings are especially important in immigrant families in which parents have low levels of schooling and are unfamiliar with the U.S. school system. School staff must be sensitive to immigrant family structures and accommodate them in their outreach efforts.

5. Instruction based on previous educational experience. Studies have shown that certain problems of immigrant children's adaptation are closely related to age of arrival and length of residence in the host country. Language difficulties, interrupted education, the conditions under which immigration has taken place, plus lack of previous school experience all affect immigrant students' school achievement. Knowledge of the English language remains one of the major educational problems of immigrant students in the United States. Other studies show that although the situation improves with time, this problem particularly affects children who enroll in U.S. schools at older ages. It takes immigrant students five or six years to get sufficient command of English to do strong academic work in that language. Pre-high-school experience is an essential factor in increasing immigrant students' high school success. Immigrant students who arrive at older ages without previous school experiences are definitely disadvantaged, both socially and academically. Both primary and secondary schools must have programs in place for older students who enroll without appropriate grade level skills. In most situations, U.S. high school teachers are not prepared to deal with adolescent students who cannot read in Spanish or English. In these circumstances, teachers need training to teach basic literacy skills to young adults.[51]

6. Reducing the isolation of immigrant students. School programs that track all low-achieving students or all immigrant students together deprive those students of the most interesting classes and the most talented teachers. Because many of the newest immigrant parents are poorly educated or lack English skills, they are likely to be tracked into the lowest level classes. A good education program will attempt to integrate immigrant children with high-achieving students in at least some classes.

7. Transitions from school to work or college. School-to-work programs that teach high-level skills are important for immigrant students who do not plan to go to college. Although most jobs offering the prospect of upward mobility require graduation from high school, the transition from school to work precedes high school graduation for many Latino immigrant students. Other programs help bridge the gap between high school graduation requirements and college entry expectations. Two examples are (1) the International High School, a collaborative curriculum project developed by New York colleges and public schools, and (2) special summer programs, such as Upward Bound, that bring immigrant high school students to college campuses for tutoring and college orientation.

Provisions that have helped keep immigrant students in school include coordinated social services, counseling, tutoring, enrichment activities, health-service referrals, job training and placement, self-paced curricula, workplace English and literacy instruction, and evening school classes. Initiatives that lead to associate degrees (or to other certification from community or technical colleges) are important options for many immigrant students. To help them plan for these postsecondary programs, students need knowledge of career options, high-quality high school programs, support services, interagency coordination, and family support.[52]

The career academy approach, another successful school-to-work experiment, forms partnerships with local employers to help keep students in school while teaching marketable skills. Small schools-within-schools combine academics with occupation-oriented courses built around themes such as business and finance, public service, electronics, and the health professions. Employers help develop the curriculum and provide internships and apprenticeships. The Manpower Demonstration Research Corporation evaluated several career academies around the country and found that they gave teachers greater opportunities to collaborate with colleagues, provided smaller classes, and created a family atmosphere that encouraged students to succeed. The career academy approach can be adapted to a wide variety of school settings and appeals to both low and high achievers. These programs appear to have been successful in keeping immigrant students enrolled in school.[53]

Migrant Students: A Special Group with Special Needs

Many migrant students enter school late in the school year and withdraw early to migrate with their families. Others drop out of school but try to return when their lives are more stable. A successful schooling experience for Mexican-immigrant and migrant students demands that teachers, counselors, and administrators have sensitivity and understanding of the mobile lives of migrant students and their families. Flexible instructional programming that allows students to drop out of school to work or take care of family responsibilities and that allows them to return and pick up their academic work without penalties is essential for migrant student success. Multiple "second-chance" opportunities for education and training—at worksites, community centers, churches, and school sites—should be made available. This flexibility also demands that these projects coordinate their instructional programs.

Flexible options, along with programs and services to combat high drop-out rates, are essential at the secondary level. The Migrant Attrition Project estimates a 45 percent national drop-out rate for migrant students. Conditions that lead to leaving school early include: (1) overage grade placement, (2) poverty, (3) interrupted school attendance, (4) inconsistent record keeping, and (5) limited English proficiency.[54]

Links to college. Texas has the largest interstate migrant student enrollment in the nation with about 110,300 migrant students identified by the Texas Education Agency. Many of these students are English-language learners. The University of Texas (UT) has enrolled over 6,000 migrant students in its award-winning Migrant Student Program since the program began in 1986.[55]

Distance learning courses—usually accessed by computer—provide enriched content designed especially for migrant students. The content is presented in short units written at a lower reading level, with extra attention paid to basic reading and writing skills. Each unit includes vocabulary development through reinforcement and practice exercises. Interactive lessons feature graphics that reinforce concepts and structure and teach study skills. All courses are approved by the Texas Education Agency, count toward high school graduation, and fulfill the Texas legislative requirements for course work. The UT Migrant Program offers college-level and high school courses that can be completed on the World Wide Web and are computer graded. Students can enroll via computer, and both students and authorized high school officials can check their progress and grades electronically. Up-to-date information about new courses, courses being planned and written, and new policies and laws affecting distance education are made available on the UT electronic mail list.

Examples of the wide range of subjects offered in the UT Migrant Program are as follows:

- The economics course covers the U.S. free enterprise system, international economics, consumer concerns, banking policies, and income taxes. Students purchase a required textbook that is used in standard university or high school classes.

- The English literature course includes nine lessons and a final exam and covers various forms of literature with an emphasis on developing writing, reading, and analytical skills. Reading selections include modern and classical fiction and nonfiction and emphasize cultural diversity. Grammar, concepts, writing assignments, and activities to develop communication skills are included in each lesson. Passing the course provides a semester credit in English.

- Some courses, such as health education, include a computer program that provides tutoring and computer-graded lessons that can be worked on as many times as needed to prepare for the final exam.

- A distance learning course, Algebra Across the Wire program, meets the special needs of migrant students by delivering primary instruction via an audio conference format. Students attend class four or five days a week, depending upon the number of weeks the course is offered at their location. Depending on the individual site, four-, six-, and eight-week sessions are offered each summer, with both daytime and evening classes. Students receive lesson plans, worksheets, and handouts designed by the instructors. The average grade in the pilot session in the summer of 1992 was 88 percent. The completion rate over the history of the course has been 95 percent.

The UT Migrant Student Program also provides support services for school districts, students, and parents. The program offers training sessions for tutors and counselors, orientation sessions for students, interstate coordination when students migrate across state lines, bilingual materials and presentations for parents, a national toll-free telephone line for assistance with work, and an annual visit to the University of Texas at Austin campus. A $125-per-course fee covers the study guide, textbook, and parent materials (study guides and textbooks also can be bought separately). A limited number of scholarships is available for migrant students who have been retained one or more times or have failed one or more sections of the Texas Assessment of Academic Skills (TAAS) test. At the option of the local school district, students can earn credit for some courses by passing an appropriate essential knowledge and skills test. Migrant students are also allowed to take exams to make up work missed because of early withdrawal or late reentry into their Texas schools. Each school district sets its own eligibility criteria for the program.

The College Assistance Migrant Program (CAMP) is a federally funded program designed to support freshmen college students from migrant and seasonal farmworker backgrounds. CAMP provides assistance in getting admitted to one of the six affiliated colleges and universities, including placement testing, tutoring, financial aid advising, career counseling, and help with summer job searches or placement. Students are eligible for the CAMP program if they or their parents have worked in migrant or seasonal farmwork for a minimum of seventy-five days during the 24 months prior to applying for college or if a student has participated in a high school migrant education program. Students must meet regular admission requirements of the college, although in some cases, a student with a General Equivalency Diploma (GED) and average GED test score of 58 (with no single test score lower than 40) may be considered. The participating colleges and universities work with students to help them get the support they need to complete college.

St. Edward's University has a special application form for CAMP that asks citizenship status, educational data including ACT or SAT scores, and recommendations from two teachers and a counselor. Students must verify family employment history and document all migrant or seasonal farmwork-related activity. They must write a 200-word composition about how they think the CAMP program and St. Edward's University can help them reach their educational and personal goals and discuss preferred courses of study and individual academic strengths and weaknesses.

Jeremias Alvarez is one of St. Edward's CAMP students. Alvarez was valedictorian of his graduating class in Presidio, a small town in west Texas along the U.S.-Mexico border. During his freshman year in the CAMP program, he maintained a perfect grade point average. In his sophomore year, he was selected as one of five distinguished Brown Scholars, an elite program for upperclassmen at St. Edward's University funded by the Brown Foundation. The honor came with a $5,000 scholarship. Each Brown Scholar carries a full class load and must put in 10-20 community-service hours each week. As part of the Brown Scholar program, Alvarez plans to develop a student-written student-designed newsletter with low-income students at an elementary school near St. Edward's University. He is majoring in international business and Spanish with a minor in communications. He has been invited to spend his junior year in China as a visiting scholar. The CAMP program helps students like Alvarez complete all the requirements for college enrollment and offers a summer orientation program. CAMP provides monthly stipends, a book allowance, and a travel allowance for winter and spring breaks. The counselors help the CAMP students seek scholarships and financial aide to finance the remaining college expenses.[56]

CHAPTER 4

Gender Issues in Mexican American Schooling

A young person's decision to leave high school without earning a diploma drastically reduces his or her chances for well-paying employment or for entering higher education and professional careers. Leaving school early particularly affects Latina females, who face greater barriers than males when seeking high-wage jobs and opportunities in postsecondary education. This chapter uses the lens of gender to look at the achievement of Mexican-immigrant and second-generation students. First, we explore gender role attitudes that strongly affect male and female Mexican immigrant students both within families and in U.S. classrooms. Peers also play a powerful role in influencing gender role attitudes—through pressures, gangs, sexual harassment, and friendships. We conclude this chapter by recommending actions that will enable schools to be more supportive of both Latino males and females.

Gender Role Attitudes

Gender role attitudes in U.S. society, our schools, and Latino families contribute to girls' and boys' educational performances. Latino family patterns, cultural practices and values, and socioeconomic integration are in a state of transition, and many real-life situations show these changes. Still, strong sex-role stereotypes representing Latinas as passive, submissive underachievers and Latinos as macho, aggressive, and dominant in male-female relationships persist and are often reinforced by family, school, and media.[1]

Traditional Catholic beliefs and values have idealized the submissive role for women and identified women as virgins, mothers, and martyrs who are altruistic and self-denying.[2] Breaking away from these traditional values may be seen as abandonment of the Catholic church and the family. The strong persistence of these stereotypical beliefs, despite changing realities of women's roles, makes it difficult for Mexican-immigrant women and men to break out of these stereotypes.

Discriminatory educational practices persist, such as tracking girls out of math and science and into low-paying "women's work" and neglecting the educational needs of girls because of their "good behavior" while rewarding boys for the academic content of their work. Omitting female experiences and perspectives in curriculum materials and textbooks also has a detrimental effect on all female students. Discriminatory practices may affect Latinas especially; they often experience "triple oppression" because of class, ethnicity, and gender. Challenges in school and in the home are even more complex for recent Mexican-immigrant girls than for mainstream girls. Mexican-immigrant females must deal with stereotypes and expectations of their particular ethnic group and also must cope with powerful gender expectations in their home cultures. Additionally, many Mexican-immigrant girls experience isolation and alienation because of limited English-language proficiency. Mexican-immigrant teenagers often must negotiate their ways through two or three cultures when grappling with gender and ethnic identity issues as they enter adolescence. To do so successfully requires family support. Close collaboration among educators, family, and community members familiar with the concerns of local Latinas is absolutely essential for Latina academic success.[3]

The role of the family. Discussions of *familism* (the behavioral and cultural patterns that reflect strong emotional and value commitments to family life) frame the research literature on Latino families. For most Latinos, the family is the dominant source of advice and assistance. Among Mexican immigrants and second-generation Mexicans, the family is a nurturing and protective unit, believed to be more important than any individual member. The family provides a sense of belonging and well-being in a cooperative environment. Even as multiple generations cease living under the same roof and as educational levels increase, the family remains the central institution in shaping the Latino experience. Even the more acculturated third-generation Mexican-origin youth continue to have high levels of contact with extended kin and report the continued importance of kin as sources of support and recreation.[4]

Over the past 30 years, there have been dramatic changes in Latino family characteristics similar to the changes occurring in all families, including lower marriage and fertility rates, fewer two-parent families, and reduced economic status for most families. The majority of Latino families are married couples, but a large percentage are female-headed families. In 1996 more than two-thirds (67.6%) of Latino families were headed by a married couple, but more than one-fourth (25.5%) were female-headed households. Although Latino families are undergoing considerable restructuring in response to demographic and cultural changes, their adaptations are not simply imitating the dominant Anglos. Mexican-origin families, regardless of social class, still provide family members with strong senses of culture, values, and worldview, although the values and cultural rituals have changed considerably from generation to generation.[5]

The women in an extended Latino family derive much culturally sanctioned power and authority from their roles as wives and mothers. In traditional Latino culture, attachments to the home are strong, and attending school or working away from the home is unnecessary for esteem. Mothers can exert powerful influences on their sons' and daughters' education and career choices, as well as their academic success. Involving recent-immigrant parents in school activities helps them feel a part of their sons' and daughters' lives outside the family, instead of feeling they are losing a child to American culture.[6]

Cultural norms in Latino families often preclude the explicit discussion of sexuality. Their relatively high birthrates, compared with non-Latino Whites, can be attributed, in part, to their lack of knowledge of contraceptives, low rates of contraceptive use, and low likelihood of seeking an abortion once pregnant. Family members often believe that proper care of children can occur only in an informal setting with a person who is familiar with the family or at least with the language and culture. It follows that a career or the pursuit of educational goals should not entail leaving children in child-care centers or with strangers. In a recent study, a larger percentage of immigrant Latina teens reported their intentions to be housewives and mothers, compared with U.S. teens. Most mothers from low socioeconomic backgrounds do not model postsecondary educational and professional career aspirations for their daughters.[7]

Traditional values can cause severe conflicts among young women and men who aspire to leave home to attend college or take well-paying jobs in cities far away from their families. Even though they value education, parents who are uncertain about the future and depressed about their own livelihood may not talk to their children about going to college. As a result, even Latino male and female students who are above average achievers may think about leaving school or may choose to work and help support their families rather than pursue higher education.

Other influences. Media and family members reinforce gender roles from the day a child is born; these roles are accentuated among teenagers. Working-class Mexican American females often experience conflicts among traditional roles of motherhood and family responsibilities and academic success. In some cases, girls deal with these conflicts by having liberal gender roles in one setting and not in another. For example, a study of Mexican-origin teens involved in a Latina mother-daughter program in Texas found that the girls had liberal attitudes toward gender roles in school. The girls believed females should attend college and were as competent as males. But within families, they were more traditional. In interviews, the girls mentioned wanting careers that allow time for families and placing careers on hold for families. Another study found that equal male-female role attitudes among high school girls contribute positively to self-image, self-esteem, sex-role orientation, and achievement and encourage girls to think of a broadened array of work, career, and family possibilities. Other studies have found that gender attitudes signal whether girls will pursue stereotypical vocations and familial paths or seek higher education and careers.[8]

Teen Pregnancies

According to information from the National Center for Health Statistics, Latina teens are most likely of all racial and ethnic groups to give birth. Among Latino groups, Mexican-origin teenage births have been the highest. Latinas are least likely to report premarital sexual intercourse, but, because they are also least likely to use contraception, they are most at risk for pregnancy. Childbearing patterns of young Latinas are also affected by the economic environments in which they live, with poor teens much more likely to become mothers than their nonpoor counterparts. Teens who become pregnant today are more likely to graduate from high school than in the 1970s, when school policies encouraged them to leave school. Now, high schools often provide day-care centers within the school and encourage young mothers to remain in school until graduation. Nonetheless, teen motherhood is difficult for the mother, the families involved, and the babies.[9]

Most teens in the United States who have had babies in the 1990s have been single mothers. In 1994, 76 percent of teen mothers of all ethnic groups gave birth outside of marriage, compared with 30 percent in 1970. Struggling to care for a child as a single parent makes it much more difficult to attend school. One group that monitors statistics on children reported in 1996 that 62 percent of high-school-age girls who had given birth had dropped out of school at some point; almost a quarter of those girls had dropped out before the pregnancy.[10]

Evidence shows that Latinas aged 15 to 19 are more than two times as likely as White teens to become teen parents. Latina teen mothers are also more likely to drop out of school than White or Black teen mothers.[11] Latinas are less likely to abort pregnancies than White or Black teens, which may be related to lack of access to abortion options or to a cultural commitment to the family and personal religious beliefs about abortion. Latinas who marry are also more likely to marry young, compared with other ethnic groups. Births among these married teenage mothers are counted as teen pregnancies.

A study by the Academy for Educational Development reported a third of the 9- to 15-year-old girls they surveyed cited pregnancy or marriage as the reason for leaving school. Latina females had the sharpest declines in self-esteem during adolescence, and a girl's role within her family was an important ingredient to her overall self-esteem. Only 38 percent of Latinas in high school felt good about themselves within their families, compared with 59 percent in middle school and 79 percent in elementary school. According to the Academy study, 83 percent of Latina high school students reported disapproval of the homemaker role, but about a third of those disapproving believed they would eventually assume that role. These results indicate Latinas are less likely than other young women in U.S. society to find support at home or in school for high educational achievement.[12]

Teen pregnancy may be linked to some teens' perceptions that few other outcomes are available to them. Most college-bound teens postpone childbearing because they perceive benefits in continuing their education without the distractions of raising a family. Students doing well in school are motivated to avoid parenthood because they believe premature pregnancies will interfere with achieving their educational goals. The opposite is true for students who are doing poorly in school. These students perceive little to gain by staying in school because they do not believe in obtaining a high-paying job or attending college are not within their grasps. In contrast, having a baby often brings rewards of marriage, higher family status as mothers, and gifts and attention to the baby. Thus, a lack of educational and occupational opportunities may produce higher teenage pregnancy rates among the Latinas. However, teenage pregnancy does not have to result in leaving school if the family is supportive of the teen mother and school programs allow her to continue taking courses toward the diploma.[13]

A study of pregnant Latina teenagers in New York revealed that Black women were more likely than Latinas to return to school once they had left, and Latina immigrants were least likely to return.[14] High educational aspirations and modern gender-role attitudes encouraged returning to school. Latinas are often left to struggle with how to respond to parental and family expectations and fit into a high school culture that emphasizes romantic love, couples, and proms.

The commonly held belief that pregnancy accounts for most female school dropouts is false. In reality, more than half of the girls who leave school before receiving a high school diploma do so for other reasons. Girls, like boys, drop out because schooling becomes irrelevant to their lives or too uncomfortable to stay. Nonetheless, discrimination against pregnant teens and teenage mothers is still common in schools across the country.

The research on gender roles shows clearly that gender identities are continually being socially constructed within a diversity of contexts and institutions. Gender roles are constrained by workplaces, households, and communities. They are affected by social-class differences, age differences, immigration status, and racial and ethnic realities. Yet, even as families change over generations, Latino family roles continue to exert strong influences on Latino youth. These adolescents feel a sense of obligation to family, common among immigrants and second-generation youths. This sense of obligation remains strong even among adolescents exposed to the dominant American culture, which is more oriented toward individualism. Some research suggests several reasons for these differences. Immigrant parents often rationalize their material sacrifices by anticipating a better future for their children, and, because the children understand the many sacrifices and hardships endured by their parents, this awareness might influence the children's sense of obligation to their parents. As second-generation youths become more Americanized, they experience increased tensions between parental authority and peer pressures. Still, for Latino youth, the family remains a key institution, and, as a result, peers do not necessarily achieve the powerful influence that they do in the lives of Anglo American adolescents.[15]

Several studies suggest that bilingualism and a firm sense of ethnic identity help Latina teenagers overcome some gender barriers, enhancing school success. Both Latino males and females draw on their cohesive families and their language and culture as sources of strength. Latino families foster values and behaviors conducive to achieving in school, but that achievement motivation is tempered by many experiences within and outside the family. Often, first-generation Mexican-immigrant youths become skeptical and ambivalent about school as they perceive diminished opportunities to do well.[16]

School Factors

As discussed above, the family plays a key role in encouraging or discouraging modern gender-role attitudes and school persistence.

But an alienating school also can be a strong contributing factor to school leaving. Other school factors include tracking and inadequate counseling and classroom biases.[17]

Tracking and inadequate counseling. Vocational education enrollments clearly show that Latinas have been steered into jobs with little career or income potential. In Denver, for example, young women made up 44 percent of the total vocational enrollment, but 90 percent of these students ended up in home economics and clerical jobs with low pay and little career potential. In Texas, Latina high school students frequently have enrolled in cosmetology classes or have been tracked into general education non-college-prep programs. A recent study found that few vocational programs encouraged Latinas to enter nontraditional fields or offered them reasons to remain in school. Limited choices were evident even when Latinas expressed interest in nontraditional fields, such as medicine, law, or academia. They tended to consign themselves to internal occupational segregation in specialties such as nursing, pediatrics, family law, child development, and elementary education. They saw their salaries as "helping" to support the family and their careers as secondary to those of their future husbands.[18]

Research also shows that counselors have acted historically as social selectors to influence which students attended college, often with biases against individuals of low socioeconomic status, minorities, and women. Sociological studies of counselors and tracking have raised public awareness about these issues and may have dissuaded counselors from engaging in biased guidance. Also, the growth of community colleges has dramatically increased opportunities to go to college; as a result, many more Latinos attend some form of college. A criticism now is that counselors may provide too little guidance. Students may not be getting the needed information, advice, and preparation to help them make good decisions about college or work. Latinos may have very little help in making realistic life choices and future plans. Also, many students may be arriving at college unprepared to complete college and without the benefit of discussing the high costs of college tuition, forgone wages, and the sacrifices and commitment that college requires.[19]

Classroom biases. A number of studies indicate that instructional materials frequently reflect sexual stereotypes and that such materials play a part in generating and maintaining disadvantages that girls experience in schools and society. A review of literature on instructional materials reaches the following conclusions: (1) many commonly used instructional materials are sex biased, (2) sex-biased language distorts students' perceptions of reality, (3) gender-equitable instructional materials can broaden attitudes about gender roles and can also increase motivation to learn, and (4) gender-equitable instructional materials influence students' sex-role behaviors. For example, when children hear stories or see films that present stereotyped behaviors, they may imitate these behaviors. The same is true when they see equitable sex-role behaviors and nontraditional gender roles—they may learn and imitate more equitable behaviors.[20]

Despite a narrowing of the "gender gap" in verbal and mathematical performance in high schools across the country, girls continue to trail boys. Even girls who take the same mathematics and science courses as boys and perform equally as well on tests are much less likely to pursue scientific or technological careers than their male classmates. Girls are more likely to be exposed to biology-related classes and are less likely to have experiences with mechanical activities and electronics. Boys use more scientific instruments. Girls are more likely than boys to doubt themselves in math. Perceptions about being good at math decrease as girls move up in high school. One result of this lack of confidence is that girls tend to drop out of higher-level math and science courses, even though they can do the work. In one study, for example, Latina girls took more Advanced Placement (AP) *courses* than boys but took fewer Advanced Placement *exams*. Latinos overall were more likely to attend poor schools with fewer resources and took fewer AP classes because fewer AP classes were available at their schools. Another recent study found increasing numbers of girls taking advanced math and science classes, but a serious gap remained in technology. Girls tended to take data-entry computer classes, while boys took advanced computer applications that lead to careers in technology.[21]

New York Times writer Carey Goldberg discusses how the recent attention to girls has stimulated scholars also to address the cultural threat to boys as they learn to be men. The article quotes Carol Gilligan, the Harvard psychologist, who reported that highly self-confident preadolescent girls begin to lose their sense of competency as they enter adolescence. Gilligan has recently begun observing four-year-old boys, arguing that just as adolescent girls struggle with their socialization toward cultural constructions of femininity, boys may experience a similar struggle in early childhood, when they are faced with pressures to conform to cultural constructions of masculinity. The article quotes other researchers who have found that "boys are not as successful in school as girls because girls read faster and sit more nicely and boys are more physically restless and impulsive." Dan Kindlon, a Harvard Medical School psychology professor, claims that in the seventh, eighth, and ninth grade, boys learn that being vulnerable is akin to death. When Latino and Black boys act tough to impress peers, White adults often see them as threatening and dangerous. Teachers and parents are advised to accept and interpret boys' rough play as rowdiness rather than troublemaking. Teachers can encourage boy-friendly activities that allow students to act out dramatic stories and involve learning-by-doing activities.[22]

Classroom organizational patterns and practices within schools can also affect achievement. The classroom environment becomes less personal, more competitive, and more ability-centered as young people progress through school. Competitiveness may lead many Latinos to lean increasingly toward peer social networks for nurture and support in middle school and high school. School changes toward competitive, ability-based norms may be less compatible with the ways girls learn in general. Girls tend to be more committed to social ties than academics at early adolescence. The strong emphasis on competition and individual accomplishments at the secondary level diminishes the value of group and family cooperation.

Several studies noted earlier support the hypothesis that girls experience conflict between achievement goals and social goals during early adolescence.[23] Early adolescent school transitions are disruptive to all young people's social networks. Perhaps because of gender-role pressures, girls, more than boys, are negatively affected by the disruptions of peer networks that occur with these transitions. Girls tend to focus attention on reestablishing social ties at these transitions, which may compete with their focus on school achievement. This is especially true at the transitions from elementary school to junior high or middle school. Girls' commitment to school declines, and they tend to like school less.

Peers

Peer relationships are important and influential in children's development at all ages, but adolescence is when peers probably have the most influence. Peers influence choices of clothes, hairstyles, music, and TV shows, and the way adolescents talk, what they do for fun, and how they behave.

Peer attitudes toward achievement. A large-scale study provides evidence that it is not enough to improve student achievement by improving schools. These researchers suggested that peers have more influence on adolescents than schools or families. Particularly for teenagers, peers are more influential than parents in day-to-day school activities, such as completing homework, behaving in class, and their attitudes toward school. Laurence Steinberg and colleagues gathered data from questionnaires administered to 20,000 high school students over three years. The participating students represented rural, urban, rich, poor, and middle-class communities, with 40 percent drawn from ethnic minorities. The researchers found that an extremely high proportion of American high school students did not take school seriously. More than a third reported they got through the school day primarily by "goofing off with their friends." The researchers found that many students spent their time outside of school in activities that competed with their studies. The majority worked and often took easy classes so their jobs would not interfere with their grades. About 20 percent said they did not try as hard as they could on their schoolwork because their friends would tease them or think less of them. More than half believed their parents would not get upset about poor grades, and nearly a third reported their parents had no idea how they were doing in school. A large percent reported their parents never consistently attended school events. Only the "unpopular brains" considered school important.[24]

According to other research, female students' perceptions of social support from peers deteriorates significantly by the end of the first year in high school. Students—but particularly Latina females—with close friends who are school oriented are more likely to graduate and consider attending college than those students who have best friends who are not school oriented. Another work shows boys tease Latina girls in junior high school about being smart. When asked in open-ended interviews what boys thought of smart girls, terms such as "nerd," "schoolgirl," "smarty-pants," "stuck-up," "dork," and "brainiac" were reported. "Pretty" girls had fewer problems with being teased about being smart than girls who were not considered pretty.[25]

Gender roles supported by peer groups strongly influence the school orientation of both males and females. The main concerns of male adolescents during middle school are an awareness and an aspiration toward the *cult of masculinity*. According to Patricia A. Adler and Peter Adler, Latino youths prosper in the established popularity system through a successful expression of maleness. Many Latino males adopt elements of a machismo posture displayed through their toughness and defiance of adult authority, challenging prescribed rules and roles in class, and distancing themselves from academics. To gain admiration and popularity among their peers, Latino males often brag about exploits in sports, experiment with deviant behavior, and boast of success with girls and dominance over other boys. To be popular, they must be competitive and dominating, physically involving themselves in competitive sports and fights with other boys to test masculinity and establish dominance. They act "cool" by distancing themselves from all things "feminine" or "nerdy."

Adler and Adler, whose research focused on girls in general, note that a girl's peer culture in adolescence is very different from that of boys. Girls become more concerned with compliance and conformity. They become romantically interested in boys. Attracting the attention of boys gains them higher status among other girls. Even girls whose mothers have careers internalize the beliefs that careers are secondary to family concerns and domesticity. Thus, both boys and girls actively participate in responding to general social norms of their peers and gender roles as they perceive them in the larger society.[26]

In many junior high and high school environments, adolescents separate into discrete ethnic group cliques and friendship groups, isolating themselves from other ethnic groups. There are some opportunities to form cross-ethnic friendships in classroom settings and other structured activities, but for spontaneous activities, students often come back together with their ethnic groups. Latinos have their "school" friends and "neighborhood" friends and very seldom socialize with the "school" friends outside of school settings. These two groups of friends often have quite different orientations toward school.[27]

Latino youth who maintain close connections and positive relationships with family members are less likely than some other students to be influenced by peers. Even second- and third-generation Mexican students maintain strong family orientations that can shape boundaries guiding behaviors and attitudes. The presence of extended family members, such as grandparents, aunts and uncles, cousins, and godparents, provides additional adults to supervise and guide adolescents toward school achievement. Latino extended family members often identify strongly with the interests and welfare of the young people within the family. Family networks become a form of social capital that provides supportive relationships among adults and children and that promotes shared norms and values. If parents or other relatives have at least a high school education, they can provide role models and support from having "made it" through the public education system.[28]

The disengagement from school that characterizes the majority of American students can particularly hurt Latinos who do not have strong families. Latino families have increasingly experienced the stresses of divorce, single parenting, and long work hours that rob children of resources, time, and attention. Students may actively demonstrate school disengagement by skipping school, hanging out in the cafeteria instead of attending class, or misbehaving. Latino students, particularly females, may also manifest their alienation with passivity and quietness in the classroom. They may, as they become more acculturated, defy their parents and family members. One immigrant father complained that his high school son had walked out of the home dressed in neatly pressed khaki pants and a shirt for school, only to stop at the home of a friend to change into more "appropriate" baggy pants or gang colors. His younger sister reported his behavior to his parents.[29] As immigrant youth become more a part of the American youth culture, peers are an important area of concern in promoting academic achievement.

Gangs. Several researchers have studied Mexican-origin gangs in Los Angeles and Chicago during the 1980s and 1990s. They have found a number of characteristics distinctive to these gangs:

- They are territorially based.

- They have a strong age-graded structure, and fighting occupies a central place in gang life.

- Cliques of boys and girls of the same ages form the primary sources of gang activity.

- Over time, gangs become more institutionalized in neighborhoods, exert greater influence over the lives of gang members, and become more deviant and aggressive.

- As first- and second-generation Mexican youth become more marginal in respect to mainstream institutional life and culture, gang membership becomes more attractive.

- Gang members often share school failure, family stress, and lack of interest in legitimate activities.

- Gang participation insulates members from negative assessments of their worth by schools and even their own families.

- The primary reason for joining gangs is "to be with one's friends."[30]

Most studies of Mexican-origin gangs characterize female gangs as satellites of male gangs, but Joan W. Moore has found that female gangs operate independently. Female gang members may serve as attachments to male gangs, sex objects submissive to the will of male gang members; or the female gangs may emulate the typical male gang activities of fighting, committing crimes, and "hanging out." Anne Campbell reported that the highest approvals for female Mexican gang members come from other girls rather than gang boys.[31]

Relations with girlfriends are more important than relations with boyfriends in determining gang membership. Other gender responsibilities also influence girl gangs. Female gang members often have family responsibilities of housekeeping, baby-sitting their brothers and sisters, or rearing their own children, which insulate them from serious gang involvement. Lack of legitimate social institutions in neighborhoods, low levels of parental involvement, lack of good jobs, peer pressure from fellow gang members and friends, and violence-prone schools all contribute to pressures on Mexican-immigrant and second-generation males and females to join gangs. Scott H. Decker and Barrick Van Winkle found that gang membership further isolates youths from schools, nongang peers, families, and relatives. Although brothers and sisters are likely to know about a sibling's gang involvement, mothers, grandparents, and other family members often are unaware of the adolescent's membership. Decker and Van Winkle's research shows that families experience considerable stress when a family member is in a gang and often become victims themselves of gang relations and violence. Against a weakened family structure and declining family influence, gangs are a potent force in shaping behavior in Mexican-origin neighborhoods. Adolescents are also strongly influenced by the behaviors and attitudes of the peers with whom they would like to be friends. Gang members influence many students, even if they are not close friends, because the "wannabes" aspire to be friends with these youths and try to imitate their behaviors.[32]

Many gang contacts for membership recruitment and many of the gang fights take place on or near school grounds. Gang members may wear gang colors, sign gang signs, write graffiti messages to other gangs, recruit new gang members, and insult members of rival gangs right under the supervision of school administrators and teachers. Students harassed by gang members may be so intimidated that they are afraid to come to school. Thus, gangs are not only a problem for the criminal justice system, they are also school problems. Gang members involved in a fight on or near school grounds will likely be expelled or transferred to an alternative school. Frequent absences because of these expulsions result in failed classes and, ultimately, school failure. School policy often demands expelling anyone even suspected of being involved in a gang to prevent discipline problems. In this manner, gang members and even those harassed by gang members are pushed out of school.

Many gang members "mature out" of gang membership. The ease or difficulty of getting out of a gang depends on the nature of the gang and the nature of the individual's relationship with the gang. Moore notes that gang members involved in serious criminal activities seldom leave the gang. Another study gives examples of "temporary gang members" who were only casual participants and who sometimes decided to leave the gang activities because they had rejected some of their violence or begun to seek steady employment.[33]

When girls become interested in romantic relationships, according to other researchers, they often become self-conscious and leave gangs. For most girls, leaving a gang occurs at the end of adolescence. For many, it coincides with the birth of a child and the realization of the constraints of motherhood. Some girls experience more ritualized exits from gangs and are "jumped out" or badly beaten by gang members when they decide to leave. The method of leaving seems to depend on the girl's previous relationship with the gang, her reason for leaving, and the formality of the departure. Most girls just diminish their involvement over time. Sometimes, family pressures cause a gang member to rethink gang membership and "phase out." Several students actively involved in gangs told me that once a young person becomes a member of a gang, it is almost impossible to quit.[34]

Good friends. The majority of Latino youth "hang out" with groups of friends who are *not* gang members. Much of the verbal interaction among adolescents involves teasing, joking, and "put downs" or "ritual insults." The way someone looks, something unusual about a family member, romantic relationships, and embarrassing incidents are the targets of teasing. Nicknames are also used to pick out an individual's distinctive characteristics, sometimes in an affectionate way and sometimes in a derogatory way, such as calling a friend "*Gordito*" (fatty) or "*Flaco*" (skinny). Often what begins in a playful way becomes a cruel and painful interaction. Ridicule and teasing are used to express disapproval and pressure peers to act in certain ways. Many fights involving teenagers begin with these jokes or "ritual insults." Adolescents also use indirect gossip about peers who are not in their close group of friends to convey information about behaviors of which they approve or disapprove. For example, Latina students may criticize other girls' hairstyles, makeup, sexual behavior, or classroom behavior as ways of pressuring conformity to peer values. Much of what teens learn about appropriate behaviors with teachers, acceptable responses in classrooms, ways to interact with other adults, ways to dress, and acceptable and unacceptable behaviors related to school are learned in these casual verbal interactions with peers. Some observers argue that doing well in school is not a result of some mysterious innate ability, luck, or the positive biases of teachers. It is explainable based on student attitudes, values, and behaviors, which are highly influenced by best friends and peers.[35]

Peers can be "bad" friends who belittle academic orientations and doing schoolwork, or "good" friends who encourage doing well in school and planning for college and a career. While we generally think of peer influences as being negative, particularly those involving gangs, good friends can have positive impacts on student behaviors. For example, if an average student is good friends with a group of peers who aspire to go to college and strive to do well at school, the average student may try harder in school to keep up with the achievements of friends. Friends can provide support and encouragement that may persuade an adolescent to stay away from gang members, attend school more regularly, or stop smoking or drinking. The disapproval of a valued friend may be sufficient persuasion to keep an adolescent from engaging in unsafe and unhealthy practices. Adolescents are much more likely to listen if a peer tells them that skipping school can lead to trouble or that other peers are having a negative influence on their behaviors, than when the same message comes from a concerned adult, teacher, or parent.

Extracurricular activities associated with high schools provide opportunities for Latino adolescents to form positive, school-oriented friendships. But it is not uncommon in urban and rural areas for teens to see their school friends only at school. Outside of school, church groups, 4-H clubs, sports teams, and community-based organizations can also sponsor youth activities that provide alternatives to negative peer groups.

Many Latino students feel that doing well in school, particularly making high grades, will, under the present system, have little or no impact on their future educational or occupational success. Many teenagers have inadequate information when making important decisions, such as which classes to take or whether or not to remain in school. Relying primarily on peers as information sources for making those decisions may result in poor decisions. Many adolescents conform to peer behaviors because they want to be accepted.

During adolescence, students begin to form long-lasting friendships. The best friends—or those with whom a teenager spends the most time and seems to have the closest relationships—will also have the most influence on attitudes, beliefs, and behaviors.[36] If an adolescent's best friend is involved in drugs, sexually active, or participating in gang activities, he or she is more likely to be drawn into these activities as well. A young person with strong moral beliefs or strong convictions about right and wrong may be able to resist peer pressures and make independent decisions without family, friend, or peer influences. But it is important to remember that when attempting to increase Latino school achievement, peers have a powerful influence.

Sexual harassment. Latina students may also leave school because of sexual harassment and the refusal of school administrators to correct it. Sylvia Cedillo, at the University of Texas Law School, worked with the Stop Harassment in Public Schools project (SHIPS) to help schools prevent harassment. The behaviors SHIPS attempted to eliminate included sexual comments or jokes; sexist terms; spreading sexual rumors; graffiti; leering; sexually graphic notes; and physical sexual harassment, such as touching, grabbing, or pinching in a sexual way. The Texas Civil Rights Project published a report of an investigation of sexual harassment in Texas schools. The project surveyed 1,860 students and found that peer sexual harassment was rampant and cut across class, race, and ethnic lines. Typically, sexually harassing behavior begins in middle school, but many students reported such behaviors before the seventh grade.[37]

Boys also are subject to sexual harassment. Ritual insults— such as "wimp," "pussy," "girl," or "fag"—imply some form of weakness and associated lack of toughness connected with femininity or homosexuality. These names have been used when boys fail to meet certain standards of combativeness. Some boys are continuously challenged to be tough, mean, and aggressive; girls as well as other boys ridicule them if they do not measure up. Through this culture of sexual aggression, boys may begin to view girls as sexual objects and find it easy to discount their feelings of discomfort and humiliation when they are harassed. One researcher found that sexual harassment was a frequent occurrence in elementary and secondary schools in small towns, as well as in large cities.[38]

The Texas Civil Rights Project published *Sexual Harassment in Schools* about what schools should do to stop harassment. This report provides information about student rights under Title IX and a school's legal responsibility to address sexual harassment. The report also includes preventive strategies for schools, a list of resources for educating students about harassment, and suggestions for parents and students about organizing to prevent harassment. The report urges parents to talk with their children about sexual harassment, to reassure the child being harassed that he or she did nothing wrong and has no reason to feel guilty, and to help the child develop a safety plan. Parents are urged to talk with teachers and administrators about problems, organize volunteers to ride on buses, or to have lunch in school cafeterias to supervise students' behaviors. Teachers are urged to be alert to what happens in classrooms, and when they witness harassment, they should take advantage of the "teachable" moment to discuss cultural standards, gender inequity, and sexual harassment. Teachers are encouraged to take sexual harassment seriously and intervene immediately when they see examples of it. There are opportunities to address sexual harassment in ongoing classroom instruction. For example, the report suggests social studies teachers can compare gender roles across cultural groups. In a literature class, students can read a story or poem about gender issues or inequities and discuss peer sexual harassment. Administrators should take sexual harassment seriously, develop and implement a policy on peer sexual harassment on the campus, and train school employees on sexual harassment, and violence awareness and prevention. Teachers can provide information to students and make filing a complaint nonthreatening. Intervening immediately and communicating with parents are important preventive strategies.[39]

Competition and conflicts among cliques of girls can also result in harassment and affect Latina girls' attitudes toward school and their abilities to learn. Students who experience peer conflicts or sexual harassment often do not want to attend school and may stay home, cut class, or not participate in class. Thus, harassment can have serious consequences for achievement when students experience difficulty in concentrating on schoolwork, suffer lowered self-esteem, and feel less confident.[40]

Some Practical Approaches

The support of family, schools, and peers is very important to Latino youth in completing high school and taking nontraditional career paths. Successful Latina women in higher education reported family and community involvement have provided important positive measures of personal worth and academic success. Survival skills, political involvement, pursuit of social justice, and being bilingual were identified as characteristics that promote positive self-image and leadership.[41]

Research shows that programs that inspire self-efficacy and promote self-confidence and high expectations are as important as school programs that provide opportunities for academic and career success. Mentors and role models from backgrounds similar to the girls, help Latinas, especially immigrant students, to establish a grounding in their families and home cultures while exploring nonstereotypical roles and nontraditional roles and life choices. Events on high school and college campuses that feature successful Latinos in nontraditional fields inspire young Latinos to think about new career options. Academic Outreach, Upward Bound, Community of Scholars, and Bridge programs—designed to improve students' academic performance at an early age and help them set and work toward academic goals—have been found to counter academic barriers, such as teachers or counselors who discourage Latinos from taking advanced classes. These programs also help Latino students maintain their goals for academic success while retaining ties to friends who may not be school oriented.

MIJA. *Mija* is a term of endearment in vernacular Spanish meaning *my daughter*. The term connotes Latino pride and familial support and caring. The acronym *MIJA* stands for *Math Increases Job Aspirations*, a program initiated in 1991 by the Intercultural Development Research Association (IDRA) in San Antonio, Texas, and funded by the U.S. Department of Education as part of the Women's Education Equity Act.[42]

The program reached out to girls before adolescence, which is a key turning point in a girl's self-concept and an age when changes in personal visions of success usually occur. The project originally targeted sixth-grade Latinas and followed participants into the seventh grade. Goals included (1) developing mathematical knowledge and skills, (2) broadening knowledge about math-related careers, (3) providing training and technical assistance to schools on gender equity and Latinas' achievement, and (4) assisting Latino parents in providing academic-related encouragement and support. The program served mostly Mexican-immigrant and Mexican American girls and addressed the problems of leaving school early, gender equity in math education, and career opportunities. At the time MIJA was initiated, IDRA estimated that the school-leaving rate among Latinos was 45 percent, with more than half leaving school before they entered the ninth grade.

The MIJA curriculum component consisted of Friday sessions one day a month, seven Saturday sessions, and a summer institute. The lessons developed math competence through creative lessons, "brain teasers," games, and manipulative and hands-on activities organized around cooperative learning approaches. The girls were encouraged to share strategies for solving problems, tutor one another, and develop self-checking and test-taking skills. The project incorporated program elements that the Quality Education for Minorities in Mathematics, Science, and Engineering Network had recognized as common characteristics of effective K-12 mathematics and science strategies: early identification of at-risk students and a clear target population; a sound, self-paced, and individualized curriculum; quality instruction that includes cooperative learning strategies and that links school to real life problems; staff with high expectations; support services, including peer and family counseling when needed; and referrals for help with basic skills, parental involvement, and community partnerships that provide financial and human resources and that help expose students to career options and role models.

The MIJA staff developed materials for the program but also used *Add-Ventures for Girls*, a curriculum developed at the University of Nevada, and *Math for Girls*, a curriculum developed by the *Math/ Science Network* at the University of California. The program included a five-day summer institute with several field trips to local colleges, the University of Texas Health Science Center Dental School in San Antonio, and other science-related sites. Sessions included interactive teaching and discussions about college preparation. The second summer institute involved Latinas who had careers in math and science. Among them were aerospace engineers, a registered nurse, a statistician, and a computer programmer.[43]

Throughout the school year, the girls heard guest speakers who talked about benefits of careers in engineering, medical, educational research, accounting, law, gem cutting, and other scientific careers that use math skills. The students also attended math and science conferences sponsored by universities in San Antonio; they interacted with female engineers, scholars, and scientists participating in various workshops. Training and technical assistance was provided to school personnel, particularly counselors and teachers, to help them identify ways to encourage and support mathematics learning among Latinas and to increase their awareness of gender equity and student achievement. Teachers were provided materials focusing on achieving gender equity in the classroom.

IDRA staff helped teachers assess teacher-student interactions in the classroom and in counseling sessions. Parents were also provided training to increase their awareness of gender equity issues, inform them of math-related careers available to their daughters, and develop their skills in communicating and demonstrating support for their daughters' math achievements. MIJA staff showed the American Association of University Women video titled "Shortchanging Girls, Shortchanging America," which alerted parents to messages girls might hear that could encourage or discourage them from studying science and math. The parent sessions were designed to support and encourage parents, even when they could not provide help with math and science content.[44]

IDRA used a number of outcome measures to determine the effectiveness of the MIJA program. For example, IDRA administered a survey to the girls about their inclination for taking more math classes before and after their participation in the program and about their relationships with their teachers and parents. After completing the program, participants reported they liked working with computers, and 95 percent felt they could do well in mathematics if they had help, compared to 45.5 percent at the beginning of the program. They showed significant increases in their appreciation of their parents' and teachers' support for their math abilities. The participants also had higher rates of passing the Texas Assessment of Academic Skills (TAAS) test than girls in general at their schools and had an increasing awareness of math-related careers. Parents of these MIJA participants also gave the program a high rating.[45]

In 1996 the program expanded to reach more Latinas and include science and engineering. The new program, Engineering, Science and Mathematics Increases Job Aspirations (ES-MIJA) is based on the goals and organization of the original MIJA program and is funded by the National Science Foundation. Through role modeling, meaningful direct instruction, participation in math and science conferences, and visits to places where they could see both men and women using science and math in their daily activities, the program has been effective in changing Latina girls' relationships with mathematics and science. The MIJA program demonstrates that support for nontraditional academic pursuits, such as math, science studies, and technical fields, helps girls begin to counter stereotypes about Latinas.[46]

Many examples of gender bias exist in our classrooms from preschool through graduate education. Teachers need to counter these biases and support the achievement of Latinas through strategies such as increasing physical or eye contact with girls, allowing ample time to answer questions, creating a sense of community and participation in the classroom, using examples in the classroom that include Latinas, listening carefully and respectfully to students' questions and comments, and coaching students who seem reticent to speak. The placement of Latino students in rigorous academic courses is a fundamentally important ingredient in their success in math and science as well as other academic areas. But placement in and of itself is not sufficient. Support systems to work with students without previous experience in high-level classes may also be necessary. Institutional and community support must be in place to ensure that students who have not had previous experience with academically oriented classes succeed in them.[47]

PEP. The Pregnancy, Education, and Parenting (PEP) program addresses pregnancy and parenthood, two of the most common reasons students drop out of school. The Texas Legislature has authorized the distribution of funds to school districts to fund PEP programs to help students who become pregnant or become parents to achieve academically and work toward graduation. The program also provides occupational or job training, access to available community resources, and information about child development, parenting, and home management. One of the most critical factors that can promote Latino student success is the involvement of school staff who believe that all students can succeed. This is especially important for teen mothers and fathers. When teens discover they are going to be parents, they need adults to confide in and go to for support. The PEP programs are designed around these success factors.[48]

The PEP programs value students' languages and cultures, hold high expectations, make education a priority, offer academic courses on parenting and counseling, and provide staff training to help teachers serve Latino students more effectively. The emphasis is on keeping students in school. Once a teenager has dropped out of school or started a family, the barriers to graduation are great. Given the difficulties faced by "reentry" teen mothers, it is not surprising that few Latina teenage mothers complete or even begin higher education programs once they have left high school. Many large urban high schools have special programs to help teen mothers complete their diplomas, but many such programs are separated from regular high school campuses and offer only basic and remedial level classes.

The PEP program was established by the Texas Legislature in 1988, when data showed that Texas had one of the highest teenage pregnancy rates in the United States. The program was designed to be voluntary, and a school district or an individual campus could apply for the funding by submitting a proposal that met several requirements. Implementers could not use self-contained instructional arrangements for students but instead had to integrate the PEP program into the regular high school curriculum. At least 30 percent of the participants had to be eligible for a free or reduced lunch. The districts had to use other federal, state, and/or local funds to match the PEP funds. In addition, the districts had to coordinate with governmental agencies, such as the Department of Health, Department of Human Services, and Attorney General's Office. In 1990 requests for applications were sent to school districts, and 26 districts were awarded grants for pilot programs.

The PEP program has been successful in providing child care and parenting classes that help keep teen parents in school. According to information provided by the coordinator of PEP, the program's average of second pregnancies is about 5 percent compared to a 25-65 percent average of second pregnancies for teen mothers nationally. Between 30 and 40 percent of the students in any second year PEP program are students who have previously dropped out of school and have been encouraged to return. In 1998, 264 programs were funded statewide, mostly in high school settings, but also in alternative schools, GED programs, and other facilities. The programs enroll both males (2,119 enrolled) and females (19,511 enrolled). Most participants (57%) are Latina teen mothers. About 20 percent of the participants have completed their high school degrees. Each funded program is required to provide counseling, child care, transportation of students' children, transportation for teen parents to and from the campus or child care facility, instruction in skills and knowledge for parenting, and assistance in obtaining services from government agencies, including prenatal and postnatal health and nutrition programs.[49]

The Hays Consolidated Independent High School in Kyle, Texas, and the San Marcos Independent School District in San Marcos, Texas, have collaborated with the Community Action, Inc. Early Head Start Program to develop successful PEP programs. These PEP programs offer parenting classes that apply toward academic credit for a high school degree. Teen fathers as well as teen mothers are encouraged to enroll. The PEP program and Early Head Start staff offer a child care center in each high school so parents can bring their babies while they attend classes. The programs meet all the quality standards required of Early Head Start, including staff training in child development, low adult-child ratios, and numerous high standards for providing health and social services.

Early Head Start funds family advocates who provide case management for teen parents below the poverty level who qualify for Early Head Start. The family advocates make home visits and work with the teens, grandparents, and children to provide the best possible educational environments for the children. High school PEP child-care centers evolved from baby-sitting centers where infants spent most of their time in cribs to well-furnished child-development centers with staff certified in child-development training. Staff organized support groups for grandparents to help them find positive ways to support their pregnant teenage granddaughters. The students may take honors classes as part of the regular school program.

The PEP programs have been so successful that there are waiting lists for teen parents who want to enroll their children at the childcare centers. Parents are required to take a parenting class and spend lunch hours with their babies. They must continue to work toward their diplomas or a GED to participate in the program. The PEP programs have succeeded in identifying teen mothers during their pregnancies and helping them to obtain prenatal care and to continue in school. The San Marcos program staff has reported that some school districts are reluctant to apply for the funds because school board members believe that providing such programs would encourage more teen pregnancies. The research presented in this chapter contradicts that belief and suggests that to help Latino teen parents in the long run, programs must help them obtain enough education to allow them to find work in higher-paying jobs. This means giving them as much help as needed to meet educational goals, providing quality child care while they work toward their diplomas, and offering training in nontraditional fields that pay high wages.

Hispanic mother-daughter programs. A number of Hispanic mother-daughter programs have been successful in targeting high-risk Hispanic sixth-grade girls and their mothers in families where no family member has graduated from college. The programs consist of activities to help girls and mothers maintain interest in school and raise educational and career aspirations. Mothers become better role models and more involved in their daughters' education. These programs extend family networks and provide mentors of university and professional women in the community. An evaluation of the University of Texas at El Paso Hispanic Mother-Daughter Program showed that by tenth grade, all of the 150 girls participating had remained in school, were active in school activities, and were planning for college. The mothers played active roles in their children's education. Mothers and daughters were closer, and the mothers reported higher expectations for their daughters and for other children. A study of a similar program at the University of Texas at San Antonio explains the effects of intergenerational academic aspirations among grandmother-mother-daughter triads. The research shows that daughters perceive their mothers as key in forming their educational aspirations. Mothers and daughters credit their mothers as providing the most support and encouragement to achieve in academics. The researchers show that daughters' academic achievement is significantly related to their mothers' levels of aspirations for them. The academic aspirations of the mother-daughter program participants has increased with mothers from each successive generation urging higher education for their daughters.[50]

Moving beyond stereotypes. Patricia Zavella emphasizes the importance of understanding differences among Latino groups and incorporating differences as well as similarities across groups in our curricula. She urges moving beyond stereotypes and paying attention to the varied histories of Latino groups, regional cultures, and generational differences. Educators must address gender bias schoolwide, including program design, curriculum development, and staff training, taking into account differences across generations and how these issues play out for immigrant students. Whether a Latino is first generation (born outside the United States) or of subsequent generations born in the United States will affect how "American" he or she feels. Social class origins also affect school experiences. Zavella proposes a curriculum that includes comparisons between Latina and non-Latina women of different cultural backgrounds who are similar in other ways, such as generation or social class. Frequent opportunities for immigrant girls to communicate and collaborate closely with U.S.-born girls, especially girls of their same ethnicity, are important and should be designed into our school programs.[51]

With families and schools working together, Latino youth can achieve higher graduation rates. By considering home, community, school, classroom, and student factors when designing effective instructional practices for all Latino students, schools can help students feel appreciated and respected.[52] A 1992 American Association of University Women (AAUW) study reported that public schools shortchanged girls, with routine discrimination by teachers, textbooks, and male students. The research shows that girls and boys begin school with equal skills, but by high school, girls fall behind, particularly in math and science.

A 1998 AAUW report found that both boys and girls do better when the elements of good education are present, including small classes, focused academic curricula, and gender-fair instruction. One factor that seems to benefit girls is when their self-worth is based less on appearance and more on academic skills. The study is clear on one thing: both girls and boys did better in school when the classes and schools eliminated sexism and stopped enforcing stereotypical roles for girls and boys.

An expanded knowledge base of Latino school success and identity development can help educators and parents determine the effectiveness of specific school and community-based strategies, the context variables, and the school structures that contribute to school success. Those strategies can then be shared with various schools and community groups serving Latino students. Successful completion of early schooling and then high school means that Latinos are more likely to continue in postsecondary education programs, as well as get higher paying jobs. The 1992 AAUW report provided a comprehensive literature review concerning the condition of public schooling for girls. The report examined relevant research on gender inequities and documented a number of ways that schools have failed to meet the needs of girls. The report also highlighted the paucity of research on minority girls in general and immigrant girls in particular. A major conclusion is that gender adds another layer of complexity to the impact of cultural, racial, and linguistic differences on Latinas' and immigrant girls' school experiences.

The study *How Schools Shortchange Girls* documented disturbing evidence that girls receive an inferior education—in quality of instruction, types of courses taken, opportunities for growth and academic development, and school climate—compared with boys. The report has stimulated local, state, and national agencies to provide more equitable treatment for girls in public schools.[53]

A 1998 study *Gender Gaps: Where Schools Still Fail Our Children* by the same group, American Association of University Women Educational Foundation, reconceptualized the problem and identified new issues in gender equity. The study documented progress of public schools toward more equitable treatment of boys and girls.

The report describes gender equity as quality education and equal opportunity for all students, recognizing variables such as sex, socioeconomic class, socioeconomic status, race, and ethnicity. The report urges that new equitable education approaches to teaching and learning should benefit both girls and boys and must address the needs of both.

The *Gender Gaps* report argues against a deficit-model approach that focuses on what is wrong with girls and that views boys as the norm against which girls are measured. The report proposes instead that we focus on institutional changes in how we think about learning and how we deal with gender relations. *Gender Gaps* points out that girls are not a homogeneous group and that differences among the population of girls by race, ethnicity, and social class may be as great as differences between boys and girls. The report urges that we compare boys to girls and compare girls against their own prior performance instead of limiting comparisons to areas that emphasize traditional male strengths.

The *Gender Gaps* report encourages us to recognize that girls and boys as individuals are diverse and often defy the statistical norms, and, in general, girls and boys are more alike than different in skills, competencies, and achievement. The report urges high educational standards for all students and a recognition that different groups may have varying needs to enable them to reach those standards. For example, emphasis on technology as a masculine domain discouraged many girls from taking the high-level computer classes that lead to technology careers. School actions put boys at greater risk of being retained, but more girls who had been retained eventually drop out. The study also concludes that schools limit gender equity when they fail to discuss risk factors for students, such as violence, sexuality, and health concerns. The cumulative effects of poverty, abuse, and other serious problems take a higher toll on girls' health than boys'.

For example, school initiatives dealing with pregnancy and sex education tended to place primary responsibility on girls, giving little attention to males' behavior and responsibility. The study points out that rigid definitions of gender roles in schools and careers create barriers for both boys and girls. Both girls and boys will likely experience conflicts between career and family obligations, and because girls will likely work for pay outside the home, boys will likely be married to a woman who works for pay outside the home. Thus, gendered assumptions about career options affect both girls' and boys' futures.

The *Gender Gaps* report also notes that Latinos are predicted to become the largest racial/ethnic group in the United States, so it is crucial that Latinas receive an education that does not limit them to unskilled, low-paying jobs. As discussed in this chapter, Latinas face unique struggles and risks linked to culture, language, compatibility of home life with schooling, and family support for their success. When working with immigrant families, U.S. schools have to confront an even greater complex array of gender values and cultures that may create stress and cultural strains on immigrant girls.[54]

Regional differences and differences in the experiences of girls from rural and urban areas create additional cultural conflicts. The report points out that gender has been largely overlooked in the literature on school reform and successful practices. The research on equity, which has focused mostly on racial/ethnic and social class equity, should be extended to consider gender as well. This requires that data on educational outcomes must be available on all students. Thus, research must recognize sex as a variable, and data must be disaggregated by race, ethnicity, gender, and social class to help us better understand the issues and concerns of Latina girls and boys in our schools.

CHAPTER 5

Creating Family-School Partnerships

P ersonal connections between families and schools, when developed with respect and care, bring parents into closer contact with their children's schooling. As a result, educational outcomes for recent immigrant and second-generation Mexican-origin children are usually enhanced.[1] We begin our examination of families and schools with a brief review of what researchers have learned about the roles of poverty, parents' education, and family structure in children's educational outcomes. These three family variables are most often linked with student achievement outcomes. This chapter then turns to an in-depth look at what my fieldwork with the Mexican immigrants and Mexican families has shown about the perceptions of parents, family strategies, and resources, and ways to establish family-school relationships that can help children do well in school. We also look at positive parent-school partnerships, the school's role in involving parents. This examination features projects that have successfully included parents in the formal education of their children. I have included recommendations about how to help parents become stronger partners in their children's early education and, at the upper levels, how to involve parents in encouraging their children to enroll in postsecondary institutions.

Family Poverty and Children's Educational Outcomes

Poverty research has important implications because recent Mexican-immigrant and second-generation families experience high poverty rates and because long-term poverty has serious consequences for children, strongly correlating with educational outcomes. Poverty can directly and indirectly influence child development, high school graduation, college enrollment, and years of schooling completed. Low-income parents can, however, overcome these influences by being effective parents and by being involved in their children's schooling.[2]

A recent study shows that family poverty has significant effects on the cognitive abilities of young children. Three types of assessment—IQ, verbal ability, and achievement tests—detected effects of income for children ages two to eight. Children from persistently poor families scored lower on all three assessments of cognitive ability than children who had never been poor. The researchers note differences in effects of poverty among children whose families were very poor (family income below 50 percent of poverty level), those with slightly higher incomes, and the near-poor. The cognitive well-being of children improved as family income increased.[3]

Many researchers have been concerned about the increasing number of mother-only families. Although Mexican-origin families are more likely to be two-parent families than mother-only families, there are increasing numbers of Latina mothers who choose not to marry or are in situations where the child's father is absent or not supporting his child. Recent data show that household structure—whether or not a child lives in a single- or two-parent home—has almost no effect when income is considered. However, mother-only families tend to have low incomes because mothers of young children usually find it difficult to work full time and manage child care, and women tend to earn less than men. But research shows that poverty, and not single-parent status, affects children most. Two-parent families who have recently immigrated into the United States also tend to live below the poverty level. A head-of-household worker can work full time, all year at minimum wage and remain below the poverty level. Many Mexican-immigrant and Mexican American families are large and among the working poor who cannot earn sufficient wages to rise above the poverty level.[4]

Income matters for several reasons. First, it is associated with the ability to provide a rich learning environment for children. Additionally, low-income jobs almost never provide medical benefits, so children from low-income families have little or no access to well-baby care, dental care, or other medical services. The economic pressures of low income can also lead to depression or family conflicts that can affect the harshness or responsiveness of parenting. In turn, family conflicts and financial stress can affect adolescents' self-confidence and achievement. Researchers studying these relationships concluded that family household factors may become more salient when children are older, such as when supervising and monitoring adolescent youths becomes important (two parents can usually provide better supervision). They also concluded that increasing the income of poor families is likely to raise the performance of young children.[5]

Mothers' educational levels have also been linked to positive school outcomes for children. In part, this link has to do with the ways in which education may influence interactions with children and the literacy environment of the home. One research team suggested that mothers' educational levels and income have independent effects on child cognitive development. Raising the educational levels of parents, as well as increasing household incomes, could improve the well-being of young children. To help improve the readiness and cognitive ability of young children, these researchers propose programs emphasizing educational strategies. Such strategies could include helping mothers learn to read, encouraging them to read more to their children, and teaching mothers about intellectually stimulating learning activities they could do with their children at home. The recommendations of these researchers form the foundation for many components of successful early childhood education programs, such as those sponsored by AVANCE (discussed in Chapter 2). The researchers concluded that the consequences of policies or social service practices that deny assistance to children born to teenage mothers, unmarried women, or various immigrant groups are troublesome because the income of these families may fall dramatically. The consequences of poverty are serious for Mexican-immigrant and first-generation families. Many of these families have young children, and the parents must take low-paying jobs because they lack proficiency in English, literacy skills, or official immigration status that allows them to work legally. The research emphasizes that young children appear to be most vulnerable to the consequences of deep poverty. The mothers of young children are least able to support themselves or add to the support of their families by working.[6]

Other research shows that family income has less effect on children's development once children enter school. Parental income does influence where a family lives, which often is connected to the quality of schools. During the school years, parents' aspirations for their children, encouragement from teachers, and the influence of children's friends have significant impacts on educational outcomes. As the influence of parental income declines, the influence of family-school relationships increases. Thus, as children enter formal schooling, the link between schools and families is critical.[7]

Parent-School Relationships

Extensive research on families and schools shows that the relationship between the primary caretaker of a child and the schools is extremely important. Most education and child development experts agree that when families get involved in their children's lives through school or community programs, the child, the program, and the family all benefit. Head Start, for example, has produced numerous studies on the importance of the partnership between the family and the child in early childhood programs.[8]

Research shows that parental involvement in schools positively affects a child's motivation and self-confidence. Parents' support at home for the school's efforts and a supportive tone for education enhance parents' abilities to socialize their children academically, that is, to socialize them to behave in ways that teachers and schools expect and reward. When parents express confidence in their children's ability to do the work expected in school and have high expectations for success, their children do better in school. Parental involvement has also been shown to improve parents' optimism about their children's school success.[9]

Some parents use the knowledge of school processes gained through their involvement in classroom activities to intervene positively in their children's education. A study of working-class and middle-class Anglo parents revealed that the parents who volunteered in classrooms saw the level of work expected, observed how teachers treated children, and were able to discuss school problems informally with teachers. Other research indicates that teachers' attitudes toward parents as a whole are positively influenced by the participation of even a small number of parent volunteers in the school.[10]

Most research on parental involvement and educational outcomes has focused on young children; yet what parents do to motivate their children and assure that they receive a strong educational foundation also helps prepare their children for middle school, high school, and college. As children move into middle and secondary schools, it becomes more difficult for parents to be involved. Adolescents are often embarrassed when their parents come to school. At higher grade levels, parents must face other school-related and adolescent issues, but involvement in their children's education is still important.

Parental Involvement in School Programs

The following section of this chapter draws from my studies of Latino parent involvement and from my classroom teaching and extensive fieldwork with Mexican-origin families over many years.[11]

Helping early childhood and elementary school programs function in ways that truly support families is a difficult challenge. A group of early childhood researchers identified four main philosophies that tend to affect practices of programs attempting to involve parents.[12] One philosophy, the deficit model, tends to view families as "victims" of poverty and ignorance, and professionals are the experts who can try to fix the families. A second philosophy views families and schools as two separate worlds: families take care of basic needs and schools take care of education. A third philosophy is one in which parents are education consumers. The intent on the part of the schools is to keep satisfied customers, but the customers have little say in running the business of education. The fourth philosophy is to view parents and schools as partners who must work together for the benefit of the child.

In programs operating under the first philosophy, parents are often blamed for rearing their children badly in deficient home environments. School- and parent-oriented programs that reflect this philosophy believe that professional experts can "rescue" a child through education. School and program staff tend to treat families paternalistically. They view themselves as experts who have the knowledge needed to "educate" family members to be more effective parents. This deficit model approach does not view families as sources of parenting strengths or take into account cultural values and family dynamics. Practitioners operating from this approach do not rely on parents and families to determine the services they need and the roles they wish to play in their children's education. Instead, this group of practitioners takes a condescending attitude that professionals are needed to improve the lives of children and families. Many intervention programs with good intentions are examples of this model. Parenting programs in which the "experts" tell families how to be good parents and provide "correct" ways of parenting reflect this philosophy.

The second broad philosophy views families and schools as separate entities with little need to be linked. According to this philosophy, teachers are experts exclusively responsible for the education of children. They may call a family in from time to time to tell them what their child and the teacher have been working on, but families are not seen as taking active roles in the education of their children or having much to contribute to the education program. Parents may be involved in teaching their children at home, but there is little effort to include parents in decisions about curricula or the school environment. Many teachers have this philosophy. The growth of professionalism in schools has resulted in teachers who consider themselves as "experts," and are reluctant to view parents with little formal education as having much worthwhile to contribute to the schooling of their children.

The third philosophy views parents as consumers of services provided by schools, child-care centers, and teachers. Parent involvement is considered important, not so much because it helps enhance the learning and development of a child, but because parents need to be kept informed and happy as consumers of services. With this perspective, schools do not share information about what is going wrong in the schools, and parents generally have little choice but to send their children to their assigned schools. They have little real influence in effecting changes or directing the education of their children. An extreme example of this occurred recently in Texas. A major school district was discovered to have changed test scores of students so the rankings of several schools would be higher. Instead of involving parents in identifying and fixing the problems that resulted in lower scores, the school administrators resorted to cheating to present a more positive image of achievement.

A fourth philosophy, the preferred one, views families as partners. In this model, the relationship between parents and teachers is nonhierarchical, with parents and staff contributing equally to decision making about programs, the teaching process, and the development of their children. Communication between parents and professionals is essential for this philosophy to work effectively, and parents must have many options for getting involved in their child's growth and development. Parents are involved as decision makers and must take active roles in their children's education. The professional's role is that of enabler: helping and supporting parents as equal partners in the education of their children. At its best, this way of involving parents develops mutual trusting relationships, respects family beliefs and values (even when they differ from those of the professionals), helps families understand the developmental processes of their children, provides access to classrooms, and involves families in decisions about policy and practice.

The goal in this chapter is to present information that can move us more toward the fourth philosophy. Although schools are in the process of changing, many school staff and programs still reflect some of the discredited first three philosophies regarding family-school partnerships. Both school staff and families need extensive training and support to enter into full partnerships. Programs have to be built with sensitivity to the real life circumstances of families and children. Successful partnerships must be grounded in honoring the cultural and linguistic practices in students' homes and supported through respectful and trusting interpersonal relationships.[13]

Barriers to participation. Families face many pressures and circumstances that detract from their involvement in their children's education. Time constraints—particularly work schedules and demands of young children—influence levels of involvement. Socioeconomic background and educational levels of adults may also affect family involvement. Immigrant parents may have problems with the English language or may be illiterate in Spanish, factors that create additional barriers to participation. Differences in culture and ethnicity, short time of residence in the community, high rates of transiency for some families, lack of understanding of how U.S. schools work, and hostile school environments also prevent Latino parents from participating in schools. Involvement in their children's education may not be a priority for families who are struggling to provide food, clothing, and housing for their children. Parents with more education may be more active in making decisions about curricula and staffing than parents who have had few opportunities for formal education. One study notes that Latina mothers' education and acculturation are key to understanding parent involvement. Latina mothers with higher levels of education typically have more familiarity with the school system and more awareness of roles expected of them in their children's education. These researchers found, however, that while many recent immigrant parents or parents with less knowledge about schools face many barriers to involvement, these parents reported high levels of perceived efficacy relevant to parental involvement. That is, they believed their culture and beliefs had served as resources for their children. These parents had higher educational expectations than some parents who were more acculturated.[14]

Early childhood education research has isolated key components of family-centered practices for schools: positiveness, responsiveness, a family orientation, friendliness, and sensitivity. Strategies to involve parents must be sensitive to local interests, a child's and family's needs, and cultural differences.[15]

Parental involvement during adolescence. Parental involvement is much more difficult when students move into middle and high school than when children are in early elementary grades. Laurence Steinberg suggests that families undergo a great deal of stress when adolescents begin to assert their independence and make their own decisions about friendships, leaving school, enrolling in college, or planning careers. Conflicts over what a teenager can and cannot do and frequent disagreements over rules cause families with adolescents to experience high levels of tension. The difficulty of this transition period is compounded when immigrant families are struggling economically or coping with serious family disruptions. The transition is also more difficult when immigrant parents know less about the school culture than their children do. While adolescent transformations may take a toll on the psychological well-being of parents, for most families, adolescence leads to a redefinition of the parent-child relationship from one of parental authority to one that is cooperative and reciprocal.[16]

My colleague Toni Falbo and I conducted a longitudinal study chronicling the experiences of Mexican-origin students identified by their schools as "at-risk of dropping out of school." We compared dropouts and students who had overcome numerous problems to graduate. Parents of the adolescents who had managed to earn high school diplomas were able to remain in charge as parents: they set limits; monitored their children's actions, whereabouts, and feelings; and drew the line when their children became involved with peers who negatively affected school achievement. These parents recognized that adolescents need to be involved in effective two-way communication with adults and in negotiations about their behaviors. The parents provided positive encouragement even when the children "messed up" or became embroiled in serious problems. Parents encouraged students in their schoolwork even when the parents themselves lacked the skills to help, and they stayed involved in school activities affecting their children. One mother with a second-grade education sat at the kitchen table with her teenage son until 2 a.m. as he worked on his homework. She could not help him, but she provided moral support.

We found that active parental involvement in schools is also key to helping adolescents graduate from high school. Parents who visited classrooms and took the initiative to contact school staff to demand assertively that they be informed about their children's academic progress were more likely to help their adolescents stay in school than parents who waited for school staff to call if there were problems or assumed that all was well if they did not hear from the school.[17]

Background knowledge that facilitates involvement. Other research confirms that most Latino families have high educational aspirations for their children and provide strong family support. But most of these parents are rarely involved in their children's schools.

Latino parents often have insufficient knowledge about the U.S. school system or inadequate resources to help their children reach their educational goals. One family in our study wanted their daughter to go to college, but, because the father had dropped out of school in the sixth grade and the mother had attended only primary school in Mexico, they had no idea about how to pursue college actively for their daughter. The daughter was not enrolled in college preparatory courses in her high school. She chose lower-level courses to keep her grade point average high. The counselor's messages about college delivered to the honors and upper-level tracks did not reach her. The parents logically thought they should begin to think about college after their daughter graduated from high school. They did not know their daughter needed to take particular high school courses to prepare her for college admissions nor did they recognize the importance of the SAT exam or early applications deadlines. The daughter had the potential for success at a four-year college but lacked an information network to help her enroll.[18]

A large body of research explains the inability of Latino students to enroll in college; most is based on a deficit model. Deficit models emphasize educational and financial problems and fail to recognize the many strengths of Latino families. The models discount the importance of ethnic group experiences and the various structural contexts in which different groups find themselves. Achievement differences among groups are the result of social processes with long histories; this is also true among families. Different Latino families have had experiences that add or detract from their abilities to help their children academically. For example, a young Mexican American mother whose parents were immigrants from Mexico and had never had the opportunity to attend school lamented, "I didn't know kids could learn their ABCs and numbers at this young age. If I had known that, I could have taught my daughter more." Another young mother, a high school graduate, had many academic skills she could have taught her young children but did not think of herself as a "teacher." She explained, "I thought that the schools would teach him how to read and write. I didn't know I was supposed to be doing it, too." Latino parents who had their own models of home teaching or had parents with better understandings of child development were able to help their children develop cognitive skills. Parents who did not have such opportunities often did very effective jobs of parenting, teaching their children social skills, and fostering self-esteem and motivation, but their children arrived at school with fewer academic skills than their peers.[19]

Monitoring schoolwork. Many Latino children may be disadvantaged because their parents cannot monitor their progress in school. For example, parents in our study who had not earned a high school diploma could not determine whether the level of their children's schoolwork was appropriate to prepare the youths for postsecondary education. Many parents believed their children were being prepared for college, when, in fact, they had been tracked into vocational or noncollege preparatory courses. One mother explained she could not read English and could not determine the level of homework assignments for her son in junior high school. She requested to see his homework and checked the dates on the papers. She calculated that if his work had the correct date on it, her son was keeping up with his assignments. She had no way of telling if the work would prepare him for college. Another parent faced a similar dilemma and suggested, "I think from day one the school should preach 'You are all going to college.' Not more or less, 'Can your parents afford college?' or 'Do you think you might want to go to college?'" This mother proposed doing away with a tracking system that identified students in the early grades as "college" or "vocation" oriented. Untracking would minimize the influence of parental educational background and prepare more Latino students for college.[20]

"Cultural match" theories, often applied to students, may also relate to parents. When parents' expectations about school involvement match those of the schools—as is the case for many Anglo, middle-class families—their children have better chances of succeeding.[21] Some research indicates, for example, that among middle- and working-class Anglo families, the levels and quality of parent involvement are linked to the social and cultural resources available to parents in the different social class positions. In a study by Annette Lareau, Latino parents who had attended only a few years of school, had been unsuccessful in school, had attended school in another country, or did not speak English, often had limited understanding of how American schools function. The Hispanic Dropout Project held committee hearings around the country and listened to parent and school staff testimonies about the high drop-out rates of Latino students. Many Latino parents said that they often had to overcome school resistance and hostility to be involved in their children's education. Many reported that their children's schools did not take them or their concerns seriously.[22]

Immigrant parents who do not understand the basic social and cultural organization of U.S. schools are at even greater disadvantages. A high-achieving Latina student whose parents had been born in Mexico explained, "They can't relate to what I'm doing. I mean, they don't know what it is. They know classes, but to them, it's 'Don't take any hard classes,' but, I mean, I have to take hard classes because I want to go to college. Basically, my whole life is at school."[23]

Mexican American as well as Anglo American and African American school staff, most of whom are middle class, are often far removed from the social and cultural experiences of recent immigrants and poor families. The staff may not always be sensitive to the barriers they face in engaging in partnerships with the schools. For example, in a rural school district serving many Mexican-immigrant families, school staff did not understand the anxiety many parents had about approaching American institutions. A mother from rural Mexico described her fear of going to her daughter's school because she could not determine where she was supposed to enter the building. She had come from a rural part of Mexico where the school was a one-room building with one entrance. She took her daughter to school each morning and watched her enter the building, but the school had a number of entrances. She was afraid she would choose the wrong door and not be able to find her daughter or someone who spoke Spanish. Indeed, the building had several large wings of classrooms, portable buildings, and a number of formidable entrances. There were no signs in Spanish to direct parents to the main office or to indicate that parents were welcome at the school. There was no obvious receptionist area where one might go for directions or assistance. Teachers and parents who have attended U.S. schools take this cultural knowledge of schools for granted.

A synthesis of research culled to identify factors that support healthy development and educational success of children shows that, after classroom practices, the *home environment and parental support* are the second most influential factors affecting learning.

Parents foster motivation to master the environment, help children develop competence, and build self-esteem—all essential factors for school success. Parents provide knowledge about careers, opportunities to learn, models of behavior, and social connections to the larger community. Again, *when parents' knowledge is congruent with that of teachers and other school staff, children are more likely to be successful in school and participate in postsecondary education.* Many family attributes associated with school achievement, such as reading to young children regularly and helping with homework, are significantly related to the parents' own educational experiences and academic skills. A tenth-grade student who had made straight A grades appreciated her family's support but noted the disadvantages she felt when her parents could not help her: "I'm in classes where it's like I'm the only Latino there. It's just like they [the other students] have tutors to help them and their parents are doctors or whatever. But, I mean, my parents can't help me because they only went to school up to the third grade. So, I mean, they can't help me with algebra or anything like that."[24]

School attitudes. Effective parenting strategies can help overcome *some* obstacles presented by low income, limited parental education, and lack of other resources to help children. But schools must also assume responsibility for working with parents and helping students learn. Many immigrant parents do the best they can for their children, given the resources they have. Schools must assume responsibility for children's successful academic achievement.[25]

One important challenge schools must face in reaching out to parents of all social classes is the reality of demanding jobs that leave parents little time to monitor the activities of their children or for active involvement in school activities. Very few families have one parent at home who can devote long hours to school projects or help their children with schoolwork. Parents may work two or more jobs or work irregular hours that preclude attending school functions. In rural areas, parents may drive long distances to their jobs, which lengthens the workday. Most working-class parents do not have jobs with flexible hours that allow for attending school meetings or functions without losing their pay. The Hispanic Dropout Project heard testimony from a number of parents who had left work only to wait several hours for a school appointment or be told the appointment had been postponed. Other parents said they were afraid of losing their jobs because of taking time off to try to resolve school problems.[26]

In a growing number of cases, children are taken care of by single parents, grandparents, extended family members, or foster parents. Students may be left on their own to make most school-related decisions, often in response to peer pressures. The changes that families of all types are experiencing means that planning for parental involvement may have to include nontraditional ways of working with families. Home visits allowing teachers to meet parents and establish positive relationships, mentoring programs that provide positive role models, and tutors to help with homework and academic problems can increase positive achievement outcomes. In some cases, schools may have to provide more support services for students to compensate for parents' inability to be involved actively in the schools.

Schools could also do a better job of getting accurate information to parents in a timely manner. During two years of participant observations and interviews with parents, I observed few opportunities for parents of older children to gain important information about what was happening in schools. For example, at one middle school opportunities for parents to address the content of classes and the school's expectations were limited to an open house at the beginning of the school year and parent-teacher conferences. Parents who missed the open house because of work or other obligations had no other opportunity to gain an overview of the school program or course requirements. PTA meetings focused primarily on fundraising. Most teacher contacts with parents were to discuss academic or behavior problems of individual students. Overall, parents had few opportunities to be involved in ways that contributed directly to helping them understand school policies or programs or helping their children succeed in school and prepare for college.[27]

Increasingly, in urban areas, Latino students are bused to schools away from their neighborhoods. Long distances are common in many rural areas where children must be gathered together in centrally located schools. When this happens, transportation is an additional problem for many parents who want to be involved in school activities. Long distances also mean that Latino parents probably do not know others in the school neighborhood, which diminishes parents' spheres of influence on their children's performances in school. Long distances also affect parent-teacher communication. Many of the informal exchanges of information between parents and teachers occur when parents bring children to school, pick them up, or drop by a classroom to leave something for their child; when parents live long distances from the school, these informal contacts are limited.

Latino parents may hold positive attitudes toward schooling in general and take pride in their child's accomplishments, but they may hold negative attitudes toward their child's school in particular. A school's environment may discourage parental participation and distract children from academic learning. Parents dissatisfied with their child's school are less likely to be involved. My interviews with parents revealed a number of reasons for dissatisfaction, including perceptions of prejudice, feelings that "teachers don't care," lack of attention because the school was too large, policies and discipline applied inequitably, and poor communication between the school and parents. Parents were eager to meet with program staff and other parents to discuss appropriate rules, how to help their children stay out of trouble, how to maintain authority as an assertive parent, and how to help their children do well in school. They were more likely to attend school-sponsored functions when staff treated them with respect.

School staff also must overcome some barriers to effective partnerships with families. Teachers and administrators often assume that parent involvement, or lack of it, is a reflection of the concerns of parents regarding their children's school success.[28] Teachers who do not involve families tend to have stereotyped perceptions of single parents and minority families and fail to see the value of working closely with parents. In reality, schools themselves often create obstacles that inhibit parental involvement, especially at upper-grade levels.

Despite the emphasis in popular media on the need for parents to be involved in their children's education, many working-class Mexican-origin parents perceive that schools do not desire their participation. In a two-hour workshop I conducted for Title I Latino-migrant parents from school districts throughout Texas, it became obvious from parent responses that the schools and parents had different perceptions of parents' roles in the schools. These differences often led to misunderstandings. One parent explained that her children's school in a small rural town had labeled parents as hostile or friendly. She reported that she was seen as a hostile parent because she demanded to visit the classrooms and wanted the principal to address her concerns about low passing rates of Mexican-origin children on the state-administered test required for graduation. Friendly parents were those who brought snacks for the staff and helped teachers photocopy materials. Although her school district had a majority of Mexican-origin students and a number of Mexican American teachers and principals, she felt the teachers and principals considered the schools "their territory" and did not see parent involvement as a positive factor in student achievement.

Other parents shared similar experiences regarding their efforts to participate in the schools. One parent reported that when she had gone with her seventh-grade son to the middle school on the first day of classes, she was told by the Anglo teachers not to interfere but to let her son find his own classes. The principal met with this mother and explained that the school staff expected teenagers to be independent in middle school. The teachers reprimanded her for being overly protective. The parent explained that she wanted to know where her son's classes were, meet his teachers, and see the type of environment he would be dealing with in the school. She and her husband believed that as parents, they should be knowledgeable about the school and monitor their son's behavior; she did not consider herself overly protective. The misunderstanding left this parent feeling that the teachers were "trying to tell me how to raise my children," and it discouraged her from participating at the school.

In both of these situations, the school staff perceived the parents' roles differently than the parents perceived them. The parents did not share the institutionalized attitudes and behaviors in the schools. In the first example, the school staff saw the parent's questions about low achievement and her desire to visit classes as an intrusion and perhaps a threat. In the second, the school staff were not sensitive to this Mexican family's cultural relationships with their children, which were expressed in close, protective supervision. In both incidents, more open communication about the school's goals for the children and the parents' desire for information could have minimized the conflicts.

Community Support for Parent-School Partnerships

Neither families nor schools can educate children alone. Effective partnerships of families with community-based organizations may be site specific, but there are some generalizations to consider. My tape-recorded interviews with Latino parents provide evidence that parents worry that there are few safe, adult-supervised activities for teenagers in the community that promote school achievement and college preparation. Parents do not know how to deal with negative peer groups or peer cultures that glorify drug use, poor academic achievement, and delinquent behavior. They want to learn about effective parenting strategies. Students not involved in school-sponsored extracurricular activities that foster positive peer groups and college-oriented activities have few community organizations as alternatives. Parents with limited incomes cannot afford to send their children to private, family-funded activities that offer educational advantages, such as summer programs on college campuses, summer classes, camps, travel, and even community-sponsored athletic teams and clubs. These activities charge high registration fees or require transportation. Many low-income families depend on the earnings of adolescents from after-school and summer jobs and cannot encourage their participation in the types of activities that provide experiences and information helpful to postsecondary enrollment.

In the interviews, parents expressed a need for Latino role models and community members to encourage students to do well in school and continue on to postsecondary education. They stressed that many children lacked role models at home who had attended college. Parents wanted their children involved in well-organized, well-staffed community programs that encourage and promote school achievement. Some families participated with their children in a number of activities that competed with school-related activities but had the potential of supporting school-oriented goals. Parents felt that religious activities were among the few opportunities for teens to learn right from wrong and that those types of activities offered help with the serious problems facing both urban and rural children today. Sports teams provided opportunities for parents, especially fathers, to be involved actively in their children's lives. School sports teams gave parents an opportunity to get to know their children's coaches and peers informally. If parents were persistent—and if their child was a talented athlete—athletic staff took an interest in the child's academic progress as well. Coaches often checked with teachers about academic achievement and reported to parents when their players fell behind in their schoolwork, so they could improve and remain eligible to play.

Community-based activities linked and coordinated with school activities provide powerful incentives for parental involvement and helpful support for student achievement. Parent support groups formed around community activities are underused means of providing information to parents who do not know where to seek help about school programs and colleges.

Reaching a Larger Pool of Hispanic Youth

In my research, I found that parents believed schools had given up on many students who did not share the behaviors and attitudes of "gifted and talented," "honors," and "college prep" students. Parents complained that school staff often lacked the will and energy to discipline and teach students who dressed and behaved differently. Parents protested that the schools shifted too much responsibility to parents for disciplining students' misbehavior at school.

Latino parents who were interviewed believed that only adolescents in serious trouble or the "superstars" received help. "Average" youth who behaved well and did not get into trouble did not get any special attention. Parents complained that school staff waited for students to fail before providing after-school programs, mentors, or assistance with schoolwork. One mother explained, "By the time I get a progress report from the school, it's like those six weeks have gone by and plus you've got maybe four more that have gone by. I'd like to see a little bit more communications of the teachers and parents to have a little more time to do something before the grades are slapped on you and you can't do anything. Because you can't go back and change this six weeks." All students can benefit from programs that deal with life skills, such as how to manage money, and how to plan a high school course schedule that prepares them for college.

Parents complained that the vast majority of contacts with the schools occurred following *negative* reports about children. School staff waited until students were in serious trouble to notify the parents about school problems. Parents said they wanted to be alerted earlier so they could work with school staff to intervene before the student created a negative record. Parents said many adolescents skipped classes because they did not see the connection between what they were learning in high school and their futures. Many of these same students did not see the serious consequences of negative behaviors in high school. Conversely, parents wanted school staff to help their children see the benefits of academic achievement. They wanted greater access to programs that push students to do well in school and that help them make plans to attend college.[29]

Opportunities at the High School Level

While many parents in our study were involved in school activities when their children were in primary school, parental involvement decreased once the children entered middle school and high school. Even working-class parents who volunteered reported they had not been called to work at the school or to participate in school functions in a meaningful way. PTA seemed to concentrate on fund-raising or activities in which parents provided food or services. The parents also said the PTA seemed to be run by "cliques" of parents who knew one another. The policy of setting appointments to see school staff or for parent conferences troubled working Latino parents and low-income parents who often had limited access to telephones or transportation and preferred to meet with school staff whenever they managed to get to the school. Parents wanted school staff to make greater efforts to reach out to parents. One positive approach they suggested for involving parents was adult education classes. Parents reported that when they tried to improve their own skills, they provided positive role models for teens. Many adult education classes also became forums for discussing college requirements and application procedures, financial aid, and ways to help adolescents prepare for college.

In focus groups with parents of teens, parents identified a need for more radio and TV public service announcements regarding school activities. Many low-income parents did not read the newspapers and often did not know of community or school activities that would benefit their children. Parents suggested a community newsletter to describe programs available in the community and how to enroll youth. They suggested working with adolescents to prepare and update the newsletter as a way of providing meaningful activities for youth. Parents also felt they lacked information about education agencies, what they do, and the services they offer. They suggested that agencies must do a better job in public relations so families know what services are available to students. Grocery store bulletin boards, public notices, posters in libraries, and other public announcements were suggested as effective ways to bring information about the school to the community.[30]

Characteristics That Make Programs Attractive

An analysis of data from interviews and focus groups suggests that successful programs involving parents as partners include several characteristics: they (1) deal with time and resource constraints; (2) provide information and training to parents and school staff about parental involvement; (3) restructure schools and programs to support family involvement; (4) bridge family-school cultural differences; and (5) draw in external supports from the community, government, agencies, and institutions.

Overall, parents expressed positive feelings about being involved in programs that help their children do well in school. Parents felt most comfortable with warm, supportive staff who quickly established rapport, allowed parents to talk about their feelings and concerns, and were knowledgeable about parents' home conditions, backgrounds, and experiences. While parents indicated that school-sponsored sessions providing information on adolescent development, sexuality, substance abuse, and parenting skills were important, the majority of parents showed little enthusiasm for traditional PTA meetings and did not attend regularly.

A broader definition of parent involvement may be needed to include the various activities parents can do with their families. For example, school staff and counselors might develop shared program activities designed explicitly to foster parent-child interactions and positive home-based activities to build academic skills. Promoting activities such as weekend college campus tours for entire families could respond to the time constraints imposed by other family demands. Parents have insightful ideas about the types of activities and programs helpful to their children, but few parents are involved in planning parental involvement activities aimed at promoting achievement.

Using peers, siblings, and other relatives to shape students' attitudes toward school can also be effective. Peer advice has a powerful influence on teenagers' attitudes about school. When peers, siblings, and relatives succeed in school and are supportive of education and the school's social standards, students are higher achievers. Older siblings are often actively involved in younger siblings' schooling in elementary school—tutoring in reading and math, helping establish realistic school expectations, and assisting with homework. But older siblings play lesser roles in middle school/junior high school. Research suggests that the decline in older siblings' involvement often occurs in upper grades when older siblings are not doing well in school. As a consequence, younger siblings rely on them less, or the older siblings are less willing to assist.[31]

The problem is not lack of parental support. Latino families promote strong family values and try to prepare their children for adult lives by encouraging their children to get a good education and stay in school. One mother explained, "I've always instilled in them the importance of their education, and I don't want them to just go to school just to be going to school because it's something that they have to do. I want them to understand that education is a fact of life. You need to know these things in order to get ahead in life."[32] This parent, like many of the Latino parents interviewed, expected her children to strive for something better than what they currently had. The majority believed that this goal could be achieved through obtaining a good education. Our schools, at all levels, can do more to maximize Latino parent-school partnerships.

Positive Programs of Parental Involvement

The Hispanic Dropout Project reported that the most successful schools aggressively recruited parents to work with them in educating their children. Parent roles were authentic and appropriate. The following programs involve Mexican-immigrant and second-generation parents in positive and effective ways.[33]

Kyle Family Learning and Career Center. The Kyle Family Learning and Career Center (KFLCC) is a collaborative effort in Kyle, Texas, to provide basic adult education, GED preparation, English language instruction, job readiness skills, computer literacy, and career planning assistance to the parents of Hispanic children in the local school district. Several agencies have shared funds and expertise to provide a professionally staffed adult learning center that can address multiple needs of families:

- Hays Consolidated Independent School District provided an abandoned bank building situated on the main street of Kyle for the KFLCC site and provided computer connections to get the center on-line;

- a prison located near Kyle provided day labor to clear out the former bank building;

- Community Action, Inc., a nonprofit, community-based organization that manages Head Start, Early Head Start, and Even Start programs, provided funds to refurbish the building, has paid the salaries of the Family Educators and ESL teachers, and has provided child care through early childhood education programs;

- an Adult Education Co-op housed at the state university near Kyle has provided additional staff to teach adult education computer classes and GED preparation;

- the Texas Workforce Commission relocated a staff person to the KFLCC to provide job search assistance and job training referrals;

- the local Job Training Partnership Act agency provided funds to run the center and staff to help link adults on welfare to job training opportunities.

Many recent Mexican-immigrant families participating in Head Start and Early Head Start attend KFLCC to learn English or prepare for the GED while their children participate in educational activities. Teachers at KFLCC coordinate their lessons with activities in the early childhood education and job training programs so parents can learn about the concepts their children are learning and can learn skills needed for job interviews. KFLCC has placed advanced adult learners in internships in schools as cooks and servers in cafeterias, secretaries and data-entry personnel in school offices, and teacher aides in classrooms. Senior staff at KFLCC hold master's degrees in adult education. They use cooperative learning techniques and engage adult learners in community-oriented projects. For example, a group of adult learners decided to prepare a survey for students at the middle school about barriers to school success. The adult learners conducted the survey, compiled the results, and prepared presentations in which they went to the middle school, spoke to students about their own life experiences, and encouraged the students to stay in school. KFLCC organized and helped sponsor a countywide graduation ceremony for adult learners who had earned the GED.

The center has sponsored evening computer classes and driver education workshops that have attracted male and female learners. The center has successfully provided well-trained staff and adequate resources for adult learners and offered services adults in the community want and need. Parent participation at parent-teacher conferences at the local elementary schools has been 100 percent because of combined school district and KFLCC efforts. A consistent number of participants has earned the GED, progressed in learning English, and gained skills and confidence in participating in school-based activities involving their children. KFLCC has received statewide recognition for its success in forging school, family, and community agency partnerships.[34]

Incorporating family histories into the curriculum. Catholic University of America recently involved families and children in an after-school project in inner-city schools. The program encouraged families to tell, write, and then type stories on computers. The program was built on the idea that all families have stories about their families' lives that, when passed on to children, help children establish a sense of cultural identity, a confirmation of self-worth, and a documentation of their faith and resiliency. The families (including grandparents, cousins, and other relatives, as well as parents and siblings) and children worked together to share family histories through storytelling and literacy activities. Families rotated through four different centers—a talking center, a writing center, a drawing center, and a computer center. The families talked about their stories and recorded them. Then, they wrote their stories with help from teachers and university volunteers. The children drew pictures about the stories, and the families typed the stories on the computer with help from computer troubleshooters. The family stories were shared in the schools. The program built trust and communication between families and schools, broadened family involvement beyond the normative mother-only participant, and provided ways for families to collaborate with teachers in improving children's learning.[35]

ALAS. ALAS, which means *wings* in Spanish, is an acronym for Achievement for Hispanics through Academic Success. The targeted students in this project were in middle school and had shown low motivation, poor academic skills, and the greatest need for teacher supervision. Many parents were Mexican immigrants from rural areas with limited knowledge of and no direct experience in parenting a child in urban America. They were learning English, had low levels of literacy, and could not receive information from traditional communications through mainstream newsletters or reports in English. According to researcher Patricia Gándara, this highest-risk group of students represents as much as 40 percent of the Latino population having difficulties with school. They also are the least likely to be affected by general school reform and traditional drop-out prevention programs.[36]

The ALAS program emphasized interventions to help students change disruptive behaviors, such as truancy, fighting, rule breaking, classroom discipline problems, and vandalism. Research shows that these behaviors are clearly related to low grades and dropping out of school. The program was based on the premise that the student and all service providers (including parents and teachers in this category) must be addressed simultaneously if the student's negative school behaviors are to be successfully changed. About half the students were English-language learners, and two-thirds were males. The ALAS program had four components: (1) *the adolescent*, who was provided problem-solving training and counseling, student recognition, and enhanced school affiliations; (2) *the school*, which provided frequent teacher feedback to students and parents, attendance monitoring, and training for teachers to help them work effectively with the students and families; (3) *the family,* which received access to community resources and parent training in school participation and guiding and monitoring the adolescent; and (4) *the community,* which focused on building collaboration among community agencies to provide family services and enhance student skills.

Teachers and students participated in ten weeks of problem-solving instruction, and students received two years of follow-up counseling and assistance in applying the problem-solving strategies. Students were given frequent positive reinforcement and recognition for achievement. Teachers made positive phone calls to parents when students met goals for improved behavior, attendance, and schoolwork. Students were made to feel cared for and looked after. The school contacted parents daily regarding truancy and attendance. Teachers provided weekly and sometimes daily feedback to students and parents about the student's school progress. Parents were provided direct instruction about how to be involved in the schools, how to monitor their adolescents' behavior, how to provide positive sanctions and reinforcements, and how and when to contact school staff and participate in school activities. Gándara emphasizes that the most difficult part of the program was working with the culture of teachers and administrators who were prone to "disown" these students and reluctant to share decision-making power. Also, teachers tended to know how students were doing in their own classes but did not coordinate with other teachers and, therefore, did not have an overall picture of particular students' academic work. The project had its own staff of administrators and counselors who spent most of their time building relationships.

The program succeeded in keeping twice as many at-risk Latino students in school and on track toward graduation, compared to a similar project. The positive results did not continue after the program's intensive involvement ended, suggesting that schools need to be accountable for students' progress, attend to students' needs, and individualize procedures and policies throughout students' school careers. The positive outcomes were attributed to the comprehensiveness of the ALAS interventions and the focus on youth, family, school, and community.

The ALAS program ran from 1990 to 1996 and was funded by a

federal research grant. Robert Slavin at Johns Hopkins University reviewed drop-out research nationally and found only three programs with comprehensive evaluation designs that provided empirical evidence of program success. ALAS was one of those programs. The evaluation involved a treatment group and a comparison group randomly assigned from the same school populations. Both groups were identified based on need for supervision, level of motivation, academic potential, social interaction skills, difficulty to teach, and need for special education. The groups were similar in reading scores, teacher ratings, and English-language proficiency. About half of each group was English-language learners, and two-thirds of each group was below the 25th percentile on the reading component of the Comprehensive Test of Basic Skills.[37]

The 36 ALAS participants received the full program: (1) development of positive social and task-related problem-solving skills; (2) recognition of accomplishments and activities that promote bonding with school; (3) intensive attendance monitoring; (4) frequent teacher feedback to parents and students; (5) parent education in school participation and teen management; and (6) an integration of community services. The 45 comparison group students, randomly assigned from the same school, received only the regular school program during grades seven, eight, and nine. Due to attrition, about 25 percent of the ALAS students were lost over the three years of implementation. According to the evaluation data, 75 percent of the ALAS students (27 out of 36) were on track to graduate after three years of the program, compared to 44 percent of the comparison group students (20 out of 45). ALAS also dramatically improved school grades and reduced the number of classes failed by the participants.[38]

The major expenses of the ALAS program, estimated at about $800 per student, were the start-up costs of staff training and additional personnel, including a half-time program supervisor, three counselor advocates, and a half-time office staff person.[39] Most of these costs were paid by the federal grant. Increased attendance of students who might have otherwise dropped out added money to the school district, which helped sustain the program during the project. Gándara concludes that to be effective over the long run, programs like ALAS must become part of the school institution. Otherwise, the programs will become targets when school districts or government agencies decide to reallocate resources.

The evaluators of the ALAS program determined that key components were establishing personal relationships with students and their families, closely monitoring students across the secondary school curriculum, increasing the aspirations of students, and increasing their basic academic skills. In the ALAS program, at least one (and sometimes more) adult was responsible for the social and academic welfare of each student. The program included specific components directed toward building positive and school-oriented peer relationships. The ALAS staff also helped find resources in the community to enable the families to provide for the basic needs of their children.

The program was consistent, intensive, and well coordinated from grade to grade. Students received constant positive messages about staying in school and doing well. The ALAS students were grouped heterogeneously with students who were doing well in school. They experienced increased time in classroom activities that reinforce achievement and promote collaborative learning. The language and cultural practices of the students were recognized and incorporated into the ALAS curriculum. The evaluation results of the ALAS program demonstrate that students with many risk factors can be kept in school, their test scores can be raised, and they can graduate from high school. When the federal grant funding the ALAS project ended, however, the school district determined that the program was too expensive and too complex to continue. According to Katherine Larson, who helped design the ALAS program, modified versions of ALAS incorporating the core curriculum of the program have been implemented in other school districts.[40]

Mobilization for Equity. In San Antonio, Texas, the Intercultural Development Research Association (IDRA), a nonprofit, community-based organization, is part of a network of projects seeking to build an informed constituency of parents and community leaders nationwide to support school reform efforts on behalf of children. One of the first activities of the IDRA project involved Latino parents from throughout San Antonio in organizing a parent conference. The conference brought together parents with many years of experience in raising children and volunteering in schools for the purpose of sharing their knowledge and learning about school reform efforts. The parents invited speakers and led workshops themselves.

Sixteen organizations from across the country (Arkansas, California, Massachusetts, Michigan, Mississippi, New Jersey, New York, North Carolina, Ohio, and Washington, D.C.) belong to Mobilization for Equity. The organizations train parents to work within school systems to understand the policy process and organize for better schools. Parents begin by analyzing specific problems and then consider more broadly what educational reforms need to occur to fix the problems. Organizations have begun dealing with tracking, school financing, equity in testing, and student support services.

The focus is on low-income families, especially Latinos and African Americans, because their children face problems of overcrowded classrooms, decaying school buildings, and inequities in access to technology and computers. The purpose of the organizational activities is to engage parents in learning about school problems, school reforms, and how those reforms affect them and their children. The community organizations are connected via the Internet to a Mobilization for Equity resource center that can access the latest information about nationwide school reform and parental involvement. A central database connected to Harvard University provides information from mainstream and ethnic news media about schools, school policies, and school reforms. For example, parents in New Jersey studied the state takeover of the Newark school district. The Education Law Center of Newark informed parents about their roles in the district's governance and what the takeover meant for their children.

Parents learn about their rights in workshops and seminars so they can participate in running the schools and examining school reform efforts. Parents receive training in monitoring the reform efforts in their schools. The San Antonio conference featured workshops on parental and student rights, bilingual education, gangs, multicultural education, and other areas of interest to the parents. The parents learned about the governance of schools, district policies, how the system works, and how they can advocate for change. Parents in New York studied student suspensions, testing, and transfers in their school district. Some centers have sponsored intensive training sessions for parents on crucial issues affecting their schools. The goal is to empower parents to move beyond the case-by-case issues of school problems and become advocates for policy changes and school reforms. These organizations work on the philosophy that school change comes about because teachers, parents, and community members work together to promote change. They believe parents need information about what constitutes academic success and failure. They also believe parental involvement should mean more than working in the lunchroom, selling candy for fund-raisers, and copying papers for teachers.

Industrial Areas Foundation: The Alliance School Initiative. Industrial Areas Foundation (IAF) is an organization committed to helping poor families gain access to power to improve their lives. The foundation has branches nationally and focused on building parent organizations that can demand change and work with school personnel, teachers, principals, counselors, and school district staff at all levels to change schools. The organization is founded on the philosophy that parents care deeply about their children and their children's education. IAF organizers acknowledge, however, that many parents are unaware of the rise in skill requirements for getting good jobs. Thus, helping parents to recognize low achievement as a problem is also an important goal of IAF. Many parents are unaware of their children's levels of academic achievement, what test scores mean in terms of achievement, or how the scores of their children and their children's schools compare with those of others.[41]

A second principle of Industrial Areas Foundation is to get parents in a position of power so they can actively participate in school governance. The definition of school participation according to the foundation is much more than attending PTA meetings and visiting classrooms. IAF involves parents in determining changes in the curriculum, making recommendations about how the curriculum is taught, and helping school staff make decisions that promote greater student achievement. This means that organizing parents have received adequate resources to provide quality education at their children's schools. IAF has organized parents to participate in school-bond elections, lobby school districts for new facilities and policies, pressure the legislature for more funding for schools, and monitor how funds are spent at the local level.

IAF uses many of the tactics used by labor union organizers. The Texas Industrial Areas Foundation organizes individual meetings with parents to find out which issues they care most about in their children's schools. IAF organizers use those meetings to identify potential parent leaders in each local community. IAF does not endorse any particular curriculum or program; instead, it works to empower parents in the local communities to identify issues and work toward systemic change. Teams of parents and teachers organized and trained by IAF walk the neighborhood and meet with the parent or guardian of each child enrolled in the neighborhood school. The teams and parents then identify school concerns and how the parents would like to participate. IAF and the teams hold meetings to discuss the parents' concerns. Meetings of parents and teachers build trust and serve as discussion forums for strategies to address identified concerns.

IAF organizers and parent leaders hold rallies around key issues to build commitment and spirit. IAF also organizes workshops for parents to help explain test scores and other indicators of achievement so parents can monitor their children's achievement and the progress of their schools. Parents and teachers learn how they can make their concerns known to decision-making bodies, such as school boards and district administrators. They attend meetings of these groups, make presentations about the needs of their schools, and seek support for the changes they envision.

IAF was instrumental in bringing together a network of parental organizations working with schools in the *Alliance Schools Network* in 1992. The alliance is composed of community-based organizations and schools, and the members include teachers, parents, and administrators working together with IAF organizations to improve individual schools. The Alliance Schools learn from one another. Every year, the Texas Interfaith Education Fund (allied with IAF) organizes a conference bringing together the parents and teachers from the Alliance Schools to meet with nationally recognized educators who have researched issues in educational change. At the conference, parents and teachers begin to recognize low student achievement as a serious problem they need to address together. The parents, teachers, and students in Alliance Schools develop confidence in their own competencies and learn to relate to one another in new and more positive ways.[42]

In 1997 the Alliance had 89 schools serving 62,673 students participating in the network. Eighty percent of the students were Latino, 36 percent were English-as-a-second-language learners, and 84 percent were economically disadvantaged. According to the data reported by the school district on student achievement and attendance, 65 percent of the 89 Alliance Schools met or exceeded their district's rate of students passing one or more sections of the 1996 Texas Assessment of Academic Skills (TAAS) test required for graduation. Since 1993 the Alliance Schools have increased their percentage of students passing all sections of the TAAS by an average of 20 percent. In 1996, 71 of the 89 (79.8%) Alliance Schools reached or surpassed the Texas average attendance records. Several Alliance Schools have made exceptional progress in improving the achievement of students and changing the school climate at their schools.[43]

The Alliance Schools also invited Texas Education Commissioner Mike Moses to meet with 600 Industrial Areas Foundation leaders from around the state as part of the ongoing dialogue with state leaders about continuing and increasing funding for Alliance School reforms. Following these dialogues, in 1993 IAF leaders and Commissioner Moses convinced the Texas Legislature to provide $2 million in extra funds for low-performing schools that had become motivated to change dramatically through direct parent and community involvement. The extra funding resulted directly from the efforts of parents, teachers, and other educators. A number of the leaders from the Alliance Schools had testified before the legislature about the importance of the funding and the progress the restructuring initiatives had brought to their schools. Houston leaders had testified about several Alliance Schools that had won the Mayor's Award for Excellence and the creation of alcohol-free zones around a number of schools and health clinics in other schools. Parents and teachers had testified about the importance of parents, teachers, and administrators working together to improve the schools.[44]

One of the schools that exemplifies the positive changes accomplished through the alliance is the Ysleta Elementary School in El Paso, Texas. Another is Zavala Elementary School in Austin, Texas.

Ysleta Elementary School used aggressive parental participation strategies to improve student test scores dramatically. In 1992 the Texas Education Agency identified Ysleta Elementary as "low performing" because only 14.3 percent of the Ysleta students had passed all three sections of the Texas Assessment of Academic Skills (TAAS). By 1997, 70 percent of the students had passed the reading component of the TAAS, 76 percent had passed the math section, and 71 percent had passed the writing section. In 1997, according to the Alliance School's statistics, 66 percent of the Ysleta Elementary students had passed all sections of the TAAS, a 51.7 percent improvement between 1993 and 1997.

Ysleta Elementary School is located along the El Paso, Texas-Juarez, Mexico, border in a low-income neighborhood. Nearly all (98%) of the students are of Mexican origin. Ninety-five percent qualify for free or reduced-price school lunches, an indicator of poverty level. Many families are first-generation Mexican immigrants who work in the *maquiladoras*, manufacturing plants located in Juarez and El Paso. Spanish is the primary language in most of the homes in the school community.

The El Paso Interreligious Sponsoring Organization (EPISO), an affiliate of Industrial Areas Foundation, worked with the Ysleta Elementary staff and parents to organize parent-staff partnerships in an effort to improve students' education. The school invested in a new staff position: parent educator. Parent members were placed on all school improvement committees, and parents were invited to participate in all professional development opportunities provided for staff. Organizers from EPISO went door to door to discuss school issues with parents and recruit them to become involved in the school. Parents and teachers held meetings to discuss high standards for teaching and learning. Parents' involvement in defining academic standards and expectations for the school encouraged teachers to promote higher quality teaching and learning at the school. Parents requested more precise standards of achievement so parents, students, and teachers could determine how well students were progressing.

As part of the achievement standards, teams of parents and teachers devised scoring guides for different grade levels and subject areas. Once parents and teachers clearly understood the goals and high outcome measures expected in the school, they worked together to achieve them. Both parents and teachers began to expect higher quality academic work in the school. Teachers, parents, and other family members continued to work together in teams organized to include representation across grade levels K-6, ensuring accountability and continuity in academic achievement as the students moved up through the grade levels.

One issue that emerged from the door-to-door discussions with parents and interviews with staff was traffic safety around the school. The parents and staff convinced the school board and the city to change the traffic patterns around the school and install new stop signs to protect children walking to and from school. Having accomplished this, the parents and staff felt empowered. They also convinced the school board to construct a new state-of-the-art school facility to replace the old inadequate building the school had previously occupied.

The community organizing facilitated by EPISO and supported by the Ysleta school administration and staff led to a number of significant changes at Ysleta and demonstrated the effectiveness of parent-school partnerships and the involvement of parents in school reform. The team efforts built on the strengths of parents, students, teachers, and local community organizations. Together, these groups were able to plan program development and implement higher academic standards. The results were demonstrated improvement in student test scores and attendance.[45]

Zavala Elementary School in Austin, Texas, is another Alliance School that has made significant improvements in the educational achievements of its students working with the Texas Industrial Areas Foundation. The improvements Zavala Elementary made resulted in the school moving from the last of 66 Austin elementaries in test-score ranking in 1991 to among the elite schools recognized for academic achievement.[46]

At Zavala, groups of parents and teachers met to discuss what they liked and disliked about the school and agreed upon a number of steps to raise student achievement. They changed the organization of instruction to include more cooperative-learning techniques and eliminated ability grouping. All children, even those with special needs, were assigned to heterogeneous classrooms. Teachers incorporated peer tutoring and other activities that made every child responsible for learning. Committees of parents and teachers identified new language arts and math curricula with a successful record of improving achievement for disadvantaged students. Teachers were provided planning time so they could coordinate instruction across grade levels. The school sponsored an after-school program that offered a variety of academic courses and popular extracurricular activities, including math clubs, karate, creative writing, and other classes and activities led by parents. The staff and parents obtained permission from the school board to start a "Young Scientists" program to prepare top-achieving students for the district's nationally recognized math and science magnet schools at the middle and high school levels. The school attracted outside support from computer companies, the National Science Foundation, and The University of Texas at Austin.

Participation in the Alliance Schools project eliminated the high rates of teacher turnover that had plagued Zavala Elementary because teachers were enthusiastic about the changes occurring. Student attendance improved so much that Zavala vied for the district champion school in student attendance. Student TAAS scores in reading and math raised higher than citywide averages.

The project was successful because the parents and teachers recognized that the status of student achievement at the school was too low and agreed that it could be much better. They agreed to work toward improving achievement together. The school implemented new governance structures that allowed parents and teachers to contribute toward solutions together. They had concrete measures of progress in student TAAS scores, attendance, and admission to the high-level programs in the district. Parents participated in hiring decisions and on committees that made decisions about funding and services to be offered to children. Parents felt at home at the school and visited the school to talk with teachers for positive reasons, not just when their children were having problems or misbehaving.

Parents and teachers recognized the difficulty of implementing systemic change and made mistakes along the way. The trusting relationships parents, teachers, and administrators had established allowed them to discuss successes and setbacks and learn from their mistakes without blaming one another. IAF continued to work with Zavala Elementary attempting to institutionalize the positive changes.

IAF staff are developing leadership among the parents, teachers, and local community members in various church parishes to assure that numerous groups are committed to reaffirm efforts to change institutional practices. All groups recognize that persistence and remaining motivated to continue monitoring student achievement and progress are keys to maintaining their accomplishments.[47]

Defining Success

Successful programs that involve Latino parents view families as having their own resources to bring to a partnership with schools. Programs are designed to promote family self-efficacy and value parental involvement. Many parents do have barriers to overcome—lack of formal education, economic needs, child-care problems, transportation, language differences, and negative attitudes toward schools—before they will become active participants in school activities. Many school staff also have barriers to overcome—not knowing how to work with parents or how to incorporate parental resources into the curriculum.

All parents want a good education for their children. Many are involved in home activities that support their children's education. If the climate is supportive and the programs meet their needs, most families will also participate in school-based efforts to help their children. Extended family members and "significant others" can also play important roles in children's academic development. As educators and teachers, we need to move beyond traditional notions of parent involvement and involve families in meaningful experiences with their children. Most important, schools and universities must support families' efforts to assist their children to succeed in school.

CHAPTER 6

Political, Social, and Pedagogical Issues Impacting Early Childhood Education and Public Schools

The challenges posed by increasing diversity in our communities and schools will be with us for decades to come. By 2050, Marcelo M. Suárez-Orozco predicts, the United States will be the only postindustrial world power with ethnic minorities constituting nearly half of the total population.[1] The difference today is that immigrants are much more socioculturally diverse than ever before. For example, public schools in New York and Los Angeles enroll children who speak more than 150 different languages. In terms of education and skills, immigrants are among the *most* and the *least* educated and skilled people in the United States. Immigrants are overrepresented among people with doctorates, Nobel prize winners, and those without a high school education. Suárez-Orozco predicts high rates of immigration will continue, despite increased border patrols and immigration laws that require new legal immigrants to have incomes 125 percent of the U.S. poverty level. This trend will continue because we live in a "transnational" age, a result of borderless economies fueled by communication technologies and systems of mass transportation.

Immigration and Education Policy

A recent study reported that immigrants now constitute more than a quarter of California's residents and workers and are responsible for more than half of the growth in the state's population and labor force. The immigrants are largely from Mexico and Central America, are less educated, are younger, and have more children than immigrants from elsewhere. The researchers found that the rate at which immigrants and their children succeed economically and socially directly depends on how educated they are. They concluded that because education is the most important determinant of the success of immigrant children, we must make special efforts to promote high school graduation and college attendance for these children, many of whom are born in the United States.[2]

Court action affecting immigrant children: _Lau v. Nichols_, 1974. Over the past 30 years, several significant court cases have addressed the lack of educational opportunities for immigrant children. The 1974 U.S. Supreme Court decision in the _Lau v. Nichols_ case, although based on the experiences of Chinese immigrant students in California, has had direct impacts on Latino immigrants and other English-language learners throughout the United States. In the _Lau_ decision, the justices decided that the failure of the San Francisco school system to provide English-language instruction to Chinese students who did not speak English denied those students a meaningful opportunity to participate in the public education program. The Court reasoned that merely providing the same facilities, textbooks, teachers, and curriculum for students who did not understand English was not equal treatment. The court ruled that when the schools provided only regular English-language instruction for English-language learners, those students were effectively shut out from any meaningful education. The ruling did not specify how the school district was to meet the special needs of these children. The decision stated, "Teaching English to the students of Chinese ancestry who do not speak the language is one choice. Giving instruction to this group in Chinese is another. There may be others."[3]

The interpretive guidelines for the _Lau_ decision published by the Office for Civil Rights of the U.S. Department of Health, Education, and Welfare clearly stated that "school districts had to take affirmative steps to rectify the language deficiency in order to open their instructional program" to immigrant students.[4] The *Lau v. Nichols* decision required schools to open up instruction benefitting students who did not speak English.

Further, the Office for Civil Rights offered specific remedies to eliminate past education practices ruled unlawful under the *Lau v. Nichols* decision. Those remedies included identifying the student's primary or home language, diagnosing the student's educational needs, and selecting an appropriate program. The remedies specified that secondary students could receive instruction in subject matter in the native language and receive English-as-a-second-language (ESL) instruction as a class component, or they could receive required and elective subjects in the native language and bridge into English, learning English in a natural setting. The regulations also allowed secondary students to receive high-intensity language training in English until they could operate successfully in school in English and then bridge into the school program for all other students. While recognizing that programmatic approaches would vary from school district to school district, the *Lau* remedies recommended bilingual education as the best way to provide special aid to limited-English-proficient (LEP) students, especially in elementary grades.

The intent of the *Lau v. Nichols* decision was clearly to include immigrant children in the education system by providing special English-language instruction and bridging into the academic curriculum. Still, the education of immigrant students remains controversial. Most recent court cases have attempted to exclude immigrant children from U.S. schools.

Undocumented immigrant children. Migration streams flow from places of origin where economic opportunities are limited, to destinations where economic opportunities are greater. Illegal immigration occurs when the receiving country adopts restrictive immigration laws that conflict with these economic situations. Many immigrants are *legal residents*, having entered the United States through official U.S. immigration processes, and they live under the protection of legal immigration status. Other immigrants are officially designated as *refugees* with transitional support services and assistance provided by the U.S. government. For example, many

Cuban immigrants have come to the United States as refugees and received financial assistance for relocation expenses, English-language instruction, and other benefits. Many other immigrants come to the United States without documentation, or they overstay official visas and are labeled as *illegal* or *undocumented* immigrants. These immigrants take great risks getting across the border and live in fear of being identified and deported. Mexican immigrants make up the largest group of undocumented immigrants, although many Central American immigrants and, in some parts of the United States, some Irish and Asian immigrants, are also undocumented. Children living in the United States illegally often experience increased instability, fear, and insecurity in their lives. Living as an undocumented immigrant also means living without legal protections, social services, and assistance available to most people in the United States. Undocumented status has been shown to be highly correlated with dropping out of school, interference with schoolwork, and physical and mental health problems. Undocumented immigrants tend to move frequently, hampering children's attachment to and achievement in school. Parents are reluctant to come to school meetings or protest unfair treatment of their children because they fear they will be deported. Currently, undocumented children are legally assured of free access to public education, but they and their families are not always clear about this right, and it has been challenged in the courts.[5]

Texas Education Code 21.031. States responded in various ways to the *Lau v. Nichols* decision. For example, shortly after, the Texas Legislature passed legislation to deny undocumented children access to free public education at local schools that had previously accepted these children.[6] The 1975 Texas legislation limited free public education to citizens and legally-admitted alien children. While the law did not directly prohibit undocumented children from attending public schools, it clearly denied them the opportunity. For example, as a result of the legislation, the Houston Independent Public Schools would not enroll undocumented children unless they paid $90 a month tuition. The Austin Independent School District required undocumented children to pay tuition ranging from $1,300 a year for elementary school to $1,729 a year for senior high school students. Because most undocumented children in Texas were from poor Mexican families and could not afford to pay tuition, the legislation effectively prevented these children from attending public schools.

Proponents of the legislation argued that undocumented children were inundating the public schools and adversely affecting the education of other students, as well as burdening Texas taxpayers. However, research conducted at the time demonstrated it was impossible to determine the impact of undocumented children on education services because often these students could be served by teachers and programs already in the schools. Some schools where student enrollments had declined in the wake of the legislation actually earned more money from the state through the average daily attendance of undocumented students. With regard to the tax burden, undocumented parents, like citizens, paid property taxes through high rental payments. They also paid state and federal taxes. Some, in fact, paid more taxes than required because they did not file for refunds, or they paid social security taxes and did not receive benefits.[7]

Another comprehensive study in the mid-1980s concluded that undocumented immigrants contributed more to the revenue of the state of Texas than it cost the state to provide services. Education was the most costly service at both the state and the local level, but health services were the most frequently used public services. Undocumented persons used few other social services. The study concluded that because undocumented immigration was such an emotionally and politically charged issue, unsupported, exaggerated figures were frequently used in arguments. It also determined that the methodology of studies about education and immigration should be carefully scrutinized before drawing conclusions.[8]

In the wake of the 1975 legislation, many districts throughout Texas began systematically excluding undocumented children. The districts' actions took the forms of refusing admission to children without documents proving citizenship or legal residency or, as mentioned earlier, requiring undocumented children to pay tuition as a condition for their enrollment. A number of concerned parents and interest groups filed suit against the districts in a direct attack on the policies. A case against the Austin Independent School District determined that students who were legally within the United

States based on specific definitions spelled out in the *Silva v. Levi* injunction could attend school. The *Silva* ruling prohibited deportation of aliens entering the United States before 1977, until final adjudication of their lawsuits.[9] A case against the Houston Independent School District was appealed to the Texas Supreme Court. At that time, the court upheld the constitutionality of the exclusion policies regarding undocumented children.[10]

Victory in *Plyler v. Doe*, 1982. In 1977 U.S. District Court Judge William W. Justice struck down the state and local exclusionary policy as it applied to the Tyler Independent School District. Judge Justice based his decision on the "lack of rationality" of the exclusions and argued that the Texas Education Code was unconstitutional because it violated the equal protection clause of the Fourteenth Amendment. A number of other cases involving Houston, Baytown, and the Pasadena Independent School District were consolidated with the *Plyler v. Doe* case and brought to the U.S. Supreme Court.[11] During these years of contention, large numbers of undocumented immigrant children remained out of school. An important consideration in the case was the effect on the future life achievements of the children who had been denied educational opportunities for months or years. The Civil Rights Division of the U.S. Justice Department filed a brief in support of the children noting that the Texas law penalized children for the actions of their parents, depriving the children of a critically important social benefit.[12]

In 1982 the *Plyler v. Doe* case was decided by the U.S. Supreme Court. By a 5-4 vote, the U.S. Supreme Court struck down the Texas statute as violating the Fourteenth Amendment arguing that the equal protection clause was intended to cover any person physically within a state's borders, regardless of the legality of that presence. The court argued that while public education was not a right guaranteed by the U.S. Constitution, it was certainly more important than other social welfare benefits. Denying children an education would make them illiterate and would prevent them from advancing on their individual merit and becoming useful members of U.S. society. The court also rejected the argument of Texas attorneys who claimed that undocumented children were less likely than other children to remain within the state and put their education to use there. The court found nothing in the record to suggest this was true.[13]

California's Proposition 187. The issue of schooling for un-documented immigrant students resurfaced in November 1994, when California voters passed Proposition 187, "Illegal Aliens, Ineligibility for Public Services Verification and Reporting Initiative Statute."[14] This initiative made undocumented immigrants ineligible for all public education. It required various state and local agencies to report persons *suspected* of being illegal aliens to the Immigration and Naturalization Service. Opponents of this proposition argued that it was unconstitutional and that it was contrary to the 1982 U.S. Supreme Court ruling in *Plyler v. Doe.* According to some observers, the crafters of Proposition 187 were well aware of the direct conflict between the education provisions of 187 and *Plyler v. Doe.* Their political goal was to challenge the U.S. Supreme Court case.[15]

Opponents argued Proposition 187 violated parents' due process rights because families were not given the right to contest being reported as suspected illegal aliens. Others argued that the reporting requirement of Proposition 187 might encourage discrimination based on race, color, or national origin. The implementation provisions of Proposition 187 also appeared to violate the restrictions of obtaining personal information about a student without prior consent of a parent. Educators argued that the proposition imposed a law enforcement function on schools that would adversely affect the learning environment for all children. Supporters of Proposition 187 claimed that the ultimate objective of the initiative was to curtail undocumented immigration by making the process of immigration less attractive. The implementation of Proposition 187 was challenged in the courts by the Mexican American Legal Defense and Education Fund (MALDEF) and other civil rights organizations.[16] In March 1998 a federal district judge found Proposition 187 unconstitutional (Proposition 187 proponents have appealed the decision to the Ninth Circuit Court of Appeals). The judge ordered written notice sent to state and local agencies and education workers telling that Proposition 187 was invalid and should not be enforced.

As shown in the following section, depriving immigrant children of education is not likely to cause their parents to return to their countries of origin. It is more likely to cause members of the second generation to become further marginalized from educational access than they already are.

Increased Immigration and Demands on U.S. Schools

Despite the negative climate, increasing numbers of immigrant students—with or without their families—have entered the United States in search of advantages associated with life and work in this country. Increases in both legal and illegal immigration to the United States in the 1970s and 1980s, together with increases in the proportion of immigrants coming from Latin American and Asian countries in the 1990s, have generated renewed interest in the impact of immigration on schools.[17]

The public education of immigrant students is of particular concern because schools have historically been the key institutions responsible for integrating immigrants and their children into the larger society. Also, in California and Texas, education is the public service arena within which immigration has had the most pronounced effect.[18] Nevertheless, little of the literature on the impact of immigration focuses specifically on education. Most studies have addressed the complexity of counting undocumented immigrants, immigrants' impact on the U.S. workforce, their use of health and social services, and the effects of changes in the immigration laws on immigrant flows to the United States.

The amnesty provision. Many analyses of the 1986 *Immigration Reform and Control Act* (IRCA) suggest that immigration restrictions do not substantially reduce the influx of immigrant students.[19] Through a general amnesty provision for those able to demonstrate continuous residence in the United States after January 1, 1982, IRCA allowed about 1.7 million persons to apply for legalization immediately. Experts estimated that 87 percent of those applying for the general amnesty were Mexican. Other experts in the early 1990s noted that as immigrants obtained legal status in the United States, they were more likely to send children to public schools. Thus, they predicted that the use of public school services would increase significantly as a result of the amnesty provision. These observers estimated that five years after legalization, about 42 percent of all amnesty recipients would enroll children in U.S. public schools. Given that the number of amnesty recipients was in the millions once family members were included and that those qualifying for amnesty were highly concentrated in California (55 percent) and Texas (18 percent), the enrollment of Mexican-immigrant children in public schools was expected to increase sharply in those states. This sharp increase may have provided the impetus for the legislation in Texas and California that attempted to withhold services to undocumented immigrants.[20]

Increased legal immigration. Several other factors about immigration added to the growing school-age population in the 1990s. Increased *legal* immigration quotas added more numbers. The family reunification components of immigration legislation gave priority to children of immigrants already in the United States. The 1990 *Immigration Reform Act* left virtually intact the family unification provisions of previous laws and provided for legalization of sizable numbers of family members of persons already legalized under the 1986 *Immigration Reform and Control Act.*[21]

With the family unification provisions, undocumented migration among Mexican women and children increased to even higher levels than those preceding the passage of the *Immigration Reform and Control Act*. Once these immigrant families settled in the United States for the long term, they began actively constructing and consolidating relationships within their new communities. Women established ties with other families, friends, and institutions. Through family members, they were drawn into various organizations and social interactions, participating in church groups, parents' school groups, and groups with their coworkers. Friends and neighbors visited frequently and planned and organized celebrations that tied together different households. The result over time was the formation of strong community ties that fostered settlement. Undocumented immigrants became homeowners, taxpayers, and small-business owners. They continued to register in schools and colleges.[22]

Increased naturalization. Efforts to cut services to immigrants, such as Proposition 187, have actually helped to stimulate an unprecedented boom in naturalization. Many immigrants who had neglected to become citizens felt that they should take steps to make their positions in the United States more official. Once naturalized, the immigrants were legally able to claim full social and economic benefits of U.S. citizenship for themselves and their families.[23]

By the early 1990s the impact of immigration on some cities had become proportionately greater than the impact of the "Great Immigration" of European immigrants a century before. For example, in

Los Angeles, San Francisco, Dallas, Houston, and Miami, foreign-born residents made up between a fifth and a third of the population. Immigrants' concentration in urban centers and their relatively high fertility rates have contributed to the growing population of students in American urban public schools. A 1990 portrait of immigration patterns showed that recently-arrived populations had relatively low levels of education. The large numbers of immigrant children who speak little English and arrive with differing levels of education pose a tremendous and growing challenge to schools.[24]

The ability of immigrants to participate in U.S. society as future citizens depends on the quality of the instruction and training their children receive and the measures taken to incorporate immigrants into U.S. society. Low education levels bring low wages and lead to greater employment instability, which may last over the duration of an immigrant's entire working life in the United States. A recent study shows that Latino immigrants and their children are losing ground in educational attainment, compared with other immigrant groups and U.S. citizens. Uneven access to preschool programs and low expectations of those Mexican-immigrant students who do attend school perpetuate the low educational attainments of large numbers of second- and third-generation Mexican Americans.[25]

Assimilation or exclusion? Historically, approaches to the education of immigrants in the United States have ranged from total assimilation to exclusion, reflecting different beliefs about how society should be structured. Before passage of the *Immigration Act of 1965,* immigration had been regulated by the 1924 *National Origins Act*, which set quotas on national groups allowed to immigrate based on the percentage of these groups already in the United States. The *National Origins Act*, passed during a particularly racist period in U.S. history, had the openly stated purpose of limiting immigration of non-White populations. During this time of primarily White immigration, U.S. educational policy was assimilationist. The mission of schools was to "Americanize" immigrant children. The immigrant education programs of the 1920s emphasized the teaching of English and the American way of life, including pledging allegiance to the flag, eating American foods, and acknowledging the superiority of the U.S. form of government.[26]

Social and political responses to immigration following passage of the *Immigration Act of 1965* reflected a much more exclusionary attitude. Debates in 1968 to place further limits on immigration represented a clear desire to restrict Mexicans, Black English-speaking and Creole-speaking West Indians, and other Caribbean and Latin American peoples.[27] In the 1970s much of the public and political concern over immigration centered on Latinos who had entered in growing numbers after 1965. In 1974 *U.S. News and World Report* wrote about the "newest Americans," claiming that the United States was experiencing "a second Spanish invasion."

State government responses to the question of how to educate the children of these recent immigrants has been complicated by court decisions and political divisions on the issue of language use in the classroom. In the states that continue to fund bilingual education, schools struggle to implement quality programs for all children who could benefit from bilingual instruction. Public support and funding for bilingual education has emphasized the early elementary grade levels, especially kindergarten through third grade. In 1992 only 22 states provided funds designated specifically for instructional services to limited-English-proficient students. Only 17 percent of the schools offering services offered intensive services that included significant native language use.[28]

Today, most middle school and secondary bilingual programs offer only a few core subjects of reading, writing, and basic math. Few high schools offer an expansive list of courses or college preparatory courses in the bilingual track. A shortage of certified bilingual teachers in many secondary school subject areas adds to the difficulty of implementing effective secondary-level bilingual programs. By failing to provide adequate instruction to students with limited-English proficiency, we may be shifting from the era of assimilating immigrants into the American way of life to a new era in which immigrants are excluded from educational success and, consequently, have difficulty gaining entry to the American middle class.

The Politics of Early Childhood Education

Mexican-immigrant families generally have a strong commitment and interest in education but often lack familiarity with U.S. institutions. These families often suffer from confusion about U.S. school programs and receive misinformation about what happens and what works and does not work with their children.[29]

Controversies over early education. Early childhood education and education programs, such as Early Head Start and Head Start, can be ways of beginning the inclusion process for immigrant children as soon as possible. Recent research emphasizes that early child care and education play important roles in nurturing children's development through kindergarten for a variety of cognitive, social, and emotional outcomes. One group of experts believes the effects of early child care influence long-term development, provide support for positive preschool experiences, and promote school readiness.[30] Early schooling has always been controversial, and it becomes even more controversial when discussing immigrant children. There has been a long-term conflict among those who believe young children should be cared for in their homes by their parents and those who believe center- or school-based care could provide a loving and supportive environment for healthy child development and perhaps add resources lacking in the family households. Immigrant families often prefer to keep their children at home. In home settings, immigrants can maintain their ethnic language and immigrant culture. In center- or school-based settings, the intent has been to socialize children into appropriate school behaviors, speaking English and learning American mainstream culture. The debate is intensified when the home and center cultures and languages are distinctly different from each other.

Mexican mothers with small children may be less likely to work outside the home than Anglo American and African American mothers, but recent estimates are that more than half of all women with children under six years old participate in the paid workforce.[31] As Mexican-immigrant women increasingly join in the paid labor force, out-of-home child care and early childhood educational experiences have become more common.

Even among those who agree that early schooling is important, there is strong potential for conflict over the *aims* of such schooling. Many people believe early education should focus on teaching cognitive and social skills. For immigrant children, the debate focuses on the language of instruction. Should it be the language the child has learned at home or English? Other people believe early education should provide a safe, stimulating place for children to explore their own interests. This perspective also brings forth the argument that the home language and culture of the children should be part of this exploration.

Another serious conflict is over the reality of what most early education programs can provide. Many programs do not have sufficient funding to create appropriate learning environments, hire well-trained staff, and maintain appropriate adult-child ratios. This is cause for concern because children in higher quality care are more likely to have better classroom environments and warmer teacher-child relationships. Policies promoting better quality child care for Mexican-immigrant students can have benefits that last into the early school years.[32]

Underrepresentation of Latino children. The President's Advisory Commission on Educational Excellence for Hispanic Americans reported that, in general, Latino children are underrepresented in quality preschool programs. From 1973 to 1993 there was very little increase in Latino three- and four-year-old enrollment in preschool, while non-Latino White preschool enrollment almost doubled, growing from 18 percent to 35 percent. Even as recently as 1995, first- and second-generation Mexican-origin three- and four-year-old children were less likely to be enrolled in any kind of preschool program, including Head Start, than were non-Latino White or African American children. Early school experiences help prepare children for school by teaching school-related skills. Children who do not participate in preschool programs tend to be less able to identify colors, recognize letters of the alphabet, count up to 50 or more, and write their names. They arrive at school behind other children who have experienced preschool. They may have also missed out on other advantages of preschool, which often include early identification of health problems, dental screenings, and access to available resources and support services.[33]

We have begun to focus more on the issue of availability of quality early childhood programs for Latino children as the numbers of first- and second-generation Mexican and Asian infants and toddlers have increased. The numbers of Mexican-origin and Asian first- and second-generation very young children have increased at higher rates than White and Black infants and toddlers, especially among the poor and near-poor. For example, during the 1980s, the number of poor White infants and toddlers increased by 12 percent, and Black infants and toddlers increased by 23 percent, while the number of Latino poor infants and toddlers increased by 60 percent, and poor Asian infants and toddlers increased by 121 percent.[34]

According to the report *The Future of Children*, a disproportionate number of Mexican first- and second-generation immigrant children are likely to be poor. While many immigrant children experience short-term poverty while their families are getting established in the United States or when families are disrupted by divorce, death, or the immigration process itself, others experience the more severe effects of long-term poverty lasting throughout their childhood years. Economic inequality and younger parents are two key reasons for long-term poverty. The poverty experiences of first- and second-generation Mexican-immigrant children have been ignored in much poverty research, although poverty has devastating effects on their educational experiences. Donald J. Hernandez has begun to analyze the incomes and economic employment experiences of various immigrant groups (by country of origin) over time and has focused on the impact of poverty on young immigrant children. Low birth weight, poor nutrition during developmental years, crowded housing, learning disabilities, developmental delays, and emotional and behavioral problems are among the many serious effects of poverty on very young first- and second-generation Mexican-origin children.[35]

Head Start. Although Head Start has been identified as one of the most successful poverty programs on record, research has not proven conclusively the program's national impact. Most reviews of Head Start's effectiveness have focused on long-term gains.[36] Critics of these reviews have pointed out that a one- or two-year program, no matter how well implemented, may not be sufficient to protect low-income children from other risks. Indirect benefits of quality early childhood programs, such as positive influences on parental child-rearing practices, parental employment opportunities, and positive links with the schools, have not been sufficiently documented.

Still, most agree that Head Start is one federally funded program that has been successful in improving the lives of many low-income children and their families. In the 1990s Head Start received additional financial support to reach out to more families, particularly Latinos. An Advisory Committee on Head Start Quality and Expansion was created in June 1993 to review the program and make recommendations for improvement and expansion. Since Head Start began in 1965, new knowledge has emerged about the types of services and supports that are effective for long-term positive outcomes for children. In addition, recognition of the importance of promoting family literacy and building on family strengths has increased. The Advisory Committee recommended that Head Start programs focus on staff development, improve management of local programs, provide better facilities, and strengthen the role of research in improving programs. The Committee also recommended increasing the number of children served and expanding the scope of services provided. It urged Head Start to forge partnerships with community and state institutions to improve early childhood and family support services for all children.[37]

One of the most recent extensions of Head Start has been the funding of Early Head Start home- and center-based programs to serve families with children aged birth to three years old. While Head Start has always involved parents in decision making and in the classrooms, the emphasis in Early Head Start is to involve families in early childhood education programs as soon as the mother knows she is pregnant. The program emphasizes child development, parenting strategies, and adult education; it is sensitive to the many varied cultures of the children Early Head Start will be serving. Still, the quality of the programs and their responsiveness to the needs of Mexican-immigrant families vary from site to site.

In recent years, Head Start has been able to serve only about a quarter of the children eligible under the federal income guidelines. Immigrant families may not know about the program or may be intimidated by the requirements to document income, employment, health care, and other information for enrollment. Many programs do not have enough qualified staff in the areas of social services, mental health services, and parent involvement to serve first- and second-generation immigrant children and families who could benefit from these programs. Both rural and urban areas struggle with high transportation costs to link children with early childhood education services. In rural areas, additional community resources are often lacking to provide dental and health screenings, health and mental health services, and social services families with young children need. Moreover, most Head Start centers do not provide full-day services and cannot accommodate parents who work full time.[38]

Encouraging reports indicate that outstanding preschool programs enhance the development of low-income, first- and second-generation immigrant students. Several studies have shown that children who participate in Head Start are less likely to drop out of school, less likely to be referred to special education programs, less likely to be retained in grade, and more likely to enroll in postsecondary education. Quality child care before participation in Head Start also has been shown to have positive long-term effects for all children, leading to better performance in kindergarten.[39]

Long-term results. Long-term results of well-implemented early childhood programs, such as Head Start and Early Head Start, are difficult to measure because many low-income children live in areas with poorly funded and inadequately staffed public schools. Once the children leave early childhood education programs and transfer into poorly performing schools, the gains they had made in preschool programs are not sustained. In general, however, data suggest that low-income students who participate in outstanding, cognitively oriented early childhood education programs subsequently perform better in school than do children of comparable background who do not participate.[40]

Research has also consistently identified the importance of a healthy pregnancy and a child's first five years of life as critical to establishing a strong foundation for learning. Within the last few years, numerous commission reports and task forces have recommended the expansion of programs for young children and additional services to families in existing programs.[41] Participation in these programs is voluntary, and the quality of the program varies from site to site and is highly dependent on the quality of the family educators and child-care providers.

Importance of nondeficit programs. It is important that models of child development be developed within specific socioeconomic, ethnic, linguistic, and cultural contexts. In this way, effective approaches for working with Latino children can be more clearly recognized, understood, and supported. Too often, program developers view Latino children as coming from deficit home environments and communities, and organize programs to change parents and homes. Continued focus on developmental deficits, rather than strengths, leads to further stigmatization of children coming from low-income ethnic-minority backgrounds. Focusing on deficits alienates the families and communities programs are intended to serve. Programs should be evaluated on how well they integrate the skills and strengths the children and families bring to the program, as well as how much progress the children make toward gaining skills that will help them be successful in school. All in all, more data are needed on school readiness and English-language learners.[42]

Training Teachers for Diversity

If we are going to encourage recent immigrant and second-generation Mexican-origin families to enroll their children in preschool programs and encourage their involvement in schools, we must have competent and caring teachers. Teachers' values, beliefs, attitudes, and prejudices affect their teaching.[43]

The impact of teachers. A recent study in Tennessee found that teacher effectiveness is the single most powerful factor affecting student academic gain. The researchers showed that as teacher effectiveness increased, lower-achieving students were the first to benefit. The best teachers were able to facilitate desirable academic progress for all students. And, regardless of ability, students with the poorest teachers made unsatisfactory gains. The researchers found that when parents and students complained about poorly performing teachers, those teachers were transferred to programs in which no one was likely to complain. Typically, these were schools or programs that served Mexican-immigrant students and had high student mobility rates and large numbers of low-income or minority students.[44]

This study has important implications for all education programs, but it is especially important for the education of first-generation Mexican-immigrant students. The Tennessee study and others suggest that teacher performance has serious outcomes for children, leading some observers to conclude that much of the low achievement blamed on children and families is actually the result of depriving the neediest students of classroom experiences with the best qualified teachers.[45]

For example, several recent studies in Texas have shown differences in achievement among students taught by teachers of varying ability. Kati Haycock reports the findings of a series of studies on the effects of good teaching. The average reading scores of a group of Dallas fourth graders who were assigned to three highly effective teachers for three consecutive years (fourth, fifth, and sixth grades) rose from the 59th percentile in fourth grade to the 76th percentile by the end of sixth grade. A fairly similar group of students was assigned to ineffective teachers for three consecutive years and their reading scores fell from the 60th percentile in fourth grade to the 42nd percentile by the end of sixth grade. The result of consistent, effective teaching was a gain of more than 35 percentile points in reading test scores. Similar effects occurred in mathematics. Beginning third graders in Dallas who were assigned to three highly effective teachers in a row improved from having average math scores around the 55th percentile to scores around the 76th percentile at the end of fifth grade. The test scores of a group of slightly higher-scoring third graders consecutively taught by three of the least effective teachers went from an average at the 57th percentile to the 27th percentile ranking by fifth grade. The researchers attributed a difference of a full 50 percentile points by the end of fifth grade to teacher effectiveness.

In another project, Haycock describes a collaborative endeavor by three school districts in El Paso, Texas. The city, the University of Texas at El Paso, and the school districts combined efforts to improve student achievement. El Paso is on the Texas-Mexico border with large numbers of Mexican-immigrant children. The goal of the collaborative is to prepare every student to be able to enter college without remediation. Over five years, the collaborative provided intensive assistance to teachers to improve instruction. Teachers received regular on-site coaching and attended summer institutes. The faculty at the University of Texas at El Paso made major changes in teacher preparation. The combined efforts of these key institutions resulted in overall improved student achievement and a narrower gap between Anglo, Latino, and African American children's achievements. Collaborative members concluded that investing in teachers really does pay dividends. The research suggests the urgency of recruiting, training, and retaining highly competent teachers for Mexican-immigrant children.[46]

According to the U.S. Department of Education, in 1992 about 80 percent of all districts reported having "some" to "a lot" of difficulty recruiting bilingual teachers of Spanish and other languages. Over half (53 percent) reported having the same difficulty hiring ESL teachers. Only ten percent of the teachers of limited-English-proficient students were certified in bilingual education and eight percent in ESL instruction.[47]

Characteristics of Good Teachers

The majority of students in teacher education programs are White, monolingual English speaking, and female. Yet, in many areas of the country, new teachers will be asked to work with students from very different backgrounds and experiences. Despite a recognition of the need to prepare teachers for diversity and a knowledge of the changing demographics in our public schools, relatively little attention has been paid to issues of social inequality and diversity in our teacher education programs. Most of the faculty who staff teacher education programs lack the interracial and intercultural experience needed to prepare new teachers for diversity. Moreover, little of the research on school and teacher effectiveness addresses diversity, although culture and context seem to be key elements of teaching that promotes the success of ethnic and language-minority students. Research has identified a number of factors that make teachers successful in teaching low-income and immigrant students.[48]

High expectations for students. A common element among effective teachers is the belief that all students can succeed. Effective teachers have the ability to communicate this belief to students.

Bridging the cultures of the home and school. Incorporating a students' culture into the curriculum can be a way to maintain the home culture and overcome the negative effects of the dominant culture. Helping students maintain a positive ethnic-cultural identity is critical to academic success. As discussed earlier, some experts encourage teachers to become researchers and conduct home visits, interviewing parents and other community members to identify the information and skills or "funds of knowledge," available to Mexican-origin households. They also urge teachers to incorporate the expertise of community members and community-based-knowledge sources into classrooms. This culturally responsive curriculum is based on empirical findings about the community and homes of their students rather than on stereotypes or generalizations.[49]

Teacher knowledge. Schools and communities with concentrations of Mexican-immigrant and second-generation students must focus on quality in teacher preparation, recruitment, assignment, and ongoing professional development. Standards must be high for entry into the profession of teaching. Assurances that teachers have adequate content knowledge, as well as skills to teach that content, are essential. Research shows that students perform best in the domains where teachers have the most expertise.[50] For teachers to include the cultures of their students in their classrooms, they need to know their students. They need specific knowledge about language acquisition, the ways socioeconomic circumstances shape learning experiences, and the cultural experiences of the students. They need to know the history and cultures of the ethnic and racial groups represented in their communities.

Effective teaching. A number of teaching strategies are considered successful for ethnic- and language-minority students. These strategies are numerous, but most include collaborative learning and the development of higher-level cognitive skills rather than factual recall. Diane August and Kenji Hakuta recognize the importance of teaching basic skills. They also argue, however, for a balance between the teaching of basic skills and the teaching of higher-level thinking skills. Effective practices identified in August and Hakuta's extensive review of studies of school and classroom effectiveness include allowing opportunities for student-directed activities, such as cooperative learning and peer tutoring; using strategies that help make instruction comprehensible to English-language learners, such as adjusting the level of English vocabulary so it is appropriate for the students' level of English proficiency; demonstrating what students will be doing, providing appropriate background knowledge, and using manipulatives, pictures, and objects related to the subject matter; building redundancy into activities; giving English-language learners opportunities to interact with fluent English-speaking peers; and using systematic student assessment to inform ongoing instructional efforts.[51]

Ongoing professional development for teachers should provide a wide variety of teaching strategies, a deep understanding of the subjects they will teach, and the ability to develop an inclusive multicultural curriculum. On-site coaching from experts is an important component of helping teachers be effective. In the El Paso school districts, where student achievement scores increased significantly, more than 50 full-time teacher coaches provided in-school assistance to teachers.[52]

Involvement of parents. Numerous studies have identified ongoing community/school communication and cooperation as an important contributor to effective schools and programs. Involvement can include a wide range of activities, from participation in formal parent-support activities to simple encouragement. An effective teacher will incorporate into the curriculum and classroom the strengths of the community and families. Homework assignments, home visits, and positive school-home communications can strengthen home-school connections. These relationships continue to be important in middle and high school, even though parents' direct involvement in their children's schooling tends to decline as their children get older. Parents can also monitor teacher assignment practices so that beginning teachers are not always concentrated in schools with low-income immigrant children or that the best teachers are not rewarded with "rights to transfer" to "easier" schools. Parents deserve to know when their children have teachers who lack expertise in assigned teaching areas. When parents know what the needs of schools are, they can become partners in helping the schools meet those needs.[53]

Appropriate assessment. Strong programs use ongoing assessment of student outcomes to monitor program effectiveness. When dealing with Mexican-immigrant students, teachers need to be knowledgeable about assessment practices and the misuses of student assessments. Teachers and counselors need to become advocates for their students in the assessment process. A central problem in assessing Mexican-immigrant students is their limited ability to perform on tests administered in English, especially if they are learning English. Many Mexican-immigrant students are exempted from national and state assessments of student achievement, or their scores on achievement tests are not disaggregated from the scores of English speakers, so it is difficult to gather accurate information about their school progress. Very few states provide assessments in languages other than English, and very few assessments provide teachers with information that can be used to enhance immigrant student learning.[54]

August and Hakuta's extensive review of studies of school and classroom effectiveness shows many studies of effective schools have not addressed factors that may be important to the success of English-language learners, a category that includes most Mexican-immigrant and second-generation children. In addition to the issues addressed above, August and Hakuta identify several other attributes that lead to effective schools and classrooms for English-language learners. Several of these attributes are discussed in the following sections.

Supportive schoolwide climate and effective leadership. Schools demonstrating supportive schoolwide climates place value on the linguistic and cultural backgrounds of the students, have high expectations for their academic achievement, and involve English-language learners in the overall school operation. The school staff value and use the language spoken by the students. The school principal is a key leader in planning, coordinating, and administering successful programs, and in making the achievement of all students a priority. Principals also recruit and retain talented and dedicated staff, involve the entire staff in ongoing professional development, provide support for effective teaching, and exert pressure when needed.

Collaboration and coordination. There is no one right way to educate Mexican-immigrant students. Different approaches are necessary to meet the diverse needs of students and the variety of conditions faced by schools and families. When a number of different programs are implemented, a smooth transition between levels of instruction is essential (for example, between native-language instruction in subject areas and content-based ESL). Coordination is the basis of the Success for All program, where ESL staff teach reading and language skills and closely coordinate their ESL efforts with efforts in the regular academic classroom programs. Content teachers also coordinate with ESL instructors. All staff cooperate to bring about success for the students. The Success for All schools develop a balance between instruction in basic and higher-order skills at all grade levels. Cooperative learning is used throughout the grades. Many studies of school and classroom effectiveness suggest that planning and providing for effective transitions from special-language instruction to mainstream classes is crucial.[55]

Intergroup Relations

The social climate in schools can undermine even the best of academic programs.[56] Newcomers soon become aware that gaining fluency in English is only one of the barriers to being accepted in the United States. Mexican-immigrant and second-generation students must also negotiate among various racial and ethnic identities and find a place in a social system highly structured by race. Existing research, based primarily on relations between Whites and Blacks, indicates that curricular interventions and school organizational factors may help develop more positive racial and ethnic attitudes and perceptions.

Racial and ethnic relations affect Mexican-immigrant students' achievement at every level of our education system. Yet, much of the research on diversity and racial and ethnic relations in America has been narrowly drawn to include mainly White and Black America. The President's Committee on Race Relations is a good example of this thinking. Native American and Asian issues were not recognized as a part of the debate in the initial stages of the committee. Certainly, in the U.S. Southwest, particularly in Texas and California, Mexicans and Mexican Americans must play a central part in this discussion. The rich contributions of many different racial and ethnic groups in the United States and the ongoing blending of cultures present diversity as an exciting and stimulating realm of experiences and opportunities.

There are, of course, growing debates about ethnicity and language, as exemplified in California's recent referendums calling for an end to bilingual education. Then, too, newspaper headlines suggest that we may soon have a less-educated, poorer, and increasingly violent society because of an increasingly diverse population. Many more headlines suggest that prejudice, stereotyping, and discrimination are still very much a part of racial and ethnic relations in the United States.

As we struggle to incorporate different groups, we have an opportunity to prove that democracy does indeed work. In fact, the very survival of democracy depends on all groups interacting in a positive way. But maintaining democracy is not easy—and positive racial and ethnic relations do not just "come about." We must pay attention to several realities. The United States is among the most diverse nations in the world. As discussed earlier, California, Texas, and New York have experienced the largest influx of new immigration and are among the most diverse states in the country. Large cities, such as New York, Chicago, Los Angeles, Houston, Dallas, and San Antonio, are good examples of the diversity in urban areas. Racial tensions, stereotypes, and discrimination disrupt our efforts to educate young people in preschools, elementary and secondary schools, and higher education. Still, research clearly demonstrates that a meaningful, productive dialogue about racial and ethnic relations can promote positive social change.

Negative racial and ethnic relations cannot be fully explained as an expression of prejudice alone. Racism is more than individual beliefs and attitudes; it is a system of advantages and disadvantages based on race/ethnicity, language, and history. The system involves cultural messages and institutional policies and practices, as well as the beliefs and actions of individuals. Racial prejudice, when combined with social power, leads to the institutionalization of racist policies and practices.[57]

Home and early school experiences. The influence of prejudice and racism begins early. Prejudice and racism are integral parts of children's socialization: books parents and teachers read to children; images on TV, in magazines, and in advertisements; songs on the radio and lullabies in our cribs; and people who come into our homes or are absent from our homes. As we discussed in earlier chapters, parenting styles differ by cultural backgrounds. Some of the most intimate ways we interact with our children, respond physically to them, communicate with them, praise them, and discipline them are largely determined by cultural patterns learned within our racial/ethnic and socioeconomic groups. At the preschool level, we can promote positive racial and ethnic relations by preventing one model of child rearing from becoming *the* correct model, and expecting all other cultural groups to conform to this model. Many parenting intervention programs have been guilty of this, and, as a result, they alienate many young parents and keep them from learning more about child development and ways they can help their children in school.[58]

Segregation at the elementary level. At the elementary school level, positive racial and ethnic relations are even more complex because our nation's neighborhoods are still very segregated. Most children grow up in neighborhoods with limited opportunities to interact with people different from their own families. Most children attend elementary schools that are racially/ethnically segregated or, if desegregated, usually only at a superficial level. In *Dismantling Desegregation: The Quiet Reversal of Brown v. Board of Education*, Gary Orfield and Susan E. Eaton give ample evidence of this trend toward resegregation. For example, from 1986 to 1991, the proportion of Black students in schools with more than half minority students rose to levels found before the Supreme Court's first busing decision in 1971. The number of Black students in intensely segregated schools (defined as 90-100 percent minority) also rose. A similar trend toward greater segregation of Latino students has also continued. According to Orfield and Eaton, during the 1991 school year, Latinos were far more likely than Blacks to be in predominantly minority schools and slightly more likely than Blacks to be in intensely segregated schools. Segregated schools are troubling because they reflect long histories of racial discrimination in many aspects of life. The benefits of desegregated schools come from access to resources and from the expectations of successful middle-class schools that routinely prepare students for college.

According to Orfield and Eaton, the level of segregation for Latino students is most severe in states where a substantial majority of all Latino children go to school: New York, California, and Texas. Compared with rankings from 1970, almost all states with significant Latino enrollment have become more segregated. "White flight" has not *created* resegregation in schools, but it is a factor. Other factors include increasing concentrations of Mexican-immigrant children enrolled in U.S. urban schools; a high birthrate among Latino families, which also increases the number of Latino children in schools; and a lower birthrate among White families, which decreases the number of White students. In fact, an overwhelming majority of Whites, Blacks, and Latinos of elementary and high school age attend public schools. Private high schools are more popular among affluent Whites, but private schools serve only one-eighth of White children.[59]

Orfield and Eaton argue that the increasing social isolation of Blacks, uncovered by William Julius Wilson, would have occurred regardless of White outmigration patterns because of prevailing trends in Black poverty and racial segregation. Other parts of the problem include the disproportionate concentration of Latino students in urban school districts with large minority enrollments and a lack of any significant initiatives for desegregation.[60]

Orfield and Eaton also point out that the majority of White children still attend public schools but lesser in number, while public school enrollment of Latinos has increased. A study by Douglas S. Massey and Nancy A. Denton argued that Mexican Americans lived in neighborhoods that were considerably less segregated, compared with Blacks. Mexican Americans in Chicago were not as severely segregated as Blacks, and their core neighborhoods remained a center of commercial activity. Thus, Latinos were not affected in the same way by the structural transformation of the economy that played a crucial role in creating the urban underclass for Blacks during the 1970s. Massey and Denton argued that Blacks experienced disproportionately more racial segregation than Latinos, and their inner-city neighborhoods lost much of the commercial activity because of the middle-class migrations to the suburbs and because of manufacturing jobs that moved to the suburbs or overseas. But Massey and Denton claimed the results were due to greater discrimination against poor Blacks, resulting in isolation of their neighborhoods, not just middle-class moves to the suburbs.[61]

Orfield and Eaton say that in 1988, 20 percent of African American students attended schools that were disproportionately minority. That figure increased to 24 percent in 1993. Among Latino students, 24 percent were in disproportionately minority schools in

1988, with an increase to 28 percent by 1993. Nationwide, in the 1991-92 school year, 73 percent of Latino students were in predominantly minority schools, and 66 percent of all African American students were in predominantly minority schools.

Amy Stuart Wells notes that part of the increased segregation of Latino students is because many Spanish-speaking immigrants to the United States do not see the issue of desegregation as a priority. They are comfortable with their children going to school solely with other Latinos and prefer dealing with schools in which the majority of the parents and students share their common Spanish language, culture, and values. Many Latino parents believe that their children are better served in predominantly Latino schools, where extensive bilingual education programs are more likely to be offered. Wells suggests that protecting the integrity of bilingual education programs, which demands a concentration of Spanish-speaking English-language learners, is a higher priority for Latinos than desegregation. Thus, she argues, successful school integration of Latino and non-Latino students has not been a concern in the Latino community. Wells also points out that data on educational attainment demonstrate that segregated schools do not always provide opportunities for school success for Latino students. She reports data from the 1985 National Council of La Raza report, which found that only 36 percent of the children identified as English-language learners had been assessed by their schools as such, and two-thirds of the children identified as limited-English-proficient students between the ages of 5 and 14 had not received special language services.[62]

At the middle/high school level. Because most children will attend racially and ethnically segregated elementary schools, the first time they are likely to have extended contact with others from different groups may be in middle or high school. Many Mexican American and Mexican-immigrant parents socialize their children to live in a hostile environment by making them aware of the prejudicial attitudes and discrimination they are likely to encounter. Many Mexican American and African American parents teach their children to confront prejudice rather than passively tolerate it. Whites also socialize their children about race, even though many Whites do not think of themselves as having race. Some White parents have

deliberately chosen to send their children to public schools to prepare them for diversity in their community and future workplaces.
Others may do so because they see no alternatives, and they may
transmit their own prejudices or stereotypes or do nothing to prepare their children to interact in diverse settings.

One study done in conjunction with a large urban school district
focused on barriers to achievement in diverse school settings.[63] Three
neighborhood elementary schools—one predominantly Black, one
predominantly Latino, and one predominantly White—fed into the
same middle school and high school. Both the Black and Latino
schools had large numbers of recent Mexican-immigrant students.
Immigrant students of several age levels were concentrated together
in bilingual classrooms and had little contact with English-dominant
students. Few children from the elementary schools had participated in classrooms with peers of different ethnic/racial groups
before making the transition into middle school. In the project, four
university faculty from different academic disciplines (a political
scientist, an educational psychologist, an anthropologist, and a soci-
ologist) worked with teams of graduate students to conduct focus
group meetings with students, administer questionnaires about racial and ethnic relations to about 1,500 students in middle and high
school, and interview parents about how they prepared their children for diversity.

The parents said they prepared their children for diversity based
on little real knowledge or understanding of members of other groups.
While the school district arranged for visits to the middle school to
familiarize students with the campus and routines, there was no
formal preparation for positive interactions with members of other
groups. The majority of the children looked forward to making friends
from other backgrounds and were excited about entering a more
diverse education setting. Once there, however, they did not know
how to approach others who were different, had few opportunities to
form friendships across racial/ethnic groups, and tended to "hang
out" with those they knew best—members of their own racial/ethnic
group from the neighborhood school. The school's academic tracking system contributed to racial/ethnic segregation. White parents
lobbied to get their children in the honors classes, even if the students were not high achieving. Latino and Black parents often did

not understand how honors classes worked and were less likely to intervene to have their children placed in those classes. The immigrant students were tracked into ESL classes. The honors classes were predominantly White, and academically talented Latino and Black children felt somewhat uncomfortable about crossing the "color line" and participating in those classes. Varsity sports and band offered some of the few opportunities for racially/ethnically mixed extracurricular activities, but teams tended to be segregated, with Latinos preferring soccer, African Americans dominating football, and White students opting for tennis, volleyball, and baseball. Most of the Latino and Black students did not stay after school for extracurricular activities because they had work or family responsibilities or lacked transportation. Students wanted more opportunities to develop positive cross-ethnic/racial friendships. Many also recognized and criticized the prejudices their parents held toward members of other groups.

School policies. Our research in this large urban school district confirmed what Janet Ward Schofield had found in other contexts. School policies can contribute to resegregation. When teachers and administrators segregate students into honors, regular, vocational, and remedial classes that create racially or ethnically homogeneous groups, the classes often magnify already existing tendencies toward stereotyping and discrimination. When immigrant students are segregated in ESL classes or bilingual tracks, their incorporation into the larger society is slowed. When teachers and administrators ignore racial acts or slurs and let complaints of harassment go unheeded, tensions percolate and boil over into violence. Further, when anxiety about dealing with members of other racial or ethnic groups is prevalent among students, behavior can be directed in ways that detract from student academic achievement.[64]

The school district in our study missed an opportunity to take advantage of the students' positive attitudes toward diversity and help them develop the intergroup skills that could have promoted more positive relations. Being able to get along with and work with people of different racial and cultural groups becomes increasingly important in light of demographic trends. Unpleasant and hurtful encounters will occur, but it is often through ethnic slights, misunderstandings, and disagreements that learning occurs. We can help

Mexican-immigrant students find a supportive community, and we can sustain our commitment in influencing positive intergroup relations for these students and in raising their levels of achievement. Finally, we can implement and enforce policies against discrimination and promote policies that support positive intergroup relations and the achievement of immigrant children. It is difficult to control people's thoughts and prejudices, but policies can set a tone and put in place the limits of acceptable behavior. Policy can provide opportunities and access for Mexican-immigrant children so they can benefit from a successful education.

Some Final Thoughts about Issues

Latinos soon will be the largest minority group in the country. Their numbers will make it impossible to ignore issues related to Latino-student achievement in the 21st century. Major cities in the Southwest and selected cities in the East and West already have sizable Latino school populations. It is imperative that communities pay attention to the needs of these students and find ways to address the issues that affect them: quality preschool and early childhood education, adequate instruction in reading and basic skills, isolation and segregation, teen pregnancies, after-school programs, positive peer relationships, high school graduation, opportunities to participate in higher education, and routes to meaningful jobs.

The chapters in this book use the lenses of culture, language, gender, family-community partnerships, and policy as variables to focus on issues of concern regarding the education of Latino children, especially those of Mexican origin. Few studies of educational equity satisfactorily disaggregate these variables. While these topics are addressed in separate chapters, the influences of each are tightly interrelated in the real-life experiences of Latino-immigrant and second-generation students. For example, among many students, differences by social class, generation in the United States, and gender may be greater than variances by ethnicity. Recent Mexican-immigrant students whose parents are well-educated and earn high incomes have little difficulty learning English and transferring the skills brought from schooling experiences in their home country to classrooms in the United States. Children whose parents are illiterate and hold unskilled, low-paying jobs may experience more barriers in school. Likewise, working-class male immigrant students may have very different experiences in U.S. schools and may encounter different expectations within their families and communities than working-class female immigrant students.

Using the lens of culture to look at educational experiences, this book emphasizes that culture permeates everyday activities, relationships, child-rearing practices, and classroom dynamics. Without understanding U.S. culture, it is difficult for recent immigrant students and their parents to participate in the school culture in a meaningful way. Likewise, unless teachers and the school community build upon the language skills and cultures students bring with them to the classrooms, little learning will be accomplished. The research available regarding culture and its influence on learning is intriguing. In many preservice teachers' conceptualizations, culture is not perceived as directly linked to learning and teaching in school.[65] Many practicing teachers also do not view school practices as culturally derived. Too often, the concept of ethnic culture is incorporated in trivial ways in the classroom: by celebrating holidays, featuring certain racial/ethnic groups for a month, preparing ethnic foods, or making cultural artifacts.

Teachers, parents, and administrators who possess little knowledge of the complexities of culture face the dangers of making generalizations and acting on stereotypes. When that happens, cultural misunderstandings become the bases of conflicts in classrooms and schools. Cultural- and language-based misconceptions are often responsible for misjudgments about the competence of immigrant students and result in lowered teacher expectations, another important determinant of Latino student achievement. The tenacity and significance of ethnic cultures in the lives of Latino-immigrant students are important in understanding the process of incorporating these students into U.S. society. Too often, our schools and teachers use a deficit model and focus on what is wrong with Latino students, families, language, and culture. Anglo American children become the norm against which Latino students are measured. This book challenges this perspective. The evidence presented in these chapters demonstrates the enduring strength of Latino families and their children as they have struggled with difficult sociocultural circumstances. Programs for Latino parents and children and teaching

strategies in the classrooms must build upon a model that emphasizes the cultural and linguistic strengths of children and their families.

Language is the primary means through which we receive, understand, and pass on our ways of life to our children and others. Often,
the very meaning of language is deeply rooted in cultural understandings. Language differences present major obstacles in school
achievement for Latino students, but the native language a student
speaks is not the overriding issue affecting achievement. Immigrant
children can learn in bilingual environments as well as in all-English
environments if the highest quality of teaching is provided, well-
coordinated programs are in place, and instruction is based on an
accurate and ongoing assessment of the students' needs. The influences of English-language learning on classroom performance and
learning to read and write have not been adequately explored. There
has been an explosion of research on reading and competing methods of teaching reading skills, but few of these studies have addressed the special concerns of English-language learners. It is difficult to imagine that language differences have been overlooked in
the highly language-related skill of learning to read.

Studies of teaching phonics, for example, make few references to
students who cannot pronounce English words or students who
speak English with an accent. Studies of whole-language teaching
methods often ignore the difficulties English-language learners confront when trying to understand the subtle or contextual meanings
of English words and phrases. In many studies of student achievement, researchers have not made explicit the principles for selecting
indicators of progress. Few of them have included influence from the
local communities to help determine priorities. Few of the studies or
programs have defined effectiveness for English-language learners
and Latino-immigrant students.

Each chapter describes components of exemplary programs that
serve Latino children, allowing readers to consider whether a particular program might be applicable for implementation at their
sites, with their student body and community. The descriptions
provide examples of positive institutional changes. They demonstrate how schools, community groups, and individuals have attempted to address the issues of language, culture, and gender to

provide a more equitable education for Latino students. Each of these programs suggests that meeting the needs of Latino students requires systemic changes rather than expecting students to adapt to the status quo. But the process of determining what is an exemplary program is not an easy task.

Effective schools and programs are commonly identified by reputation, nomination, or a few outcome measures, such as slight improvements in achievement test scores or student retention rates. Two recent works provide criteria for determining whether a program is effective and identify a list of promising programs.[66] According to Stanley Pogrow, a specialist in school reform, many program evaluations do not adequately deal with important issues of defining, identifying, implementing, and replicating exemplary programs. Few researchers make explicit the principles for selecting indicators of progress. In many cases, it is unclear whether increases in achievement occur because of modifications in curricula, leadership, school climate, instructional strategies, or because of associated student outcomes, such as improved attendance. Both Slavin and Pogrow agree that few exemplary programs are available. Pogrow also points out that programs effective in conventional learning environments may be totally wrong for other learning environments.

Pogrow emphasizes that standards for determining the success of programs must be high and proposes that exemplary programs should increase learning significantly beyond typical standards, such as national averages, and should do so consistently over time. Pogrow is highly critical of many claims made about successful programs and argues that comparing one group of participants with a control or comparison group means little if the participants improve at a slightly greater rate, but both groups remain low achieving. He also notes that we need to know the specific conditions of effectiveness, because no program can be universally successful. Pogrow points out that some programs are touted as effective because of marketing and lobbying strategies, and these programs may benefit in funding decisions, making it difficult for other equally effective programs to garner attention.

Many program evaluations are based on faulty methodologies, Pogrow also argues. Sometimes, control group comparison designs show results, but the research is based on only a few sites or only a few grade levels. Sampling participants and picking control sites are also controversial issues. A comparison site with inadequate staff and poor resources is an unequal basis of comparison for a well-funded intervention program. Determining outcome measures is also a problem. Some program evaluations are based on limited outcome measures. He further argues that effective programs should produce multiple positive outcomes. Identifying what is effective in schoolwide programs is problematic because the comprehensive programs are amorphous, which makes it difficult to determine which students are benefitting and how much. This is especially important in attempting to evaluate the effectiveness of programs for Latino and immigrant children. Many good programs might be judged statistically ineffective because the program was poorly implemented or too complex, received inadequate support in the implementation process, or the director had hired inept practitioners. Costs compared with benefits is also an important consideration, because it is expensive to implement new programs and may take several years to determine if a program is having a positive impact. For students, teachers, and families, the most important criteria are whether the program will work effectively in their schools, with their student populations, and with the resources available in their community.[67]

Improving Latino student achievement demands multiple approaches at different grade levels and key developmental stages. Preschool programs should focus on adequate care, child development, and ways of helping parents provide appropriate learning opportunities for their children. Elementary school must provide students with sound reading and math skills so they can build on those skills at the higher grades. Adolescence is a key developmental period; middle school must address peer pressures and social needs as well as academic responsibility and challenge. In high school, content enrichment, preparation for postsecondary education, and career interests take priority.

Parents must be involved in decision making and partnerships with schools at all levels, not just when their children are young. Also needed are specialized interventions, such as parenting programs; bilingual education; intensive English for English-language learners; newcomer programs; and remedial, gifted, and talented programs that target special populations or specific student needs. Equally important are schoolwide, systemic interventions and changes that address curricula, school organizational practices, teaching strategies, school climate, attitudes, and leadership.

The intent of this book is to offer information that allows practitioners to explore alternative approaches and models that are effective with Latino children and families. Few program evaluations and little of the research on school reform address the achievement of Mexican-immigrant students directly or address gender and socioeconomic differences in achievement among Latino students. Often, English-language learners are not included in outcome reports because the outcome measures are in English and the students are not proficient in English.

Sometimes, key questions are not addressed in evaluation studies. We need to know if the programs are successful with all students, including the students who are English-language learners and those who are most at risk of failing. We need to know if the programs address the needs of hard-to-reach migrant students and nonliterate families. We need to know how language and cultural diversity are dealt with in research protocols, teaching strategies, and program materials. The criteria compiled from the literature for identifying successful programs are general and rarely specific to the particular needs of Latino and immigrant children. The majority of the programs and the research studies featured in this book were designed specifically with these children in mind.

Community groups and educators must be cautious in determining which reforms to attempt in their schools. They must also be wary of conflicts of interest when individuals or companies have vested interests in promoting certain programs, training, or materials. Parents and teachers must become informed consumers of education and be able to consider opposing views and make reasoned decisions about effective strategies for change.

The roles of schools in helping families are being debated in many circles. Funding initiatives, such as Early Head Start, target early educational interventions and encourage intensive parenting programs for low-income and immigrant families. Some oppose these programs, arguing that any intervention is based on a deficit model and may destroy the cultural strengths of immigrant families. Others see these programs as ways to level the field, giving immigrant and low-income children some of the same opportunities and resources their peers experienced when they arrived at school. Some families perceive these programs as ways of gaining skills needed to improve the school achievement of their children. Others see them as an imposition of middle-class Anglo values and decline to participate. Many well-developed programs, such as those discussed in this book, involve parents actively in decision making and have been popular and successful. Latino-immigrant families are not passive recipients of unwanted education services; they value education highly and want the best for their children. They are adaptive and resourceful and take advantage of the components of education programs they value and need.

In the end, the relationships between students and teachers are more important than the types of programs implemented in a school. Teachers who have high expectations of Latino students will have students who achieve on a high level. Critically important are that school staff respect parents and students, listen to their concerns, and work in partnership with families to help students learn. Active and informed parents and teachers can influence education policies. The principles underlying the Industrial Areas Foundation's successful community-school partnerships bear repeating: (1) parents, teachers, and the community must recognize low achievement as a problem; (2) parents and school staff must agree to work together to raise achievement; and (3) communities, school boards, and state and federal governments must provide well-trained staff and adequate resources to assure quality learning opportunities for Latino students. We hope that implementing community-grounded programs will have a significant impact on Latino achievement, but the programs may have their most profound impacts on the attitudes of school staff and administrators when, perhaps for the first time, they must work as partners with the families of their students.

The best of program designs will be implemented poorly if the staff is not highly motivated and well qualified to work with Latino families and children. As currently structured, teacher education programs do not adequately prepare new teachers to work in diverse settings. Many teacher education programs pay lip service to cultural diversity but do little to help preteachers prepare to understand

and be sensitive to cultural differences. Prospective teachers are not prepared to work with families as partners in the education process. They are not trained to listen to their students and learn about the communities in which they teach.

An unusually large number of teachers currently in U.S. public schools will soon retire. The *New York Times* reports statistics from the U.S. Department of Education estimating that 2.1 million public schoolteachers will be hired over the next 10 years. Arizona, California, Idaho, New Mexico, Texas, and Utah—all states with large concentrations of Latino children—are expecting increases in elementary and secondary school enrollment of more than 10 percent. These new teachers must be prepared to work effectively with Latino students and their families.

Educators, in many cases, fallaciously believe that education occurs in a vacuum and pay little heed to the rich resources in the communities and families of their students. Historically, professionalization has tended to separate Anglo teachers from their students and the families of the students. Many professional educators assume they know all the answers to provide their students with an adequate education. When culturally diverse student populations are involved, professionalization creates an even greater chasm. Joyce E. King, Etta R. Hollins, and Warren C. Hayman remind us that schools cannot merely deliver instructional services; they must also ensure that all students actually learn.[68] That requires teachers to do more than "cover the curriculum." Teachers must enable very diverse populations of learners to develop their talents, think independently, manage complexity, find and use new technologies, and work cooperatively with others to solve problems.

The success of education programs is largely dependent on the willingness of education professionals to listen and learn from the families they serve. It is also dependent on the responsiveness of the targeted families and their motivation to claim ownership of their schools and take an active part in planning, implementing, and evaluating them.

Perhaps the lack of extensive research documenting the successful learning and teaching of immigrant students and the limited number of successful programs serving them exists because U.S. policies have not generally been supportive of immigrant education.

Legislation that limits immigrant's access to public education—such as California's Proposition 187, which attempted to exclude immigrant students from public education, and California's Proposition 227, which prohibits bilingual education—makes it difficult for teachers to provide adequate instruction for Latino students. The trends in California make clear the role of politics in the education of Latino-immigrant children. Legislation that mandates particular teaching approaches, regardless of the context, overrides concerns of parents and local communities and belittles the skills a child brings to the classroom in his or her native language. Decisions about students' learning opportunities are often politicized or based on pressing needs of the schools—such as classroom crowding or the availability of teachers—instead of assessments of students' needs. Both in the short term and in preparing students for college and careers, all children suffer when sound research, appropriate teaching and learning theory, and successful practices are not the bases for decisions that affect their education.

Resources

All contact information and Web URLs were verified before this book went to press.

Achievement for Hispanics through Academic Success (ALAS)
University of California at Santa Barbara
Graduate School of Education
Phelps Hall
Santa Barbara, CA 93106
Contact: Dr. Katherine Larson
Telephone: 805-672-2811
E-mail: larson@education.ucsb.edu

ALAS provides assistance to low-income middle school youth with emotional, behavioral, or academic problems that place them at high risk for dropping out of school.

American Association of Community Colleges (AACC)
One Dupont Circle, NW, Suite 410
Washington, DC 20036-1176
Contact: Arnold Kee
Telephone: 202-728-0200, Ext. 262
Fax: 202-833-2467
E-mail: akee@aacc.nche.edu
Web site: http://www.aacc.nche.edu

This agency publishes a journal featuring issues of transition and success in community colleges.

Annenberg Institute for School Reform
Brown University
Box 1985

Providence, RI 02912
Contact: Jeffrey Kimpton
Telephone: 401-863-7990
Fax: 401-863-1290
E-mail: AISRInfo@brown.edu
Web site: http://www.aisr.brown.edu

This institute studies public engagement in school reform.

ASPIRA Association, Inc.
National Office
1444 Eye St., NW, Suite 800
Washington, DC 20005
Telephone: 202-835-3600
Fax: 202-835-3613
E-mail: aspira1@aol.com
Web site: http://www.aspira.org

ASPIRA has conducted research studies and developed materials for parent education. It also trains parents to monitor school programs and participate in policy-making processes.

AVANCE Family Support and Education Programs
301 S. Frio, Suite 380
San Antonio, TX 78207-4425
Contact: Mercedes Perez DeColon, Vice President, Programs
Telephone: 210-270-4630
Fax: 210-270-4612
Web site: http://www.avance.org

AVANCE provides adult education and parenting materials that are culturally sensitive. The organization also provides technical assistance to other projects.

AVID Center (Advancement Via Individual Determination)
McConaughy House
2490 Heritage Park Row
San Diego, CA 92110
Contact: Mary Catherine Swanson, Executive Director
Telephone: 619-682-5050
Fax: 619-682-5060
Web site: http://www.avidcenter.org

The AVID program stresses college preparation and enrollment for underachieving students who are the first in their families to attend college. The program utilizes college-preparatory courses and tutors.

Center for Law and Education (CLE)

1875 Connecticut Ave., NW, Suite 510
Washington, DC 20009
Telephone: 202-986-3000
Fax: 202-986-6648
Publications line: 202-462-7688
E-mail: cle@cleweb.org or hn1669@handsnet.org
Web site: http://www.cleweb.org

This center works to advance the right of all students, particularly low-income students, to a high-quality education. CLE produces publications, conducts training, and engages in advocacy on behalf of students and parents.

Chicano/Latino Policy Project (CLPP)

Institute for the Study of Social Change
University of California at Berkeley
2420 Bowditch St., #5670
Berkeley, CA 94720-5670
Telephone: 510-642-6903
Fax: 510-643-8844
E-mail: clppcuclink4@berkeley.edu
Web site: http://www.clpr.edu

CLPP is an affiliated research project of the Institute for the Study of Social Change at the University of California at Berkeley. CLPP's mission is to develop and support public policy research on domestic policy issues that affect the Latino community in the United States. CLPP promotes collaborative research; encourages and facilitates the exchange of ideas; provides research and training opportunities for faculty and for graduate and undergraduate students; disseminates policy-relevant publications; and conducts outreach meetings for the general public and elected officials.

Consistency Management and Cooperative Discipline (CMCD)

University of Houston
College of Education
Houston, TX 77204-5872
Contact: H. Jerome Freiberg
Telephone: 713-743-8663
Fax: 713-743-8664
E-mail: cmcd@uh.edu

This program is designed to help students prepare for success, achieve self-discipline, and develop responsibility. The primary goal of CMCD is to create a disciplined, caring, and respectful climate focused on active learning.

Funds of Knowledge
The University of Arizona
College of Education
Language, Reading & Culture
Tucson, AZ 85721
Contact: Luis C. Moll
Telephone: 520-621-1291 or 520-621-1311
Fax: 520-621-1853

This program helps teachers and researchers to incorporate knowledge of families and communities into curricula.

Hispanic Mother-Daughter Program
The Junior League of Austin
1925 San Jacinto
Austin, TX 78712
Contact: Dorothy Garza
Telephone: 512-475-6308
Fax: 512-471-9600
E-mail: dzgarza@mail.utexas.edu

This program operates in collaboration with the Junior League of Austin and the University of Texas (UT) at Austin. Other projects operate independently at UT El Paso and UT San Antonio.

Idaho College Assistance Migrant Program (CAMP)
Boise State University
Center for Multicultural Educational Opportunities
1910 University Dr.
Boise, ID 83725
Contact: Dr. John Jensen, Director; Ms. Gypsy Hall,
Associate Director
Telephone: 208-426-1754 or 800-824-7017, Ext. 1754
Fax: 208-426-4006
E-mail: jjensen@boisestate.edu

The CAMP Program is one of six federally funded programs that help migrant or seasonal farmworkers or their children go to college. CAMP provides financial support, counseling, tutoring, and mentoring to at-risk students to ensure their success in school. Participants explore career options, visit work sites, and meet potential employers.

Institute for Educational Leadership
1001 Connecticut Ave., NW, Suite 310
Washington, DC 10036
Contact: Jacqueline Danzberger
Telephone: 202-822-8405
E-mail: iel@iel.org

The institute studies successful public engagement strategies and models of excellent practice in public schools.

Intercultural Development Research Association (IDRA)
5835 Callaghan Rd., Suite 350
San Antonio, TX 78228-1190
Contact: Aurelio M. Montemayor
Telephone: 210-444-1710
Fax: 210-444-1714
E-mail: contact@idra.org
Web site: http://www.idra.org

IDRA conducts research and development activities; creates, implements, and administers innovative education programs; and provides teacher, administrator, and parent training and technical assistance.

Kyle Family Learning and Career Center
Community Action, Inc. of Hays, Caldwell, and Blanco Counties
Box 748
San Marcos, TX 78666
Contact: Jon Engel, Community Programs
Telephone: 512-396-4564
Fax: 512-396-4565
E-mail: jonengel@itouch.net

This collaborative effort has established an adult center for education and employment. It involves Head Start, Early Head Start, Even Start, Hays Consolidated Independent School District, the Rural Capital Area Workforce Development Board, and other agencies.

Mexican American Legal Defense and Educational Fund (MALDEF)
National Parent/School Partnership Program
634 S. Spring St.
Los Angeles, CA 90014
Contact: Lucy Acosta, Director
Telephone: 213-629-2512, Ext. 120
Fax: 213-629-0266

E-mail: Lucy@maldef.org

MALDEF provides technical assistance and training for parents, teachers, and administrators in establishing parent leadership programs in their local districts; a national support network for Latino parents; a Latino parent involvement media awareness campaign; and an information advice line.

Mobilization for Equity (MFE)
National Coalition of Advocates for Students
100 Boylston St., Suite 737
Boston, MA 02116-4610
Contact: Jan Buettner, MFE Resource Center Coordinator
Telephone: 617-357-8507
Fax: 617-356-9549
E-mail: ncasmfe@aol.com

MFE trains and supports parents to participate effectively in local school improvement efforts. Ten fundamental student rights make up the MFE agenda, which, when implemented at the local, state, and national levels, improves public education for all students.

Multicultural Review
Greenwood Publishing Group, Inc.
88 Post Rd. West
P.O. Box 5007
Westport, CT 06881-5007
Contact: Gerry Lynch Katz, Managing Editor
Telephone: 203-226-3571
Fax: 203-226-6009
E-mail: gkatz@greenwood.com

This journal reviews books—including children's books—and reading and teaching materials for multicultural studies.

National Association for Bilingual Education (NABE)
1220 L St., NW, Suite 605
Washington, DC 20005-4018
Telephone: 202-898-1829
Fax: 202-789-2866
E-mail: NABE@nabe.org
NABE publishes a newsletter, a journal, and policy papers regarding bilingual education.

National Council of La Raza
1111 19th St., NW, Suite 1000
Washington, DC 20036

Contact: Charles Kamasaki
Telephone: 202-785-1670
Fax: 202-776-1794

The council publishes reports and policy papers.

National Institute for Literacy
1775 I St., NW, Suite 700
Washington, DC 20006
Contact: Communications Director
Telephone: 202-232-2025
Fax: 202-233-2051

This independent federal agency provides policy and program materials and assistance to help promote adult literacy.

National Task Force on Minority High Achievement
The College Board
45 Columbus Ave.
New York, NY 10023
Contact: L. Scott Miller, Director
Telephone: 212-713-8305 or 212-713-8195
Fax: 212-649-8427
E-mail: smiller@collegeboard.org

This task force is concerned with increasing the number of Latino and other minority students who achieve at very high levels academically at all levels of the education system.

Newcomer Program
Mains Elementary School
655 Sheridan St.
Calexico, CA 92231
Contact: Gloria Celaya
Telephone: 760-357-7410 or 760-357-7351
Fax: 760-768-1446

This program provides immigrant students with a transitional learning experience, enabling them to adjust to the changes they must make in a new country. The program uses students' primary languages to introduce a variety of instructional techniques and strategies (e.g., literature studies; use of graphic organizers; use of journals and logs for reading, writing, math, and science).

Project GRAD (Graduation Really Achieves Dreams)
1100 Louisiana, Suite 450
Houston, TX 77002
Contact: Sharon Jacobson, Executive Director

Telephone: 713-757-5162
Fax: 713-757-3144

Project GRAD is a systemic, education reform program for inner-city public education. Project GRAD emphasizes a solid foundation of reading, writing, and math; builds self-discipline and self-esteem; provides resources for at-risk children; and culminates with the possibility of a four-year college scholarship. It works in collaboration with businesses, education systems, the community, and individuals.

Sheltered English Approach (SEA)

Glendale Unified School District
Special Projects
223 N. Jackson St.
Glendale, CA 91206
Contact: Alice Petrossian
Telephone: 818-241-3111, Ext. 301
Fax: 818-246-3715

This approach-based system provides content instruction in ESL classes.

Success for All

Success for All Foundation
200 W. Towsontown Blvd.
Baltimore, MD 21204
Contact: Barbara Coppersmith
Telephone: 800-548-4998 or 410-616-2300
Fax: 410-324-4444
E-mail: sfa@successforall.net
Web site: http://www.successforall.net

Success for All is a comprehensive reform model used in more than 1,600 schools, including many serving Latino children. It incorporates reforms in reading, writing, and language, as well as tutors, family support, and other elements. It has a Spanish bilingual adaptation, Exito para Todos, and an adaptation for ESL instruction.

Teaching Tolerance

400 Washington Ave.
Montgomery, AL 36104
Editorial fax: 334-264-3121
Order Dept. fax: 334-264-7310
Web site: http://www.splcenter.org

This semiannual publication is free to teachers. It provides examples of successful school- and community-based projects that promote

positive intergroup relations and projects that focus on racial/eth-
nic, gender, religious, and economic inequities.

Texas Adult Literacy Clearinghouse

Texas Center for Adult Literacy and Learning
College Of Education
Texas A&M University
College Station, TX 77843-3256
Contact: Harriet Vardiman Smith, Materials/Research
Coordinator
Telephone: 409-845-6615
Hotline: 800-441-READ
Fax: 409-845-0952
E-mail: hsmith@coe.tamu.edu
Web site: http://www.cdlr.tamu.edu/tcall/

This clearinghouse provides a lending library, free materials, a quarterly newsletter *(Literacy Links)*, technical assistance, and professional development opportunities for teachers and administrators in
Texas adult basic education and family literacy programs.

Texas Civil Rights Project (TCRP)

2212 E. Martin Luther King Blvd.
Austin, TX 78702-1344
Contact: Sylvia Cedillo
Telephone: 512-474-5073
Fax: 512-474-0726

TCRP promotes racial, social, and economic justice. Stop Harassment in Public Schools, a project of TCRP, educates teachers, students, and parents about preventing and eliminating sexual harassment in schools. TCRP provides information and resources about
sexual harassment policies, litigation, and curricula, including the
manual *Sexual Harassment in Schools: What Students Suffer and
What Schools Should Do* in English and Spanish.

Texas College Assistance Migrant Program (CAMP)

St. Edward's University
3001 S. Congress Ave.
Austin, TX 78704-6489
Contact: Esther Yacono
Telephone: 512-448-8625
Fax: 512-464-8820
Web site: http://www.ed.gov/offices/OESE/MEP/

The purpose of CAMP is to provide migrant/seasonal farmworkers
who have completed high school requirements an opportunity to

work toward a four-year baccalaureate degree. This program offers the eligible student financial, academic, and other supportive assistance necessary for successful completion of the first two semesters of college.

Texas Industrial Areas Foundation (IAF)

1106 Clayton Lane, Suite 120 West
Austin, TX 78723
Contact: Yvonne Darrah
Telephone: 512-459-6551
Fax: 512-459-6558

IAF coordinates the Alliance Schools network, which works with the community to organize for urban school reform. IAF organizes workshops for Alliance School parents and teachers.

University of California Linguistic Minority Research Institute

University of California, Santa Barbara
Building 528, Room 4722
Santa Barbara, CA 93106-3220
Contact: Dr. Russell W. Rumberger, Director
Telephone: 805-893-2250
Fax: 805-893-8673
E-mail: imri@lmrinet.ucsb.edu

The institute publishes a newsletter and various reports on language and education.

Upward Bound Programs

Office of the Federal TRIO Programs
U.S. Department of Education
400 Maryland Ave., SW
Washington, DC 20202-5249
Contact: Office of the Federal TRIO Programs
Telephone: 202-708-4804
Fax: 202-401-6132
E-mail: Trio@ed.gov

The goal of the Upward Bound Program is to increase the rates at which participants complete secondary education. Upward Bound projects provide intensive academic instruction and support to participants in their preparation for college entrance. Services include tutoring; counseling; cultural enrichment activities; and instruction in mathematics, science, foreign languages, composition, and literature on college campuses.

U.S. Department of Education

Partnership for Family Involvement in Education
600 Independence Ave., SW
Washington, DC 20202-8170
Telephone: 202-401-3132
Fax: 202-401-3036

The Department of Education has a number of publications that describe successful local approaches for family involvement in children's education.

White House Initiative on Educational Excellence for Hispanic Americans

400 Maryland Ave., SW
Washington, DC 20202
Contact: Ana M. "Cha" Guzman, Chairperson, President's Advisory Commission; Sarita E. Brown, Executive Director
Telephone: 202-401-1411
Fax: 202-401-8377
E-mail: sarita_brown@ed.gov

This department has sponsored reports on Hispanic education.

Academic References That Provide Overviews of Research

American Association of University Women Educational Foundation

1111 Sixteenth St., NW
Washington, DC 20036-4873
Telephone: 800-225-9998, Ext. 477
Fax: 202-872-1425
E-mail: foundation@aauw.org

The foundation awards academic fellowships and grants. It publishes reports, including *How Schools Shortchange Girls: The AAUW Report* (1992), *Hostile Hallways: The AAUW Survey on Sexual Harassment in America's Schools* (1993), *Separated By Sex: A Critical Look at Single-Sex Education for Girls* (1998), *Gender Gaps: Where Schools Still Fail Our Children* (1998), and *Voices of a Generation: Teenage Girls on Sex, School, and Self* (1999). The foundation also produces videos on gender bias in education.

Handbook of Research on Multicultural Education
Banks, James A., and Cherry A. McGee Banks, eds. New York: MacMillan, 1995. This book includes 47 reviews of literature on topics related to Latino students and second-language learners.

National Center for Education Statistics (NCES)
Office of Educational Research and Improvement
U.S. Department of Education
555 New Jersey Ave., NW
Washington, DC 20208-5574
Telephone: 202-219-1828
Web site: http://nces.ed.gov

The center publishes reports on dropouts and the condition of education, as well as reviews and reports on education activities internationally.

National Clearinghouse for Bilingual Education (NCBE)
The George Washington University
Graduate School of Education & Human Development
2011 Eye St., NW, Suite 200
Washington, DC 20006
Contact: Minerva Gorena, Interim Director
Telephone: 202-467-0867
Fax: 800-531-9347
E-mail: askncbe@ncbe.gwu.edu
Web site: http://www.ncbe.gwu.edu

NCBE collects, analyzes, and disseminates information relating to the effective education of linguistically and culturally diverse learners in the United States through occasional publications, a regular e-mail newsletter, and a comprehensive Web site with a searchable on-line database and a full-text library.

National Research Council
National Research Council Committee
Board on Children, Youth and Families
2101 Constitution Ave., NW, Room HA 152
Washington, DC 20418
Contact: Michele Kipke, Director
Fax: 202-334-3829
E-mail: mkipke@nas.edu

The council copublished the report *Improving Schooling for Language-Minority Children: A Research Agenda* with National Academy Press, 1997, edited by Diane August and Kenji Hakuta.

Notes to Chapter 1

1. It was difficult to determine the appropriate term to use when referring to the children and family members addressed in this book. For editorial purposes, we decided to use *Latino*, unless the discussion refers specifically to Mexican American or Mexican-origin persons. One exception is in the discussion of statistical information produced by government agencies, which use the term *Hispanic*. Few other American ethnic groups have been more absorbed by the question, "What shall we call ourselves?" The members of this group vary widely in their specific histories, their generation of immigration to the U.S., geographical locations, and social characteristics. A term of definition adopted by one segment of the group may be considered inaccurate or offensive by others. In addition to Latino, the terms *Mexican-origin*, *Chicano*, *Hispanic*, *Mexican American*, *Mexicano*, *Spanish-speaking*, and *Spanish American* have been prominent Hispanic identifiers. Each has a specific connotation that distinguishes it. *Mexican-origin* includes recent immigrants from Mexico as well as those of Mexican heritage who are citizens of the U.S. of many generations; *Chicano* is a term used by some civil rights activists and is more popular in California than in other locations; *Hispanic* is the term used in government documents but it refers not only to persons of Mexican origin but to Cubans, Puerto Ricans, and others of Spanish ancestry; *Mexican American* is a term often preferred by third- and later-generation persons of Mexican origin, and it technically does not include recent Mexican immigrants, although Mexican immigrant children who grow up in the United States may prefer this term; *Mexicano* is the term used in Spanish, and it is strongly associated with recent immigrants; *Spanish-speaking* was an early term used in the U.S. census, but it is inaccurate because many Mexican Americans no longer speak Spanish, and many who speak Spanish are not of Mexican origin; *Spanish American* is often used in New Mexico and refers to people who can trace their ancestry back to Spanish settlers as well as Mexico; *Latino* is a term used by those who want to emphasize their roots in the Western Hemisphere and seems to be preferred by most members of this group. Other terms have also been used by various people, including *Latin American*, *Hispano*, and *Spanish surname*.

2. See Romo and Falbo, *Latino High School Graduation*.

3. See De Witt, "Rise Is Forecast."

4. See Rumbaut, "Immigrants Continue to Shape America"; Fisher and others, *Latino Education*, 6; and U.S. Department of Education, *Improving Opportunities*; and Holmes, "Black Populace."

5. McMillen, Kaufman, and Klein, *Dropout Rates in the United States: 1995*, 35. National Center for Education Statistics collected data in this report from state education agency reports.

6. See McMillen, Kaufman, and Klein, *Dropout Rates in the United States: 1995*.

7. Spanish speakers were followed by Vietnamese (3.6 percent), Hmong (2.4 percent), and Tagalog (1.6 percent), cited in Linguistic Minority Research Institute, "LEP Enrollments."

8. Information is from a study by the National Center for Health Statistics reported in Holmes, "Hispanic Births." The report also noted a high birthrate among Hispanic teenage girls.

9. Portes and MacLeod, "Educational Progress," 256.

10. See U.S. Bureau of the Census, *March 1998*.

11. See Donald J. Hernandez, "Family and Economic Circumstances."

12. See U.S. Bureau of the Census, *March 1997*.

13. See U.S. Department of Education, *Condition of Education*.

14. See Goldenberg, *Latin American Immigration*.

15. See Donald J. Hernandez, "Family and Economic Circumstances."

16. See McMillen, Kaufman, and Klein, *Dropout Rates in the United States: 1995* and McMillen and Kaufman, *Dropout Rates in the United States: 1996*.

17. McMillen and Kaufman, *Dropout Rates in the United States: 1996*, 16. Additional data included throughout.

18. Ibid., 26. See also Deborah J. Carter and Wilson, *Minorities in Higher Education*.

19. McMillen and Kaufman, *Dropout Rates in the United States: 1996*, 26, 32, 3, 34. Additional data included throughout.

20. See Deborah J. Carter and Wilson, *Minorities in Higher Education*.

21. See National Council of La Raza, *Latino Education*.

22. See Ohio Commission on Hispanic/Latino Affairs, "Annual Report."

23. See U.S. Department of Education, *Condition of Education*.

24. Ibid.

25. See Oakes, *Keeping Track*; Oakes, "Can Tracking Research"; Darling-Hammond, "Inequality and Access"; Oakes, "Tracking in Secondary Schools"; Slavin, "Cooperative Learning"; and Schofield, "Improving Intergroup Relations."

26. See Banks and Banks, *Multicultural Education*.

27. See National Council of La Raza, *Latino Education* and Kaufman, McMillen, and Sweet, *Comparison of High School Dropout Rates*.

28. See Mehan and others, *Constructing School Success*.

29. McAdoo, "Project GRAD's Strength," 9.

30. See Hispanic Dropout Project, *No More Excuses*.

31. See Wagner, "Power and Learning."

32. See Eugene E. Garcia, *Understanding and Meeting* and U.S. Department of Education, *Improving Opportunities*.

33. Alford and Brooks, "Days Away," B1, B3.

Notes to Chapter 2

1. See Spindler, *Education and Culture*; Sherzer, "Discourse-Centered Approach"; and Trueba "Culture and Language."

2. See Williams, *Mexican American Family* and Hondagneu-Sotelo, *Gendered Transitions*.

3. See Eugene E. Garcia and McLaughlin, "Meeting the Challenge."

4. See Rist, "Student Social Class."

5. See Kendall, "Learning about Diversity" and Demo and Hughes, "Socialization and Racial Identity."

6. See Marger, *Race and Ethnic Relations*.

7. See Coll, "Children of Immigrants."

8. See Phillips, *Invisible Culture*.

9. See James E. Garcia, "More Dropouts Minorities."

10. See Laurence Steinberg, "Autonomy, Conflict, and Harmony" and the literature review in Valdés, "Dual-Language Immersion Programs."

11. See Ogbu, "Variability in Minority School Performance."

12. See Ainsworth-Darnell and Downey, "Assessing the Oppositional Cultural Explanation."

13. See Hao and Bonstead-Bruns, "Parent-Child Differences."

14. See, for example, Sarah LeVine, *Dolor y Alegría*.

15. See Schieffelin and Ochs, *Language Socialization*.

16. See Harkness and Super, *Parents' Cultural Belief Systems* and Eugene E. Garcia and others, "Meeting the Challenge."

17. See Robert A. LeVine and others, "Education and Mother-Infant Interaction."

18. See Gaskins, "How Mayan Parental Theories."

19. See Eisenberg, "Teasing."

20. See Valdés, *Con Respeto*.

21. See Romo, de la Piedra, Lopez, Phillips, and Wortham, "Fathers and Families" and de la Piedra, "Mexican Immigrants' Definition of Fatherhood."

22. Valdés, *Con Respeto*, 193.

23. See Hamburg, *Today's Children* and Rothenberg, *Understanding and Working with Parents*.

24. See AVANCE Family Support and Education Program, *Final Report*. This study was funded by the Carnegie Corporation of New York and conducted by professor Dale Johnson of the University of Houston and Dr. Todd Walker of AVANCE.

25. See Sheila Smith and Sigel, "Two Generation Programs."

26. See Gonzalez and others, "Funds of Knowledge."

Notes to Chapter 3

1. See UNESCO, *Meeting of Specialists*; UNESCO, *Socio-Educational Situation*; and UNESCO, *Use of Vernacular Languages*.

2. See Ogbu and Matute-Bianchi, "Understanding Sociocultural Factors"; Cummins, *Bilingualism and Special Education*; Hakuta, *Mirror of Language*; and August and Hakuta, *Improving Schooling*.

3. Proposition 227, *English Language in Public Schools: Initiative Statute*, was submitted to the people of California in accordance with the provisions of the California Constitution, art. 2, sec. 8. Sec. 1, chap. 3 (commencing with sec. 300) was added to the *California Education Code*, pt. 1. According to the summary prepared by the California attorney general, the proposed law (1) requires all public school instruction to be conducted in English; (2) allows the requirement to be waived if the parents or guardian show that the child already knows English, or has special needs, or would learn English faster through another instructional technique; (3) provides for placement, not longer than one year, in intensive sheltered English immersion programs for children not fluent in English; (4) appropriates $50 million per year for 10 years to fund English instruction for individuals pledging to provide English tutoring to children in their community; and (5) permits enforcement suits by parents and guardians.

4. See Terry, "Bilingual Education"; Porter, *Forked Tongue;* and Cornejo, "Bilingual Education."

5. See August and Hakuta, *Improving Schooling*.

6. Examples of this research include Bankston and Zhou, "Effects of Minority Language"; Eugene E. Garcia, "Educating Mexican American Students"; Cazden and Snow, "English Plus"; Matute-Bianchi, "Ethnic Identities"; and Baker and de Kanter, *Effectiveness of Bilingual Education*. See also Hakuta and Gould, "Synthesis of Research."

7. August and Hakuta, *Improving Schooling,* 359. See also Hakuta, *Mirror of Language*; Gándara and others, *Capturing Latino Students*; and Thomas and Collier, *School Effectiveness*.

8. See Lucas, Henze, and Donato, "Promoting the Success"; Thomas and Collier, *School Effectiveness*; and August and Hakuta, *Improving Schooling*.

9. See Horn and Carroll, *Confronting the Odds*.

10. See Romo, "Mexican Origin Population's Differing Perceptions."

11. See Valdés, "World Outside."

12. See Celedon, *Analysis of a Teacher's and Students' Language Use*.

13. See San Miguel, *"Let all of them take heed."*

14. See Olsen, *Made in America* and Olsen and Dowell, *Bridges*.

15. See Portes and Zhou, "New Second Generation"; Hraba, *American Ethnicity*; and Hirshman, "Problems and Prospects."

16. Olsen, *Made in America*, 91.

17. See Portes and Schauffler, "Language and the Second Generation"; Portes and Rumbaut, *Immigrant America*; and Valdés, *Con Respeto.*

18. See Goldenberg, *Latin American Immigration.*

19. Romo and Falbo, *Latino High School Graduation*, 75.

20. See Fillmore, "Language Minority Students."

21. See Lopez, "Language."

22. Ibid.

23. See Romo and Falbo, *Latino High School Graduation.*

24. Portes and Hao, *"E Pluribus Unum*," 288. See also Portes and Schauffler, "Language and the Second Generation" and Portes and Rumbaut, *Immigrant America.*

25. See Portes and Hao, *"E Pluribus Unum."*

26. See Heath, *Ways with Words*; Delgado-Gaitan, *Literacy for Empowerment*; Fillmore, "Latino Families"; and Beck, "Understanding Beginning Reading."

27. See, for example, Gadsden, "Family Cultures."

28. See Moll and Greenberg, "Creating Zones."

29. See August and Hakuta, *Improving Schooling.*

30. See Heath, *Ways with Words*; Moll and Gonzalez, "Lessons from Research"; and Moll and Greenberg, "Creating Zones."

31. See Snow, "Development of Definitional Skill."

32. See August and Hakuta, *Improving Schooling.*

33. See Gadsden, "Family Cultures."

34. Ibid. See also Gadsden, "Understanding Family Literacy."

35. See Fantuzzo and others, "Assessment of Preschool" and Valencia, *Evolution of Deficit Thinking.*

36. See Pan, Snow, and Rowe, "Patterns of Verbal and Nonverbal Communication." This research is being conducted under the direction of Catherine Snow at the Center for Children and Families in the Education Development Center at Harvard University.

37. See Gadsden, "Family Cultures."

38. See Slavin and Yampolsky, "Success for All" and Slavin and Madden, "Success for All/Éxito para Todos."

39. See, for example, Thomas P. Carter and Chatfield, "Effective Bilingual Schools"; Eugene E. Garcia, *Education of Linguistically and Culturally Diverse Students*; Eugene E. Garcia, *Understanding and Meeting;* Lucas, Henze, and Donato, "Promoting the Success"; Moran and Hakuta, "Bilingual Education"; and Olsen and Dowell, *Bridges.*

40. See Olsen, *Made in America.*

41. I make a distinction between children who have to assimilate (give up cultural perspectives, speak English, behave like middle-class White children), which they often have to do to succeed in school, and children who have been shown to do well and are able to move amongst the school culture and their family, community, and peer cultures. These latter students acculturate (or take what they need to be successful) but do not give up the strong senses of identity, community, and support they have gained from their ethnic languages and cultures. I allow that it is necessary for immigrants to learn English and how to function in a variety of mainstream contexts to be successful; however, their ethnic identities and cultures can provide a support system, a sense of pride, and a sense of identity *also* needed to be successful. Acculturation, to me, means taking the best of both worlds. Dale McLemore, my coauthor in the *Racial and Ethnic Relations* textbook, prefers the term *incorporation.* New theories of assimilation recognize the complexity of the processes and note that it does not just mean taking on the dominant Anglo culture. As Blacks and American Indians, Whites and Hispanics, and Asians and Hispanics live in the same neighborhoods and intermarry, each takes on some of the cultural aspects of the others. Alejandro Portes and others have identified the concept of *segmented assimilation* to reflect ongoing processes among the many minorities in the United States who have little contact with mainstream Whites.

42. See Manaster, Chan, and Safady, "Mexican American."

43. See Valencia and Aburto, "Uses and Abuses."

44. See Masahiko and Ovando, "Language Issues."

45. Stevens and Wood, *Justice, Ideology, and Education*, 97. Secondary school programs also need sound ways of transferring achievement information with migrant students who move from school to school. Schools must be able to document assessment results, courses taken, and courses recommended to be taken, as well as partial and complete credits awarded for work completed during the enrollment period. This information is essential for meeting the education needs of secondary migrant students.

46. See Orfield, Eaton, and the Harvard Project on School Desegregation, *Dismantling Desegregation.*

47. See Eugene E. Garcia, "Educating Mexican American Students."

48. Delgado-Gaitan, *Literacy for Empowerment*, 1 and Valdés, *Con Respeto,* 167.

49. See Gándara and others, *Capturing Latino Students* and Romo and Falbo, *Latino High School Graduation.*

50. See Azmitia and others, "Older Siblings' Participation."

51. See Cummins, "Role of Primary Language" and Cummins, "Empowering Minority Students."

52. See Neubert and Leak, "Serving Urban Youth" and Imel, *New Work Force.*

53. See Ocasio, "Across the Nation."

54. See Salerno, *Migrant Students.*

55. See Texas Migrant Interstate Program, *Migrant Interstate Coordination Report.* In 1996 the UT migrant program won the National University Continuing Education Association's Significant Achievement in Independent Study Award and the Distinguished Credit Program Award given by the Region VII Association for Continuing Higher Education. The program offers flexibility to migrant students who may work in the fields with their families and move to follow the crops. Students set their own study schedules and choose the dates of their final examinations based on how prepared they are to take the tests. There are no enrollment limitations, and students can earn credits even if they are living in rural areas or far from their home schools. Before the growth of the Internet, students mailed completed lessons and computer cards to the UT Migrant Student Program and took paper-and-pencil exams.

56. The CAMP program maintains five other sites in addition to St. Edwards University: California State University, Sacramento; California State University, Fresno; Boise State University in Idaho; Oregon State University; and Pennsylvania State University. For more information about St. Edwards University's CAMP program, see *St. Edward's University News* 41, no. 2 (1998).

Notes to Chapter 4

1. See De Leon, "Career Development."

2. See Alcalay, "Hispanic Women."

3. See Lee and Sing, "Gender Equity."

4. See Vega, "Study of Latino Families"; Marcelo M. Suárez-Orozco and Carola E. Suárez-Orozco, "Cultural Patterning"; and Valenzuela and Dornbusch, "Familism and Assimilation."

5. See Ortiz, *Mexican American Women*; National Council of La Raza, *Latino Education*; and Williams, *Mexican American Family.*

6. See Tinajero, Gonzales, and Dick, *Raising Career Aspirations.*

7. See Solis, "Status of Latino Children" and Becerra and de Anda, "Pregnancy and Motherhood."

8. See Ortiz, *Mexican American Women*; Martinez, "High Achieving Latinas"; Valenzuela, "Liberal Gender Role Attitudes"; and Anderson, *Changing Woman.*

9. See Ventura and others, *Advance Report*; Riba and Zinn, "Childbearing among Youths Studied"; and Luker, *Dubious Conceptions.*

10. See Bianchi and Spain, "Women, Work, and Family" and Child Trends, *Summary of Facts.*

11. See Children's Defense Fund, *Teenage Pregnancy.*

12. See Academy for Educational Development, *Short Changing* and Arthur E. Hernández, "Do Role Models Influence."

13. See Romo and Falbo, *Latino High School Graduation.*

14. See Darabi, "Education of Non-High School Graduates."

15. See Carola E. Suárez-Orozco and Marcelo M. Suárez-Orozco, *Transformations.*

16. See O'Halloran, "Mexican American Female Students" and Del Castillo and Torres, "Interdependency of Educational Institutions."

17. See Romo and Falbo, *Latino High School Graduation* and Intercultural Development Research Association, *IDRA Newsletter.*

18. See Crocker, "Report Card"; Romo and Falbo, *Latino High School Graduation*; and Martinez, "High Achieving Latinas."

19. See Rosenbaum, Miller, and Krei, "Gatekeeping in an Era."

20. See Keating, "Striving for Sex Equity" and Scott and Schau, "Sex Equity."

21. See the following studies by the American Association of University Women: *How Schools Shortchange Girls* and *Gender Gaps.*

22. See Goldberg, "After Girls Get the Attention."

23. See Roberts and others, "Gender Differences."

24. See Laurence D. Steinberg, Brown, and Dornbusch, *Beyond the Classroom.*

25. See Reyes, Gillock, and Kabus, "Longitudinal Study" and Martinez, "High Achieving Latinas."

26. See Adler and Adler, *Peer Power.*

27. See Romo and Falbo, *Latino High School Graduation.*

28. See Valenzuela, "Liberal Gender Role Attitudes" and Valenzuela and Dornbusch, "Familism and Assimilation."

29. This story, told by an immigrant father, comes from a focus group graduate students and I conducted with Early Head Start fathers in November 1997 as part of a project funded by the Hogg Foundation for Mental Health. The project is called "Fathers and Families: A Study of Working Class Mexican Origin Fathers' Parenting Strategies."

30. See Decker and Van Winkle, *Life in the Gang*; Moore, *Homeboys*; Moore, *Going Down to the Barrio*; Vigil, *Barrio Gangs*; and Horowitz, *Honor and the American Dream.*

31. See Moore, *Going Down to the Barrio* and Campbell, "Female Participation in Gangs."

32. See Decker and Van Winkle, *Life in the Gang.*

33. See Moore, *Homeboys* and Vigil, *Barrio Gangs.*

34. Romo and Falbo, *Latino High School Graduation*, 69-91. See also Campbell, "Female Participation in Gangs."

35. See Laurence D. Steinberg, Brown, and Dornbusch, *Beyond the Classroom.*

36. See Savin-Williams and Berndt, "Friendship and Peer Relations."

37. See Texas Civil Rights Project, "Sexual Harassment in Schools."

38. See Eder, Evans, and Parker, *School Talk.*

39. See Texas Civil Rights Project, "Sexual Harassment in Schools."

40. See Merten, "Meaning of Meanness."

41. See Arthur Hernández, Vargas-Lew, and Martinez, "Intergenerational Academic Aspirations." See also "Why Hispanic Women Succeed in Higher Ed."

42. See Sosa and Garcia, "MIJA."

43. Ibid. See also De Luna, "Project MIJA."

44. See Sosa and Garcia, "MIJA."

45. See De Luna and Montes, "MIJA Girls."

46. See Yáñz-Pérez, "IDRA's MIJA Program Expands."

47. See Sadker and Sadker, *Failing at Fairness* and Mehan and others, *Constructing School Success.*

48. See Lucas, Henze, and Donato, "Promoting the Success."

49. Sue Kaulfus of PEP provided fax of PEP statistics to author, 1998.

50. See Tinajero, Gonzales, and Dick, *Raising Career Aspirations* and Arthur Hernández, Vargas-Lew, and Martinez, "Intergenerational Academic Aspirations."

51. See Zavella, "Reflections on Diversity."

52. See Scribner, "Advocating for Hispanic High School Students."

53. See American Association of University Women, *How Schools Shortchange Girls.*

54. See American Association of University Women, *Gender Gaps.*

Notes to Chapter 5

1. See Gándara and others, *Capturing Latino Students.*

2. See Duncan and Brooks-Gunn, *Consequences of Growing Up Poor* and Teachman and others, "Poverty During Adolescence."

3. See Smith, Brooks-Gunn, and Klebanov, "Consequences of Living in Poverty."

4. Ibid.

5. See Conger, Conger, and Elder, "Family Economic Hardship."

6. See Smith, Brooks-Gunn, and Klebanov, "Consequences of Living in Poverty."

7. See Duncan and Brooks-Gunn, *Consequences of Growing Up Poor.*

8. See Berger, *Parents as Partners*; Bronfenbrenner, "Ecology of the Family"; Comer, "Home-School Relationships"; Comer, "Educating Poor Minority Children"; Taylor and Machida, "Contribution of Parent and Peer Support"; and Zigler and Muenchow, *Head Start.*

9. See Epstein, "Perspectives and Preview"; Henderson, *Evidence Continues to Grow*; Henderson and Berla, *New Generation of Evidence*; Alexander, Entwisle, and Horsey, "From First Grade Forward"; Chavkin, "Involving Migrant Families"; Delgado-Gaitan, "Involving Parents in Schools"; and Reynolds, "Comparing Measures."

10. See Lareau, *Home Advantage* and Epstein, "Parents' Reactions."

11. I taught fifth grade in an inner-city Los Angeles school and worked directly with the parents of Mexican-immigrant students. As a postdoctoral fellow at Stanford University, I interviewed high school students about schooling and their families. In Texas, my extensive fieldwork with Mexican-immigrant families and adolescents was the basis for Romo and Falbo, *Latino High School Graduation.* From 1994 to 1996 I worked with a team of researchers and graduate students at the University of Texas at Austin's Lyndon B. Johnson School of Public Affairs to explore the ways that parents prepare their children for diversity in middle schools. I have made numerous presentations to public schoolteachers, parents, and administrators about parental involvement in schools and have been an outside evaluator for Head Start, Early Head Start, and Even Start programs. I draw from this range of work to discuss Mexican-origin parents and their efforts to help their children be successful in school.

12. See McWilliam, McMillen, Sloper, and McMillen, "Early Education."

13. See Gándara and others, *Capturing Latino Students.*

14. See Moreno and Lopez, "Latina Mothers' Involvement."

15. See McWilliam, Tocci, and Harbin, "Family-Centered Services."

16. See Laurence Steinberg, "Autonomy, Conflict, and Harmony."

17. See Romo and Falbo, *Latino High School Graduation.*

18. See Chavkin, "Debunking the Myth"; Chavkin, *Families and Schools*; Chavkin, "Involving Migrant Families"; and Romo and Falbo, *Latino High School Graduation.*

19. Examples are from interviews conducted during the author's fieldwork, 1994-97 (hereafter cited as Romo, interviews). For more information on deficit models, see Valdés, *Con Respeto* and McLemore and Romo, *Racial and Ethnic Relations.*

20. Romo, interviews.

21. Mehan and others, *Constructing School Success*, 161.

22. See Lareau, *Home Advantage.*

23. Romo, interviews.

24. See Wang, Haertel, and Walberg, "Fostering Educational Resilience." Quote is from an interview conducted by the author, 1990.

25. See Romo and Falbo, *Latino High School Graduation.*

26. See Hispanic Dropout Project, *No More Excuses.*

27. See Romo, "Multicultural Climate."

28. See Epstein, "Perspectives and Previews"; Epstein and Dauber, "School Programs"; and Valdés, *Con Respeto.*

29. Romo, interviews.

30. See Romo, Ellis, and Bell, "Parent Involvement."

31. See Laurence D. Steinberg, Brown, and Dornbusch, *Beyond the Classroom* and Azmitia and others, "Older Siblings' Participation."

32. Romo, interviews.

33. See Hispanic Dropout Project, *No More Excuses.*

34. See Romo, "Workforce Instructional Network."

35. See Catholic University of America, *First Teachers* and Hale, "Transmission of Cultural Values."

36. For a detailed description of the program, see Gándara and others, *Capturing Latino Students.*

37. See Slavin and Fashola, *Show Me the Evidence!* The evaluation was designed and conducted by Russell Rumberger, professor of education, University of California at Santa Barbara, Graduate School of Education.

38. Gándara and others, *Capturing Latino Students*, 12-14.

39. Ibid., 14.

40. ALAS project evaluator Russell Rumberger and Katherine Larson, correspondence with author, December 1998.

41. See Murnane and Levy, *Teaching the New Basic Skills.*

42. See Rips, "Alliances in Public Schools."

43. Alliance Schools statistics provided by the Texas Education Agency, 1997.

44. See Rips, "Alliances in Public Schools."

45. See Panasonic Foundation and American Association of School Administrators, "Getting Closer to the Public."

46. See Rips, "Alliances in Public Schools."

47. See Murnane and Levy, *Teaching the New Basic Skills.*

Notes to Chapter 6

1. See Marcelo M. Suárez-Orozco, "Immigration and Education."

2. See McCarthy and Vernez, *Immigration in a Changing Economy.*

3. *Lau v. Nichols,* 414 US 563 (1974).

4. U.S. Department of Health, Education, and Welfare, Office for Civil Rights, *Task Force Findings.* These guidelines were issued to clarify the federal government's position in Title VI of the *Civil Rights Act* of 1964 (42 *U.S.C.* 2000 et seq.) that provided that "no recipient of federal funds may provide services, aid, or other benefits to an individual which is different or is provided in a different manner from that provided to others under the program; or restrict an individual in any way from the advantages enjoyed by others receiving service, aid, or benefit under the program."

5. See Olsen, *Crossing the Schoolhouse Border.*

6. *Texas Education Code*, sec. 21.031 [Vernon Supp.], 1976.

7. See Cortez, *Distribution of Undocumented Pupils.*

8. University of Texas at Austin, *Use of Public Services.*

9. *Silva v. Levi,* civil action complaint 76-C-4268 (111 E.D. 1976), was filed because of irregularities in issuing immigrant visas. It enjoined the U.S. Immigration and Naturalization Service from deporting persons who possessed a Silva letter, which indicated they were members of this class of immigrants who had entered the United States prior to 11 March 1977 from an independent country of the Western Hemisphere, and who had a priority date for issuance of an immigrant visa between 1 July 1968 and 31 December 1976. The *Silva* injunction allowed immigrants with Silva letters to remain in the United States until the lawsuit was settled. Immigrant students possessing a Silva letter were not subject to the *Texas Education Code,* 21.031, which restricted undocumented children from attending free public schools.

10. *Hernandez v. Houston Independent School District,* 558 S.W. (E.D. 121 Texas 1977) was brought by the families of undocumented children living within the Houston Independent School District to challenge the exclusion of undocumented children from public schools unless they paid the cost of their education. Additional defendants in the state court action were the Texas Education Agency and the State of Texas. The Court of Civil Appeals for the Third Supreme Judicial District of the State of Texas affirmed the judgment of the district court and upheld the constitutionality of sec. 21.031 of the *Texas Education Code*, which restricted undocumented children from free public schooling.

11. Several pending United States district court cases were consolidated into *Plyler v. Doe,* 457 US 202 (1982). From the Southern District of Texas, Houston Division, the following civil actions were included: H-78-1862, *Sandra Cardenas et al. v. Dr. Lee Myers, Superintendent, Pasadena Independent School District et al.*; H-78-2132, *Gasper Garza et al. v. Billy Reagan, Superintendent, Houston Independent School District*; H-78-1797, *Mayra Martinez et al. v. Billy Reagan, Superintendent, Houston Indepen-*

dent School District et al.; H-78-1831, *Elvia Mendoza et al. v. Dr. Johnnie Clark, Superintendent, Goose Creek Consolidated Independent School District et al.* One civil action was included from the Northern District of Texas, Dallas Division: 3-79-0440-D, *A. Boe et al. v. Linus Wright, Superintendent, Dallas Independent School District et al.* Two civil actions were included from the Western District of Texas, Midland-Odessa Division: MO-79-CA-49, *J. and R. Roe et al. v. William Holm, Superintendent, Ector County Independent School District et al.* and MO-79-CA-54, *Jimmy Joaquin and Rodrigo Coe et al. v. William Holm, Superintendent, Ector County Independent School District et al.*

12. See Intercultural Development Research Association, *Education of Undocumented Children.*

13. See Emanuel, *Constitutional Law.*

14. Sec. 7 of Proposition 187 was designed to prevent illegal alien children from attending California public elementary and secondary schools. It amended California law by adding a new section to the *California Education Code* (1995). Sec. 48215 (a) requires California public elementary and secondary schools to refuse admission to children who are not citizens, aliens not lawfully admitted as permanent residents, or persons not otherwise authorized to be in the United States. Sec. 48215 (d) states that school districts must also verify the immigration status of each child's parent or legal guardian.

15. See Linda E. Carter, "Intermediate Scrutiny."

16. LEXIS, News Library, 17720 (C.D. CA 20 November 1995). Several suits challenging the constitutionality of *League of United Latin American Citizens v. Wilson*, 59 F.3d 1002, 1005 (9th Cir. 1995), CV 94-7569, Proposition 187 were consolidated into this case. Relying on *Plyler v. Doe*, many opponents considered Proposition 187 in conflict with federal immigration laws.

17. See McCarthy and Vernez, *Immigration in a Changing Economy*, Massey, "Settlement Process" (1985); Massey, "Settlement Process" (1986); Portes, *New Second Generation*; Vernez and Abrahamse, *How Immigrants Fare*; Passel, "Undocumented Immigrants"; Passel, "Undocumented Immigration"; and Massey, "Dimensions of the New Immigration."

18. See McCarthy and Vernez, *Immigration in a Changing Economy*, Vernez, *Undocumented Immigration*; and Vernez, *Mexican Labor.*

19. A version of IRCA passed the U.S. House of Representatives on 9 October 1986, more than a year after its Senate passage. The House and Senate reached a compromise version, and IRCA was signed into law by President Reagan in November 1986. IRCA's most significant consequence was the legalization of millions of undocumented workers currently residing in the United States. The majority of the legalized immigrants were from Mexico. Another provision of the IRCA makes it illegal for employers knowingly to employ aliens not authorized to work in the United States. The law requires all employers to document all employees' identities and their eligibility to work in the United States. See Calavita, "U.S. Immigration."

20. Massey, Donato, and Liang, "Effects of the *Immigration Reform and Control Act*," 207. See also U.S. Immigration and Naturalization Service, "Implementation of the *Immigration Reform and Control Act*" and Hoefer, "Characteristics of Aliens."

21. See Cafferty and others, *Dilemma of American Immigration* and Bean and Fix, "Significance of Recent Immigration."

22. See Bean, Espenshade, White, and Dymoski, "Post-IRCA Changes" and Hondagneu-Sotelo, *Gendered Transitions.*

23. See Bean, de la Garza, Roberts, and Weintraub, *At the Crossroads.*

24. See Valdez and others, *Immigration* and Portes and Rumbaut, *Immigrant America.*

25. See Vernez, *Mexican Labor;* McCarthy and Vernez, *Immigration in a Changing Economy,* and Chapa, "Myth of Hispanic Progress."

26. See McLemore and Romo, *Racial and Ethnic Relations* and Glazer, "Immigrants and Education."

27. See Reimers, *Still the Golden Door.*

28. See San Miguel, *"Let all of them take heed"* and U.S. Department of Education, *Descriptive Study.*

29. See Valdés, *Con Respeto.*

30. See Peisner-Feinberg and others, "Longitudinal Effects."

31. See U.S. Bureau of the Census, *Who's Minding the Kids?*

32. See Peisner-Feinberg and others, "Longitudinal Effects."

33. See President's Advisory Commission on Educational Excellence for Hispanic Americans, *Our Nation on the Fault Line.*

34. U.S. Senate Committee on Labor and Human Resources, *Infants and Toddlers,* 16 (hereafter cited as U.S. Senate, *Infants and Toddlers*).

35. See Donald J. Hernandez, "Family and Economic Circumstances."

36. See U.S. Senate Committee on Labor and Human Resources and U.S. House Committee on Education and the Workforce, *Head Start.*

37. See U.S. Department of Health and Human Services, *Creating a 21st Century.*

38. See U.S. Senate Committee on Labor and Human Resources, *Early Childhood Programs* (hereafter cited as U.S. Senate, *Early Childhood Programs*).

39. See Kagan and Zigler, *Early Schooling* and Peisner-Feinberg and others, "Longitudinal Effects."

40. See Carnegie Task Force on Meeting the Needs of Young Children, *Starting Points;* Kennedy, "School Readiness Act"; and Schorr, *Within Our Reach.*

41. See, for example, U.S. Senate, *Infants and Toddlers* and U.S. Senate, *Early Childhood Programs.*

42. See Valdés, *Con Respeto* and Fantuzzo and others, "Assessment of Preschool Play."

43. See Cross, "Teachers' Practical Knowledge."

44. See Sanders and Rivers, "Cumulative and Residual Effects."

45. See Haycock, "Good Teaching Matters."

46. Ibid.

47. See U.S. Department of Education, *Descriptive Study.*

48. See Zeichner, *Educating Teachers*; Delpit, *Other People's Children*; Banks and Banks, *Multicultural Education*; Darling-Hammond, "Inequality and Access"; and King, Hollins, and Hayman, *Preparing Teachers.*

49. See Moll, Amanti, Neff, and Gonzalez, "Funds of Knowledge" and Gonzalez and others, "Funds of Knowledge."

50. See Eva L. Baker, *Report on the Content Area Performance Assessments.*

51. August and Hakuta, *Improving Schooling*, 178-182.

52. See Haycock, "Good Teaching Matters."

53. See Moll, "Some Key Issues"; Eugene E. Garcia, *Education of Linguistically and Culturally Diverse Students;* Lucas, Henze, and Donato, "Promoting the Success"; Thomas P. Carter and Chatfield, "Effective Bilingual Schools"; and Stevenson and Baker, "Family-School Relation."

54. See August and Hakuta, *Improving Schooling.*

55. See Slavin and Yampolsky, "Success for All" and August and Hakuta, *Improving Schooling.*

56. See August and Hakuta, *Improving Schooling.*

57. See Tatum, *Why Are All the Black Kids Sitting Together* and McLemore and Romo, *Racial and Ethnic Relations.*

58. Phinney and Rotheram, *Children's Ethnic Socialization*; Banks, "Multicultural Education"; Tatum, *Why Are All the Black Kids Sitting Together;* Akiba, Coll, and Magnuson, "Children of Color"; and Kendall, "Learning about Diversity."

59. See Orfield, Eaton, and the Harvard Project on School Desegregation, *Dismantling Desegregation.*

60. See Wilson's work: *Declining Significance of Race*; *Truly Disadvantaged*; and *When Work Disappears.*

61. See Massey and Denton, *American Apartheid.*

62. See Wells, *Hispanic Education.*

63. See Romo, "Multicultural Climate." This project was conducted by the University of Texas at Austin's Lyndon B. Johnson School of Public Affairs.

64. See Schofield, "Improving Intergroup Relations"; Fine, Weis, and Powell, "Communities of Difference"; and Stephan, "Intergroup Relations."

65. Hollins, "Directed Inquiry," 100.

66. Slavin and Fashola, *Show Me the Evidence!* and Klein, "Response."

67. See Pogrow, "What Is an Exemplary Program."

68. See King, Hollins, and Hayman, *Preparing Teachers.*

Bibliography

Academy for Educational Development. *Short Changing Hispanic Girls: An Analysis of Hispanic Girls in the Greenberg-Lake Survey of Self-Esteem, Education, and Career Aspirations among Adolescent Girls and Boys in the United States.* Washington, DC: American Association of University Women, 1992. ERIC Document Reproduction Service No. ED 387 557.

Adler, Patricia A., and Peter Adler. *Peer Power: Preadolescent Culture and Identity.* New Brunswick, NJ: Rutgers University Press, 1998.

Ainsworth-Darnell, James W., and Douglas B. Downey. "Assessing the Oppositional Cultural Explanation for Racial/Ethnic Differences in School Performance." *American Sociological Review* 53(4): 536-53 (1998).

Akiba, Dais, Cynthia Garcia Coll, and Katherine Magnuson. "Children of Color and Children from Immigrant Families: The Development of Social Identities, School Engagement, and Interethnic Social Attribution During Middle Childhood." 1998. Manuscript under review.

Alcalay, Rina. "Hispanic Women in the United States: Family and Work Relations." *Migration Today* 12(3): 13-20 (1984).

Alexander, Karl L., Doris R. Entwisle, and Corrie S. Horsey. "From First Grade Forward: Early Foundations of High School Dropout." *Sociology of Education* 70(April): 87-107 (1997).

Alford, Andy, and A. Philips Brooks. "Days Away from First Bell, Districts Hunt for Teachers." *Austin American Statesman*, 31 July 1998, B1, B3.

American Association of University Women. *Gender Gaps: Where Schools Still Fail Our Children.* Washington, DC: The AAUW Educational Foundation, 1998.

——. *How Schools Shortchange Girls: A Study of Major Findings on Girls and Education.* Washington, DC: The AAUW Educational Foundation, 1992. ERIC Document Reproduction Service No. ED 339 674.

Anderson, Karen. *Changing Woman: A History of Racial Ethnic Women in Modern America.* New York: Oxford University Press, 1996.

August, Diane, and Kenji Hakuta, eds. *Improving Schooling for Language-Minority Children: A Research Agenda.* Washington, DC: National Academy of Sciences Press; National Research Council, 1997. ERIC Document Reproduction Service No. ED 408 377.

AVANCE Family Support and Education Program. *Final Report of an Evaluation of the AVANCE Parent-Child Education Program.* Vol. I, *Impact Evaluation.* Rev. ed. San Antonio: AVANCE National Office, 1995.

Azmitia, Margarita, Catherine R. Cooper, Edward M. Lopez, and L. M. Rivera. "Older Siblings' Participation in Mexican-Descent Students' Academic

Achievement." Paper presented at the annual conference of the American Educational Research Association, San Diego, 1998.

Baker, Eva L. *Report on the Content Area Performance Assessments (CAPA): A Collaboration among Hawaii Dept. of Education, the Center for Research on Evaluation Standards and Student Testing, and the Teachers and Children of Hawaii.* Los Angeles: School of Education, University of California, Los Angeles, 1996.

Baker, Keith A., and Adriana A. de Kanter. *Effectiveness of Bilingual Education: A Review of the Literature.* Final draft report. Washington, DC: U.S. Department of Education, Office of Planning, Budget, and Evaluation, 1981.

Banks, James A. "Multicultural Education and the Modification of Students' Racial Attitudes." In *Toward a Common Destiny: Improving Race and Ethnic Relations in America,* edited by Willis D. Hawley and Anthony W. Jackson. San Francisco: Jossey-Bass, 1995.

Banks, James A., and Cherry A. McGee Banks, eds. *Multicultural Education: Issues and Perspectives.* 2d ed. Boston: Allyn & Bacon, 1993.

Bankston, Carl L., III, and Min Zhou. "Effects of Minority Language Literacy on the Academic Achievement of Vietnamese Youths in New Orleans." *Sociology of Education* 68(1): 1-17 (1995).

Bean, Frank D., Rodolfo O. de la Garza, Brian Ross Roberts, and Sidney Weintraub. *At the Crossroads: Mexican Migration and U.S. Policy.* Lanham, MD: Rowman & Littlefield, 1997.

Bean, Frank D., Thomas J. Espenshade, T. White, and R. Dymoski. "Post-IRCA Changes in the Volume and Flow of Undocumented Migration to the United States." In *Undocumented Migration to the United States: IRCA and the Experience of the 1980s,* edited by Frank Bean, Barry Edmonston, and Jeffrey S. Passel. Washington, DC: Urban Institute, 1990.

Bean, Frank D., and Michael Fix. "The Significance of Recent Immigration Policy Reforms in the United States." In *Nations of Immigrants: Australia and the United States in a Changing World,* edited by Garry P. Freeman and James Jupp. New York: Oxford University Press, 1992.

Becerra, Rosina M., and Diane de Anda. "Pregnancy and Motherhood among Mexican American Adolescents." *Health and Social Work* 9(2): 106-23 (1984).

Beck, Isabel L. "Understanding Beginning Reading: A Journey Through Teaching and Research." In *Literacy for All: Issues in Teaching and Learning,* edited by Jean Osborn and Fran Lehr. New York: Guilford, 1998.

Bennett, Christine I. "Research on Racial Issues in American Higher Education." In *Multicultural Education: Issues and Perspectives,* edited by James A. Banks and Cherry A. McGee Banks. New York: Macmillan, 1995.

Berger, Eugenia Hepworth. *Parents as Partners in Education: Families and Schools Working Together.* 4th ed. New York: Merrill, 1995.

Bianchi, Suzanne M., and Daphne Spain. "Women, Work, and Family in America." *Population Bulletin* 51(3) (1996).

Bronfenbrenner, Urie. "Ecology of the Family as a Context for Human Development: Research Perspectives." *Developmental Psychology* 22(6): 723-42 (1986).

Cafferty, Pastora San Juan, B. R. Chiswick, A. M. Greeley, and T. A. Sullivan. *The Dilemma of American Immigration: Beyond the Golden Door.* New Brunswick, NJ: Transaction, 1983.

Calavita, Kitty. "U.S. Immigration Policy Responses: The Limits of Legislation." In *Controlling Immigration: A Global Perspective,* edited by Wayne A. Cornelius, Philip L. Martin, and James F. Hollifield. Stanford, CA: Stanford University Press, 1994.

Campbell, Anne. "Female Participation in Gangs." In *Gangs in America,* edited by C. Ronald Huff. Newbury Park, CA: Sage, 1990.

———. *The Girls in the Gang: A Report from New York City.* Oxford: Basil Blackwell, 1984.

Carnegie Task Force on Meeting the Needs of Young Children. *Starting Points: Meeting the Needs of Our Youngest Children.* New York: Carnegie Corporation, 1994. ERIC Document Reproduction Service No. ED 369 562.

Carter, Deborah J., and Reginald Wilson. *Minorities in Higher Education: 1996-1997 Fifteenth Annual Status Report.* Washington, DC: American Council on Higher Education, 1997.

Carter, Linda E. "Intermediate Scrutiny under Fire: Will *Plyler* Survive State Legislation to Exclude Undocumented Children from School?" *University of San Francisco Law Review* 31 (1997): 345-98.

Carter, Thomas P., and Michael L. Chatfield. "Effective Bilingual Schools: Implications for Policy and Practice." *American Journal of Education* 95(1): 200-32 (1986).

"A Casting Call for Teachers." *New York Times,* 5 April 1998, 28.

Catholic University of America. *First Teachers.* Washington, DC: U.S. Department of Education; Laboratory for Student Success, 1998.

Cazden, Courtney B., and Catherine E. Snow. "English Plus: Issues in Bilingual Education, Preface." *Annals of the American Academy of Political and Social Science* 508(March): 9-11 (1990).

Celedon, Sylvia. "An Analysis of a Teacher's and Students' Language Use to Negotiate Meaning in an ESL/Mathematics Classroom." Ph.D. diss., University of Texas, 1998.

Chapa, Jorge. "The Myth of Hispanic Progress." *Journal of Hispanic Policy* 4(1990): 3-18.

Chavkin, Nancy Feyl. "Debunking the Myth about Minority Parents." *Educational Horizons* 67(4): 119-23 (1989).

———. "Involving Migrant Families in Their Children's Education: Challenges and Opportunities for Schools." In *Children of La Frontera,* edited by Judith LeBlanc Flores. Charleston, WV: ERIC Clearinghouse on Rural Education and Small Schools, 1996. ERIC Document Reproduction Service No. ED 393 631.

———, ed. *Families and Schools in a Pluralistic Society.* Albany: State University of New York Press, 1993.

Children's Defense Fund. *Teenage Pregnancy in the Latino Community.* Washington, DC: Children's Defense Fund, 1991.

Child Trends. *Summary of Facts at a Glance,* October 1996. http://www.tyc.state.tx.us/prevention/facts.htm (16 June 1999).

Coll, Cynthia Garcia. "Children of Immigrants: School, Self, and Community." Plenary II presentation at the 4th National Head Start Research Conference, Washington, DC, 1998.

Comer, James P. "Educating Poor Minority Children." *Scientific American* 259(5): 42-48 (1988).

———. "Home-School Relationships as They Affect the Academic Success of Children." *Education and Urban Society* 16(3): 323-37 (1984).

Conger, Rand D., K. J. Conger, and Glen H. Elder, Jr. "Family Economic Hardship and Adolescent Adjustment: Mediating and Moderating Processes." In *Consequences of Growing up Poor,* edited by Greg J. Duncan and Jeanne Brooks-Gunn. New York: Russell Sage Foundation, 1997.

Cornejo, Richard J. "Bilingual Education: Some Reflections on Proposition 227." *Hispanic Outlook in Higher Education* 9(3): 27-32 (1998).

Cortez, Albert. *The Distribution of Undocumented Pupils in Texas Public Schools: A First Look.* San Antonio: Intercultural Development Research Association, 1981.

Crocker, Elvira Valenzuela. "The Report Card on Educating Hispanic Women." *Peer Report* 3(December 1982). ERIC Document Reproduction Service No. ED 263 263.

Cross, Beverly. "Teachers' Practical Knowledge during Curriculum Planning in a Professional Development School." Ph.D. diss., Ohio State University, 1992.

Cummins, Jim. *Bilingualism and Special Education: Issues in Assessment and Pedagogy.* San Diego: College Hill Press, 1984.

———. "Empowering Minority Students: A Framework for Intervention." *Harvard Educational Review* 56(1): 18-36 (1986).

———. "The Role of Primary Language Development in Promoting Education Success for Language Minority Students." In *Schooling and Language Minority Students: A Theoretical Framework.* Los Angeles: California State Department of Education, National Evaluation, Dissemination and Assessment Center, 1981.

Darabi, Katherine F. "The Education of Non-High School Graduates After the Birth of a Child: Final Report." 1979. ERIC Document Reproduction Service No. ED 192 242.

Darling-Hammond, Linda. "Inequality and Access to Knowledge." In *Multicultural Education: Issues and Perspectives,* edited by James A. Banks and Cherry A. McGee Banks. New York: Macmillan, 1995.

Darling-Hammond, Linda, and A. Lin Goodwin. "Progress toward Professionalism in Teaching." In *Challenges and Achievements of American Education: 1993 ASCD Yearbook,* edited by Gordon Cawelti. Alexandria, VA: Association for Supervision and Curriculum Development, 1993.

Dawson, Deborah A. "Family Structure and Children's Health and Well-Being: Data from the 1988 National Health Interview Survey on Child Health." *Journal of Marriage and the Family* 53(3): 573-84 (1991).

Decker, Scott H., and Barrick Van Winkle. *Life in the Gang: Family, Friends, and Violence.* New York: Cambridge University Press, 1996.

de la Piedra, M. T. "Mexican Immigrants' Definition of Fatherhood: A Different Perspective of Male Involvement in Schools." M.A. thesis, University of Texas, 1998.

Del Castillo, A. R., and M. Torres. "The Interdependency of Educational Institutions and Cultural Norms: The Hispana Experience." In *The Broken Web: The Educational Experience of Hispanic American Women,* edited by Teresa McKenna and Flora Ida Ortiz. Berkeley, CA: Floricanto, 1988.

De Leon, B. "Career Development of Hispanic Adolescent Girls." In *Urban Girls: Resisting Stereotypes, Creating Identities,* edited by Bonnie Ross Leadbeater and Niobe Way. New York: New York University Press, 1996.

Delgado-Gaitan, Concha. "Involving Parents in Schools: A Process of Empowerment." *American Journal of Education* 100(1): 20-46 (1991).

———. *Literacy for Empowerment: The Role of Parents in Their Children's Education.* New York: Falmer, 1990.

Delpit, Lisa D. *Other People's Children: Cultural Conflict in the Classroom.* New York: W. W. Norton, 1995. ERIC Document Reproduction Service No. ED 387 274.

De Luna, Anna. "Project MIJA: Breaking Boundaries for Young Latinas." *IDRA Newsletter* 20(9): 4-5 (1993).

De Luna, Anna, and Felix Montes. "MIJA Girls Getting Excited about Math: Assessing the Outcomes of the MIJA Program." *IDRA Newsletter* 22(2): 5-6, 14 (1995).

Demo, David H., and M. Hughes. "Socialization and Racial Identity among Black Americans." In *Race, Class, and Gender in a Diverse Society,* edited by Diana Kendall. Boston: Allyn & Bacon, 1997.

De Witt, Kristine. "Rise Is Forecast in Minorities in Schools." *New York Times,* 13 September 1991.

Donato, Katharine M. "U.S. Policy and Mexican Migration to the United States, 1942-92." Paper presented at the annual meeting of the American Sociological Association, Pittsburgh, 1992.

Dornbusch, Sanford M., P. L. Ritter, P. Herbert Leiderman, Donald F. Roberts, and M. J. Fraleign. "The Relation of Parenting Style to Adolescent School Performance." *Child Development* 58(5): 1244-57 (1987).

Dugger, C. W. "Among Young of Immigrants, Outlook Rises." *New York Times,* 21 March 1998.

Duncan, Greg J., and Jeanne Brooks-Gunn, eds. *Consequences of Growing Up Poor.* New York: Russell Sage Foundation, 1997.

Eckert, Penelope. *Jocks and Burnouts: Social Categories and Identity in the High School.* New York: Teachers College Press, 1989.

Eder, Donna, with Catherine C. Evans, and Stephen Parker. *School Talk: Gender and Adolescent Culture.* New Brunswick, NJ: Rutgers University Press, 1995. ERIC Document Reproduction Service No. ED 388 393.

Eisenberg, Ann R. "Teasing: Verbal Play in Two Mexican Homes." In *Language Socialization across Cultures,* edited by Bambi B. Schieffelin and Elinor Ochs. New York: Cambridge University Press, 1986.

Emanuel, S. *Constitutional Law.* New York: Emanuel Law Outlines, 1983.

Epstein, Joyce L. "Parents' Reactions to Teacher Practices of Parent Involvement." *Elementary School Journal* 86(3): 277-94 (1986).

———. "Perspectives and Previews on Research and Policy for School, Family, and Community Partnerships." In *Family-School Links: How Do They Affect Educational Outcomes?* edited by Alan Booth and Judith F. Dunn. Mahwah, NJ: Lawrence Erlbaum, 1996.

———. "Theory to Practice: School and Family Partnerships Lead to School Improvement and Student Success." In *School, Family and Community Interaction: A View from the Firing Lines,* edited by Cheryl L. Fagnano and Beverly Z. Werber. Boulder, CO: Westview, 1994.

Epstein, Joyce L., and Susan L. Dauber. "School Programs and Teacher Practices of Parent Involvement in Inner-City Elementary and Middle Schools." *Elementary School Journal* 91(3): 289-305 (1991).

Fantuzzo, John, Brian Sutton-Smith, K. C. Coolahan, P. H. Manz, S. Canning, and Darlena Debnam. "Assessment of Preschool Play Interaction Behaviors in Young Low-Income Children: Penn Interactive Peer Play Scale." *Early Childhood Research Quarterly* 10(1995): 105-20.

Fillmore, Lilly Wong. "Language Minority Students and School Participation: What Kind of English Is Needed?" *Journal of Education* 164(2): 143-56 (1982).

———. "Latino Families and the Schools." Unpublished manuscript, 1990.

Fine, Michelle, Lois Weis, and Linda C. Powell. "Communities of Difference: A Critical Look at Desegregated Spaces Created for and by Youth." *Harvard Educational Review* 67(2): 247-84 (1997).

Fisher, Maria, with Sonia M. Perez, Bryant Gonzalez, Jonathan Njus, and Raul Yzaguirre. *Latino Education: Status and Prospects.* Washington, DC: National Council of La Raza, 1998.

Gadsden, Vivian L. "Family Cultures and Literacy Learning." In *Literacy for All: Issues in Teaching and Learning,* edited by Jean Osborn and Fran Lehr. New York: Guilford, 1998.

———. "Understanding Family Literacy: Conceptual Issues Facing the Field." *Teachers College Record* 96(1994): 58-96.

Gadsden, Vivian L., and M. Hall. *Intergenerational Learning: A Review of the Literature.* Philadelphia: National Center on Fathers and Families, University of Pennsylvania, 1996.

Gándara, Patricia, Katherine Larson, Hugh Mehan, and Russell Rumberger, eds. *Capturing Latino Students in the Academic Pipeline.* Chicano/Latino Policy Project, vol. 1, no. 1. Berkeley: University of California, 1998.

Garcia, Eugene E. "Educating Mexican American Students: Past Treatment and Recent Developments in Theory, Research, Policy, and Practice." In *Handbook of Research on Multicultural Education*, edited by James A. Banks and Cherry A. McGee Banks. New York: Macmillan, 1995.

———. *Education of Linguistically and Culturally Diverse Students: Effective Instructional Practices.* National Center for Research on Cultural Diversity and Second Language Learning, Educational Practice Report No. 1. Washington, DC: Center for Applied Linguistics, 1990.

———. "Hispanic Children: Theoretical, Empirical, and Related Policy Issue." *Educational Psychology Review* 4(1): 69-93 (1992).

———. *Understanding and Meeting the Challenges of Student and Cultural Diversity.* Boston: Houghton Mifflin, 1994.

———. *Understanding the Needs of LEP Students.* New York: Houghton Mifflin, 1994.

Garcia, Eugene E., and Barry McLaughlin, eds., with Bernard Spokek, and Olivia N. Saracho. "Meeting the Challenge of Linguistic and Cultural Diversity in Early Childhood Education." In *Yearbook in Early Childhood Education, v. 6. Introduction.* New York: Teachers College Press, 1995.

Garcia, James E. "More Dropouts Minorities, Despite Gains." *Austin American Statesman*, 7 September 1991.

Gaskins, Suzanne. "How Mayan Parental Theories Come into Play." In *Parents' Cultural Belief Systems: Their Origins, Expressions, and Consequences*, edited by Sara Harkness and Charles M. Super. New York: Guilford, 1996.

Glazer, Nathan. "Immigrants and Education." In *Clamor at the Gates: The New American Immigration*, edited by N. Glazer. San Francisco: Institute for Contemporary Affairs, 1985.

Goldberg, Carey. "After Girls Get the Attention, Focus Shifts to Boys' Woes." *New York Times*, 23 April 1998, A1.

Goldenberg, Claude. *Latin American Immigration and U.S. Schools: Social Policy Report.* Ann Arbor, MI: Society for Research in Child Development, 1996.

Gomby, Deanna S., Mary B. Larner, and Richard E. Behrman. "Long-Term Outcomes of Early Childhood Programs: Analysis and Recommendations." *Future of Children* 5(3): 6-24 (1995).

Gonzalez, Norma, Luis C. Moll, M. F. Tenery, A. Rivera, R. Gonzales, and Cathy Amanti. "Funds of Knowledge for Teaching in Latino Households." *Urban Education* 29(4): 443-70 (1995).

Hakuta, Kenji. *Mirror of Language: The Debate on Bilingualism.* New York: BasicBooks, 1986.

Hakuta, Kenji, and L. J. Gould. "Synthesis of Research on Bilingual Education." *Education Leadership* 44(6): 38-44 (1987).

Hale, Janice. "The Transmission of Cultural Values to Young African American Children." *Young Children* 46(6): 7-15 (1991).

Hamburg, David A. *Today's Children: Creating a Future for a Generation in Crisis.* New York: Random House Times Books, 1992.

Hao, Lingxin, and Melissa Bonstead-Bruns. "Parent-Child Differences in Educational Expectations and the Academic Achievement of Immigrant and Native Students." *Sociology of Education* 71(3): 175-98 (1998).

Harkness, Sara, and Charles M. Super, eds. *Parents' Cultural Belief Systems: Their Origins, Expressions, and Consequences.* New York: Guilford, 1996.

Haycock, Kati. "Good Teaching Matters . . . a Lot. *Education Trust* 3(2): 3-14 (1998).

Heath, Shirley Brice. "Sociocultural Contexts of Language Development." In *Beyond Language: Social and Cultural Factors in Schooling Language Minority Students.* Developed by Bilingual Education Office, California State Department of Education. Los Angeles: Evaluation, Dissemination, and Assessment Center, California State University, 1986.

———. *Ways with Words: Language, Life, and Work in Communities and Classrooms.* New York: Cambridge University Press, 1983.

Henderson, Anne T., ed. *The Evidence Continues to Grow: Parental Involvement Improves Student Achievement: An Annotated Bibliography.* Columbia, MD: National Committee for Citizens in Education, 1987.

Henderson, Anne T., and Nancy Berla., eds. *A New Generation of Evidence: The Family is Critical to Student Achievement.* Washington, DC: National Committee for Citizens in Education, 1994. ERIC Document Reproduction Service No. ED 375 968.

Hernández, Arthur E. "Do Role Models Influence Self Efficacy and Aspirations in Mexican American At-Risk Females?" *Hispanic Journal of Behavioral Sciences* 17(2): 256-63 (1995).

Hernández, Arthur, Linda Vargas-Lew, and Cynthia L. Martinez. "Intergenerational Academic Aspirations of Mexican-American Females: An Examination of Mother, Daughter, and Grandmother Triads." *Hispanic Journal of Behavioral Sciences* 16(2): 195-204 (1994).

Hernandez, Donald J. "Family and Economic Circumstances of Children in Immigrant and Native-Born Families: 1910 to 1990." Paper presented at Plenary II, Head Start's Fourth National Research Conference, Washington, DC, 9-12 July 1998.

Hirshman, Charles. "Problems and Prospects of Studying Immigrant Adaptation from the 1990 Population Census: From Generational Comparisons to the Process of 'Becoming American.'" *International Migration Review* 28(4): 690-713 (1994).

Hispanic Dropout Project. *No More Excuses: The Final Report of the Hispanic Dropout Project.* N.p.: Hispanic Dropout Project, 1998.

Hoefer, M. D. "Characteristics of Aliens Legalizing under IRCA." Paper presented at the annual meeting of the Population Association of America, Baltimore, 1989.

Hollins, Etta R. "Directed Inquiry in Preservice Teacher Education: A Developmental Process Model." In *Preparing Teachers for Cultural Diversity,* edited by Joyce E. King, Etta R. Hollins, and Warren C. Hayman. New York: Teachers College Press, 1997.

Holmes, S. A. "Black Populace Nearly Equaled by Hispanic." *New York Times,* 7 August 1998, A13.

———. "Hispanic Births in U.S. Reach Record High." *New York Times,* 13 February 1998, A13.

Hondagneu-Sotelo, Pierrette. *Gendered Transitions: Mexican Experiences of Immigration.* Berkeley: University of California Press, 1994.

Horn, Laura J., and C. Dennis Carroll. *Confronting the Odds: Students at Risk and the Pipeline to Higher Education.* National Center for Education Statistics, Statistical Analysis Report. Washington, DC: U.S. Department of Education, 1997.

Horowitz, Ruth. *Honor and the American Dream.* New Brunswick, NJ: Rutgers University Press, 1983.

Hraba, Joseph. *American Ethnicity.* 2d ed. Itasca, IL: F. E. Peacock, 1994.

Huff, C. Ronald, ed. *Gangs in America.* Newbury Park, CA: Sage, 1990.

Imel, Susan. *The New Work Force: Trends and Issues Alerts.* Columbus, OH: ERIC Clearinghouse on Adult, Career, and Vocational Education, 1989. ERIC Document Reproduction Service No. ED 312 412.

Intercultural Development Research Association (IDRA). *Education of Undocumented Children in Texas: A Status Report.* San Antonio: IDRA School Finance Project, 1979.

———. *IDRA Newsletter* 21(9): 1-22 (1994). ERIC Document Reproduction Service No. ED 376 016.

Kagan, Sharon L., and Edward F. Zigler, eds. *Early Schooling: The National Debate.* New Haven: Yale University Press, 1987.

Kaufman, Phillip, Marilyn M. McMillen, and David Sweet. *A Comparison of High School Dropout Rates in 1982 and 1992.* Special report created at the request of the U.S. Department of Education. Washington, DC: National Center for Education Statistics, 1996.

Keating, P. "Striving for Sex Equity in Schools." In *Access to Knowledge,* edited by John I. Goodlad and Pamela Keating. New York: College Entrance Examination Board, 1990.

Kellogg Commission on the Future of State and Land-Grant Universities. *Returning to Our Roots: Student Access.* Washington, DC: National Association of State Universities and Land-Grant Colleges, 1998.

Kendall, Diana. "Learning about Diversity and Inequality." In *Race, Class, and Gender in a Diverse Society,* edited by Diana Kendall. Boston: Allyn & Bacon, 1997.

Kennedy, E. "School Readiness Act." *Congressional Record,* 24 April 1991, S4986-S5002, p. 279-80.

King, Joyce. E., Etta R. Hollins, and Warren C. Hayman. *Preparing Teachers for Cultural Diversity.* New York: Teachers College Press, 1997.

Klein, Susan S. "Response: A System of Expert Panels and Design Competitions: Complementary Federal Approaches to Find, Develop, and Share

Promising and Exemplary Products and Programs." *Educational Researcher* 26(6): 12-20 (1997).

Lareau, Annette. *Home Advantage: Social Class and Parental Intervention in Elementary Education.* Philadelphia: Falmer, 1989.

Lee, V. W., and R. N. Sing. "Gender Equity in Schools for Immigrant Girls." *New Voices* 3(2): 1-2 (1993).

LeVine, Robert A. "Child Rearing as Cultural Adaptation." In *Culture and Infancy: Variations in the Human Experience*, edited by P. Herbert Leiderman, Steven R. Tulkin, and Anne Rosenfeld. New York: Academic Press, 1977.

LeVine, Robert A., Patrice M. Miller, Amy L. Richman, and Sarah LeVine. "Education and Mother-Infant Interaction: A Mexican Case Study." In *Parents' Cultural Belief Systems: Their Origins, Expressions, and Consequences*, edited by Sara Harkness and Charles M. Super. New York: Guilford, 1996.

LeVine, Sarah. *Dolor y Alegría: Women and Social Change in Urban Mexico.* Madison: University of Wisconsin Press, 1993.

Linguistic Minority Research Institute. "LEP Enrollments Increase Almost 5% in 1996." *News Report and Analysis* (University of California) 6(1) (1996).

Lopez, D. E. "Language: Diversity and Assimilation." In *Ethnic Los Angeles*, edited by Roger Waldinger and Mehdi Bozorgmehr. New York: Russell Sage Foundation, 1996.

Lucas, Tamara, R. Henze, and Ruben Donato. "Promoting the Success of Latino Language-Minority Students: An Exploratory Study of Six High Schools." *Harvard Educational Review* 60(3): 315-39 (1990).

Luker, Kristin. *Dubious Conceptions: The Politics of Teenage Pregnancy.* Cambridge: Harvard University Press, 1996.

Manaster, Guy J., Jason C. Chan, and Randa Safady. "Mexican American Migrant Students' Academic Success: Sociological and Psychological Acculturation." *Adolescence* 27(105): 123-36 (1992).

Marger, Martin N. *Race and Ethnic Relations: American and Global Perspectives.* Belmont, CA: Wadsworth, 1994.

Martinez, L. "High Achieving Latinas: The Interplay of Attitudes Toward School, Self-Esteem and Gender Role Attitudes." Honors thesis, University of Texas, 1998.

Masahiko, Minami, and Carlos J. Ovando. "Language Issues in Multicultural Contexts." In *Handbook of Research on Multicultural Education*, edited by James A. Banks and Cherry A. McGee Banks. New York: Macmillan, 1995.

Massey, Douglas S. "Dimensions of the New Immigration to the United States and the Prospects for Assimilation." *Annual Review of Sociology* 7(1981): 57-85.

———. "The Settlement Process among Mexican Migrants to the United States." *American Sociological Review* 51(5): 670-84 (1986).

———. "The Settlement Process among Mexican Migrants to the United States: New Methods and Findings." In *Immigration Statistics: A Story of Neglect*, edited by Daniel B. Levine, Kenneth Hill, and Robert Warren. Washington, DC: National Academy Press, 1985.

Massey, Douglas S., and Nancy A. Denton. *American Apartheid: Segregation and the Making of the Underclass.* Cambridge: Harvard University Press, 1993.

Massey, Douglas S., Katharine M. Donato, and Z. Liang. "Effects of the *Immigration Reform and Control Act* of 1986: Preliminary Data from Mexico." In *Undocumented Migration to the United States: IRCA and the Experience of the 1980s,* edited by Frank D. Bean, Barry Edmonston, and Jeffrey S. Passel. Washington, DC: Urban Institute, 1990.

Matute-Bianchi, Maria Eugenia. "Ethnic Identities and Patterns of School Success and Failure among Mexican-Descent and Japanese-American Students in a California High School: An Ethnographic Analysis." *American Journal of Education* 95(1): 233-55 (1986).

McAdoo, Maisie. "Project GRAD's Strength is in the Sum of Its Parts." *Ford Foundation Report* (spring/summer): 9-10 (1998).

McCarthy, Kevin F., and Georges Vernez. *Immigration in a Changing Economy: California's Experience—Questions and Answers.* Santa Monica: RAND, 1998.

McLemore, S. Dale, and Harriett Romo. *Racial and Ethnic Relations in America.* 5th ed. Boston: Allyn & Bacon, 1998.

McMillen, Marilyn M., and Phillip Kaufman. *Dropout Rates in the United States: 1996.* Special report created at the request of the U.S. Department of Education. Washington, DC: National Center for Education Statistics, 1997.

McMillen, Marilyn M., Phillip Kaufman, and S. Klein. *Dropout Rates in the United States: 1995.* Special report created at the request of the U.S. Department of Education. Washington, DC: National Center for Education Statistics, 1997.

McWilliam, R. A., B. J. McMillen, K. M. Sloper, and J. S. McMillen. "Early Education and Child Care Program Philosophy about Families." In *Advances in Early Education and Day Care,* vol. 9, edited by Carl J. Dunst and Mark Wolery. Greenwich, CT: JAI Press, 1997.

McWilliam, R. A., L. Tocci, and G. Harbin. "Family-Centered Services: Lessons from Exemplary Service Providers." Chapel Hill: University of North Carolina Press, 1996.

Mehan, Hugh, I. Villanueva, L. Hubbard, and A. Lintz. *Constructing School Success: The Consequences of Untracking Low-Achieving Students.* New York: Cambridge University Press, 1996.

Merten, Don E. "The Meaning of Meanness: Popularity, Competition, and Conflict among Junior High School Girls." *Sociology of Education* 70(3): 175-91 (1997).

Moll, Luis C. "Some Key Issues in Teaching Latino Students." *Language Arts* 65(5): 465-72 (1988).

Moll, Luis C., C. Amanti, D. Neff, and Norma Gonzalez. "Funds of Knowledge for Teaching: Using a Qualitative Approach to Connect Homes and Classrooms." *Theory into Practice* 31(1): 132-41 (1992).

Moll, Luis C., and Norma Gonzalez. "Lessons from Research with Language-Minority Children." *Journal of Reading Behavior* 26(4): 439-56 (1994).

Moll, Luis C., and James B. Greenberg. "Creating Zones of Possibilities: Combining Social Contexts for Instruction." In *Vygotsky and Education,* edited by Luis C. Moll. Cambridge: Cambridge University Press, 1990.

Moore, Joan W. *Going Down to the Barrio: Homeboys and Homegirls in Change.* Philadelphia: Temple University Press, 1991.

——. *Homeboys: Gangs, Drugs and Prison in the Barrios of Los Angeles.* Philadelphia: Temple University Press, 1978.

Moran, C. E., and Kenji Hakuta. "Bilingual Education: Broadening Research Perspectives." In *Handbook of Research on Multicultural Education,* edited by James A. Banks and Cherry A. McGee Banks. New York: Macmillan, 1995.

Moreno, Robert P., and J. A. Lopez. "Latina Mothers' Involvement in Their Children's Schooling." Paper presented at the annual meeting of the American Educational Research Association, San Diego, 1998.

Murnane, Richard J., and Frank Levy. *Teaching the New Basic Skills: Principles for Educating Children to Thrive in a Changing Economy.* New York: Free Press, 1996.

National Center for Education Statistics. *Enrollment in Public Elementary and Secondary Schools by Race or Ethnicity and State, Table 44: Digest of Education Statistics 1996.* Washington, DC: U.S. Department of Education, 1996.

National Council of La Raza. *Latino Education: Status and Prospects.* Conference ed. Washington, DC: National Council of La Raza, 1998.

Neubert, Debra A., and Lawrence E. Leak. "Serving Urban Youth with Special Needs in Vocational Education: Issues and Strategies for Change." *TASPP Bulletin* 2(2): 1-3 (1990). ERIC Document Reproduction Service No. ED 326 695.

"The Newest Americans: The Second 'Spanish Invasion.'" *U.S. News and World Report,* 8 July 1974, 34-36.

Oakes, Jeannie U. "Can Tracking Research Inform Practice? Technical, Normative, and Political Considerations." *Educational Researcher* 21(4): 12-21 (1992).

——. *Keeping Track: How Schools Structure Inequality.* New Haven: Yale University Press, 1985. ERIC Document Reproduction Service No. ED 274 749.

——. "Tracking in Secondary Schools: A Contextual Perspective." *Educational Psychologist* 22(1986): 129-54.

Oakes, Jeannie U., with Tor Ormseth, Robert Bell, and Patricia Camp. *Multiplying Inequalities: The Effects of Race, Social Class, and Tracking on Opportunities to Learn Mathematics and Science.* Santa Monica: RAND, 1990. ERIC Document Reproduction Service No. ED 329 615.

Ocasio, L. "Across the Nation Parents Learn to Jump-Start Change." *Ford Foundation Report* (summer/fall): 9-11 (1996).

Ogbu, John U. "Variability in Minority School Performance: A Problem in Search of an Explanation." *Anthropology and Education Quarterly* 18(4): 312-34 (1987).

Ogbu, John U., and Maria Eugenia Matute-Bianchi. "Understanding Sociocultural Factors in Education: Knowledge, Identity, and Adjustment in Schooling." In *Beyond Language: Social and Cultural Factors in Schooling Language Minority Students*, developed by California State Department of Education, Bilingual Education Office. Sacramento: Evaluation, Dissemination, and Assessment Center, California State University, 1986.

O'Halloran, Cynthia S. "Mexican American Female Students Who Were Successful in High School Science Courses." *Equity and Excellence in Education* 28(2): 57-64 (1995).

Ohio Commission on Hispanic/Latino Affairs. "Annual Report for Fiscal Year 1996, Focus on Education." 30 June 1997.

Olsen, Laurie. *Crossing the Schoolhouse Border: Immigrant Students and the California Public Schools.* San Francisco: Rosenberg Foundation, 1988.

———. *Made in America: Immigrant Students in Our Public Schools.* New York: New Press, 1997.

Olsen, Laurie, and Carol Dowell. *Bridges: Promising Programs for the Education of Immigrant Children.* Los Angeles: California Tomorrow, 1989. ERIC Document Reproduction Service No. ED 314 544.

Orfield, Gary, Susan E. Eaton, and the Harvard Project on School Desegregation. *Dismantling Desegregation: The Quiet Reversal of* Brown v. Board of Education. New York: New Press, 1996.

Ortiz, Flora Ida. *Mexican American Women: Schooling, Work and Family.* ERIC Digest. Charleston, WV: ERIC Clearinghouse on Rural Education and Small Schools, 1995. ERIC Document Reproduction Service No. ED 388 490.

Pan, Barbara Alexander, Catherine Snow, and M. Rowe. "Patterns of Verbal and Nonverbal Communication Between Mothers and Their 14-Month-Old-Children. Paper presented at the Fourth National Head Start Research Conference, Washington, DC, 9-12 July 1998.

Panasonic Foundation, and American Association of School Administrators. "Getting Closer to the Public." *Strategies For School System Leaders on District-Level Change* 5(1) (1998). http://www.aasa.org/pubs/strategies/jan98.htm (16 June 1999).

Passel, Jeffrey S. "Undocumented Immigrants: How Many?" In *Proceedings of the Social Statistics Section of the American Statistical Association.* Washington, DC: American Statistical Association, 1985.

———. "Undocumented Immigration." *Annals, American Academy for Political and Social Sciences* 487(1986): 181-200.

Peisner-Feinberg, E., R. Clifford, N. Yazejian, M. C. Howes, and S. L. Kagan. "The Longitudinal Effects of Child Care Quality: Implications for Kindergarten Success." Paper presented at the American Educational Research Association Annual Meeting, San Diego, April 1998.

Philips, Susan U. *The Invisible Culture: Communication in Classroom and Community on the Warm Springs Indian Reservation.* New York: Longman, 1983.

Phinney, Jean S., and M. J. Rotheram, eds. *Children's Ethnic Socialization: Pluralism and Development.* Newbury Park, CA: Sage, 1987.

Pogrow, Stanley. "What Is an Exemplary Program, and Why Should Anyone Care? A Reaction to Slavin and Klein." *Educational Researcher* 27(7): 22-28 (1998).

Porter, Rosalie Pedalino. *Forked Tongue: The Politics of Bilingual Education.* New York: BasicBooks, 1990.

Portes, Alejandro, ed. *The New Second Generation.* New York: Russell Sage Foundation, 1996.

Portes, Alejandro, and Lingxin Hao. "*E Pluribus Unum:* Bilingualism and Loss of Language in the Second Generation." *Sociology of Education* 71(October): 269-94 (1998).

Portes, Alejandro, and Dag MacLeod. "Educational Progress of Children of Immigrants: The Roles of Class, Ethnicity, and School Context." *Sociology of Education* 69(4): 255-75 (1996).

Portes, Alejandro, and Rubén G. Rumbaut. *Immigrant America: A Portrait.* Berkeley: University of California Press, 1990.

Portes, Alejandro, and Richard Schauffler. "Language and the Second Generation: Bilingualism Yesterday and Today." In *The New Second Generation,* edited by Alejandro Portes. New York: Russell Sage Foundation, 1996.

Portes, Alejandro, and Min Zhou. "The New Second Generation: Segmented Assimilation and Its Variants." *Annals of the American Academy of Political and Social Sciences* 530(1993): 74-96.

President's Advisory Commission on Educational Excellence for Hispanic Americans. *Our Nation on the Fault Line: Hispanic American Education.* Washington, DC: White House Initiative on Educational Excellence for Hispanic Americans, 1996. ERIC Document Reproduction Service No. ED 408 382.

Reimers, David M. *Still the Golden Door: The Third World Comes to America.* New York: Columbia University Press, 1985.

Reyes, Olga, Karen Gillock, and Kimberly Kabus. "A Longitudinal Study of School Adjustment in Urban, Minority Adolescents: Effects of a High School Transition Program." *American Journal of Community Psychology* 22(3): 341-69 (1994).

Reynolds, Arthur J. "Comparing Measures of Parental Involvement and Their Effects on Academic Achievement." *Early Childhood Research Quarterly* 7(1992): 441-62.

Riba, M. L., and Maxine Baca Zinn. "Childbearing among Youths Studied." *NEXO: Newsletter of the Julian Samora Research Institute* 6(3): 10 (1998).

Rips, Geoff. "Alliances in Public Schools." *Texas Observer,* 11 October 1996, 13-14.

Rist, Ray C. "Student Social Class and Teacher Expectations: The Self-Fulfilling Prophecy in Ghetto Education." In *Exploring Themes of Social Justice in Education: Readings in Social Foundations*, edited by Joan H. Strouse. Upper Saddle River, NJ: Merrill, 1997.

Roberts, Laura R., Pamela A. Sarigiani, Anne C. Petersen, and J. L. Newman. "Gender Differences in the Relationship between Achievement and Self-Image during Early Adolescence." *Journal of Early Adolescence* 10(2): 159-75 (1990).

Romo, Harriett D. "The Mexican Origin Population's Differing Perceptions of Their Children's Schooling." In *The Mexican American Experience: An Interdisciplinary Anthology*, edited by Adolfo O. de la Garza, Frank D. Bean, C. Bonjean, Ricardo Romo, and R. Alvarez. Austin: University of Texas Press, 1985.

———. "Multicultural Climate and Adolescent Achievement: An Ecological Perspective." Paper presented at the 103rd annual convention of the American Psychological Association, New York, August 1995.

———. "Workforce Instructional Network (WIN) Head Start Family Service Center Initiative, San Marcos, Texas: Final Program Report and Evaluation." 1996.

Romo, Harriett D., M. T. de la Piedra, N. Lopez, J. Phillips, and A. Wortham. "Fathers and Families: Working-Class Mexican-Origin Fathers' Parenting Strategies." Poster session presented at Head Start's Fourth National Research Conference. Washington, DC, July 1998.

Romo, Harriett D., A. M. Ellis, and M. L. Bell. "Parent Involvement in Bexar County Alternatives Program." Report to the Mexican American Unity Council, San Antonio, 1996.

Romo, Harriett D., and Toni Falbo. *Latino High School Graduation: Defying the Odds*. Austin: University of Texas Press, 1996.

Rosenbaum, James E., Shazia Rafiullah Miller, and Melinda Scott Krei. "Gatekeeping in an Era of More Open Gates: High School Counselors' Views of Their Influence on Students' College Plans." *American Journal of Education* 104(4): 257-78 (1996).

Rothenberg, B. Annye. *Understanding and Working with Parents and Children from Rural Mexico: What Professionals Need to Know about Child-Rearing Practices, the School Experience, and Health Care Concerns.* Menlo Park, CA: The CHC Center for Child and Family Development Press at the Children's Health Council, 1995.

Rumbaut, Rubén G. "Immigrants Continue to Shape America." *NEXO: Newsletter of the Julian Samora Research Institute* 6(3): 1 (1998).

———. "Ties That Bind: Immigration and Immigrant Families in the United States." In *Immigration and the Family: Research and Policy on U.S. Immigrants*, edited by Alan Booth, Ann C. Crouter, and Nancy Landale. Mahwah, NJ: Lawrence Erlbaum, 1997.

Sadker, Myra, and David Sadker. *Failing at Fairness: How America's Schools Cheat Girls.* New York: Macmillan, 1994. ERIC Document Reproduction Service No. ED 386 268.

Salerno, Anne. *Migrant Students Who Leave School Early: Strategies for Retrieval.* ERIC Digest. Charleston, WV: ERIC Clearinghouse on Rural Education and Small Schools, 1991. ERIC Document Reproduction Service No. ED 335 179.

Sanders, W. L., and J. C. Rivers. "Cumulative and Residual Effects of Teachers on Future Student Academic Achievement." University of Tennessee Value-Added Research and Assessment Center, 1996.

San Miguel, Guadalupe, Jr. *"Let all of them take heed": Mexican Americans and the Campaign for Educational Equality in Texas, 1910-1981.* Austin: University of Texas Press, 1987. ERIC Document Reproduction Service No. ED 390 629.

Savin-Williams, Ritchard Charles, and T. J. Berndt. "Friendship and Peer Relations." In *At the Threshold: The Developing Adolescent,* edited by S. Shirley Feldman and Glen R. Elliott. Cambridge: Harvard University Press, 1990.

Schieffelin, Bambi B., and Elinor Ochs. *Language Socialization across Cultures.* New York: Cambridge University Press, 1986.

Schofield, Janet Ward. "Improving Intergroup Relations among Students." In *Handbook of Research in Multicultural Education,* edited by James A. Banks and Cherry A. McGee Banks. New York: Macmillan, 1995.

Schorr, Lisbeth B. *Within Our Reach: Breaking the Cycle of Disadvantage.* New York: Anchor Press/Doubleday, 1988.

Scott, K. P., and Candace Garrott Schau. "Sex Equity and Sex Bias in Instructional Materials." In *Handbook for Achieving Sex Equity Through Education,* edited by Susan S. Klein. Baltimore: Johns Hopkins University Press, 1985.

Scribner, Alicia Parades. "Advocating for Hispanic High School Students: Research-Based Educational Practices." Special issue. *High School Journal* 78(4): 206-14 (1995).

Sherzer, Joel. "A Discourse-Centered Approach to Language and Culture." *American Anthropologist* 89(1987): 295-309.

Slavin, Robert. "Cooperative Learning and Intergroup Relations." In *Handbook of Research on Multicultural Education,* edited by James A. Banks and Cherry A. McGee Banks. New York: Macmillan, 1995.

Slavin, Robert E., and Olatokundo S. Fashola. *Show Me the Evidence! Proven and Promising Programs for America's Schools.* Thousand Oaks, CA: Corwin Press, 1998.

Slavin, Robert E., and Nancy A. Madden. "Success for All/Éxito para Todos: Effects on the Reading Achievement of Students Acquiring English." Report no. 19. Baltimore: Johns Hopkins University; Howard University, Center for Research on the Education of Students Placed at Risk, 1998.

Slavin, Robert, and R. Yampolsky. "Success for All: A Summary of the Research." Paper presented at the annual meeting of the American Educational Research Association, San Francisco, April 1992.

Smith, J. R., Jeanne Brooks-Gunn, and Pamela Kato Klebanov. "Consequences of Living in Poverty for Young Children's Cognitive and Verbal Ability and Early School Achievement." In *Consequences of Growing Up Poor,* edited by Greg J. Duncan and Jeanne Brooks-Gunn. New York: Russell Sage Foundation, 1997.

Smith, Sheila, and Irving E. Sigel, eds. "Two Generation Programs for Families in Poverty: A New Intervention Strategy." In *Advances in Applied Developmental Psychology,* vol. 9. Norwood, NJ: Ablex, 1995.

Snow, Catherine E. "The Development of Definitional Skill." *Journal of Child Language* 17(3): 697-710 (1990).

Solis, J. "The Status of Latino Children and Youth." In *Understanding Latino Families: Scholarship, Policy and Practice,* edited by Ruth E. Zambrana. Thousand Oaks, CA: Sage Publications, 1995.

Sosa, Alicia, and Y. Garcia. "MIJA: Aiming for Higher Ground." *IDRA Newsletter* 19(8): 7-12 (1992).

Spindler, George D. *Education and Culture: Anthropological Approaches.* New York: Holt, Rinehart and Winston, 1963.

Steinberg, Laurence. "Autonomy, Conflict, and Harmony in the Family Relationship." In *At the Threshold: The Developing Adolescent,* edited by Shirley Feldman and Glen R. Elliott. Cambridge: Harvard University Press, 1990.

Steinberg, Laurence D., B. Bradford Brown, and Sanford M. Dornbusch. *Beyond the Classroom: Why School Reform Has Failed and What Parents Need to Do.* New York: Simon and Schuster, 1996.

Steinberg, Stephen. *The Ethnic Myth.* New York: Atheneum, 1989.

Stephan, Walter G. "Intergroup Relations." In *Handbook of Social Psychology,* 3d ed., edited by Gardner Lindzey and Elliot Aronson. New York: Random House, 1985.

Stevens, Edward, Jr., and George H. Wood. *Justice, Ideology, and Education: An Introduction to the Social Foundations of Education.* 2d ed. New York: McGraw-Hill, 1992.

Stevenson, David, and David Baker. "The Family-School Relation and the Child's School Performance." *Child Development* 58(1987): 1348-57.

Suárez-Orozco, Carola E., and Marcelo M. Suárez-Orozco. *Transformations: Immigration, Family Life, and Achievement Motivation among Latino Adolescents.* Stanford, CA: Stanford University Press, 1995.

Suárez-Orozco, Marcelo M. "Immigration and Education: Issues and Research." Speech presented at The Spencer Foundation Conference on Immigration and Education, Los Angeles, 8 October 1997.

Suárez-Orozco, Marcelo M., and Carola E. Suárez-Orozco. "The Cultural Patterning of Achievement Motivation: A Comparison of Mexican, Mexican Immigrant, Mexican American, and Non-Latino White American Students." In *California's Immigrant Children: Theory, Research, and Implications for Educational Policy,* edited by Rubén G. Rumbaut and Wayne A. Cornelius. San Diego: University of California, Center for U.S.-Mexican Studies, 1995.

Tatum, Beverly Daniel. *Why Are All the Black Kids Sitting Together in the*

Cafeteria? And Other Conversations about Race. New York: BasicBooks, 1997.

Taylor, Angela R., and Sandra Machida. "The Contribution of Parent and Peer Support to Head Start Children's Early School Adjustment." *Early Childhood Research Quarterly* 9(3/4): 387-405 (1994).

Teachman, Jay D., K. M. Paasch, R. D. Day, and K. P. Carver. "Poverty During Adolescence and Subsequent Educational Attainment." In *Consequences of Growing Up Poor,* edited by Greg J. Duncan and Jeanne Brooks-Gunn. New York: Russell Sage Foundation, 1997.

Terry, D. "Bilingual Education Facing Toughest Test." *New York Times*, 10 March 1998, A1.

Texas Civil Rights Project. "Peer Sexual Harassment: A Texas-Size Problem." Austin, TX, 1997.

———. "Sexual Harassment in Schools: What Students Suffer and What Schools Should Do." Austin, TX, 1998.

Texas Migrant Interstate Program. *Migrant Interstate Coordination Report.* Pharr, TX: Pharr-San Juan-Alamo ISD, 1998.

Thomas, Wayne P., and Virginia Collier. *School Effectiveness for Language Minority Students.* Washington, DC: National Clearinghouse for Bilingual Education, 1996.

Tinajero, Josefina Villamil, M. L. Gonzales, and F. Dick. *Raising Career Aspirations of Hispanic Girls: Fastback 320.* Bloomington, IN: Phi Delta Kappa Educational Foundation, 1991.

Trueba, Henry T. "Culture and Language: The Ethnographic Approach to the Study of Learning Environments." In *Language and Culture in Learning,* edited by Barbara J. Merino, Henry T. Trueba, and Fabián A. Samaniego. Washington, DC: Falmer, 1993.

UNESCO. *Meeting of Specialists on the Socio-Cultural and Linguistic Integration of the Children of Migrant and Former Migrant Workers.* Yugoslavia: UNESCO, 1989.

———. *The Socio-Educational Situation of the Children of Migrants.* Paris: UNESCO, 1989.

———. *The Use of Vernacular Languages in Education.* Paris: UNESCO, 1953.

University of Texas at Austin. *The University of Texas at Austin Migrant Student Program Receiving School Guide.* Austin: University of Texas, Migrant Student Program, 1992. ERIC Document Reproduction Service No. ED 352 234.

———. *The Use of Public Services by Undocumented Aliens in Texas: A Study of State Costs and Revenues.* Policy Research Project Report, no. 60. Austin: Lyndon B. Johnson School of Public Affairs, 1984.

University of Texas Migrant Student Program. http://www.utexas.edu/dce/eimc/il/migrant/ (16 June 1999).

U.S. Bureau of the Census. *March 1997 Current Population Survey.* Washington, DC, 1996. http://www.census.gov/population/www/socdemo/hispanic.html (16 June 1999).

———. *March 1998 Current Population Survey, Hispanic Data.* Washington, DC, 1998.

———. *Who's Minding the Kids? Current Population Reports, Series P-70, No. 30.* Washington, DC: U.S. Government Printing Office, 1992.

U.S. Department of Education. *The Condition of Education.* Washington, DC: National Center for Education Statistics, 1996.

———. *Descriptive Study of Services to Limited English Proficient Students.* Provided for the 1993 reauthorization of the federal elementary and secondary education programs. Washington, DC: Office of the Under Secretary, 1993.

———. *The Educational Progress of Hispanic Students: Findings from the Condition of Education.* Washington, DC: National Center for Education Statistics, 1995.

———. *Improving Opportunities: Strategies from the Secretary of Education for Hispanic and Limited English Proficient Students.* Washington, DC: Office of Bilingual Education and Minority Languages Affairs, 1998.

———. See also Horn, Laura J.; Kaufman, Phillip; and McMillen, Marilyn M.

U.S. Department of Health and Human Services. *Creating A 21st Century Head Start Quality and Expansion.* December 1993.

———. National Center for Health Statistics. *1995 Birth Statistics Released,* 23 March 1998.

U.S. Department of Health, Education, and Welfare. Memorandum. J. Stanley Pottinger to School Districts with more than five percent national origin-minority group children. "Identification of Discrimination and Denial of Services on the Basis of National Origin," 25 May 1970.

———. Office for Civil Rights. *Task Force Findings Specifying Remedies Available for Eliminating Past Educational Practices Ruled Unlawful under* Lau v. Nichols. Washington, DC: Office of the Secretary, 1975.

U.S. General Accounting Office. See U.S. Senate Committee on Labor and Human Resources.

U.S. Immigration and Naturalization Service. "Implementation of the *Immigration Reform and Control Act* (IRCA): Final Rules." *Federal Register* 52(84) (1 May 1987).

U.S. Senate Committee on Labor and Human Resources. *Early Childhood Programs: Many Poor Children and Strained Resources Challenge Head Start.* Briefing Report by the General Accounting Office to the Chairman, Subcommittee on Children, Family, Drugs and Alcoholism. GAO/HEHS-94-169BR, May 1994.

———. *Infants and Toddlers: Dramatic Increases in Numbers Living in Poverty.* Report by the General Accounting Office to the Chairman, Subcommittee on Children, Family, Drugs and Alcoholism. GAO/HEHS-94-74, April 1994.

U.S. Senate Committee on Labor and Human Resources, and U.S. House Committee on Education and the Workforce. *Head Start: Research Insufficient to Assess Program Impact.* Testimony by the General Accounting

Office before the Senate Subcommittee on Children and Families and the House Subcommittee on Early Childhood, Youth and Families. GAO/T-HEHS-98-126, 1998.

Valdés, Guadalupe. *Con Respeto: Bridging the Distances between Culturally Diverse Families and Schools: An Ethnographic Portrait.* New York: Teachers College Press, 1996.

——. "Dual-Language Immersion Programs: A Cautionary Note Concerning the Education of Language-Minority Students." *Harvard Educational Review* 67(3): 391-429 (1997).

——. "The World Outside and Inside Schools: Language and Immigrant Children." *Educational Researcher* 27(6): 4-18 (1998).

Valdez, R. B., J. DaVanzo, Georges Vernez, and M. Wade. *Immigration: Getting the Facts.* Issue Paper No. 1. Los Angeles: RAND, 1993.

Valencia, Richard R., ed. *The Evolution of Deficit Thinking: Educational Thought and Practice.* London: Falmer, 1997.

Valencia, Richard R., and S. Aburto. "The Uses and Abuses of Educational Testing: Chicanos as a Case in Point." In *Chicano School Failure and Success: Research and Policy Agendas for the 1990s,* edited by Richard R. Valencia. London: Falmer, 1991.

Valenzuela, Arturo. "Liberal Gender Role Attitudes and Academic Achievement among Mexican-Origin Adolescents in Two Houston Inner-City Catholic Schools." *Hispanic Journal of Behavioral Sciences* 15(3): 310-23 (1993).

Valenzuela, Arturo, and Sanford M. Dornbusch. "Familism and Assimilation among Mexican-Origin and Anglo High School Adolescents." In *Chicanas and Chicanos in Contemporary Society,* edited by Roberto M. De Anda. Boston: Allyn & Bacon, 1996.

——. "Familism and Social Capital in the Academic Achievement of Mexican Origin and Anglo Adolescents." *Social Science Quarterly* 75(1): 18-36 (1994).

Vega, William A. "The Study of Latino Families: A Point of Departure." In *Understanding Latino Families,* edited by Ruth E. Zambrana. Thousand Oaks, CA: Sage, 1995.

Ventura, Stephanie J., J. A. Martin, T. J. Matthews, and S. C. Clarke. *Advance Report of Final Natality Statistics, 1994.* Monthly vital statistics report, vol. 44, no. 11. supp. Hyattsville, MD: National Center for Health Statistics, 1996.

Vernez, Georges. *Mexican Labor in California's Economy: From Rapid Growth to Likely Stability.* Palo Alto, CA: Stanford University Press, 1993.

——. *Undocumented Immigration: An Irritant or Significant Problem in U.S.-Mexico Relations?* Labor and Population Program, Reprint Series 94-18. Los Angeles: RAND, 1994.

Vernez, Georges, and Allan Abrahamse. *How Immigrants Fare in U.S. Education.* Santa Monica, CA: RAND, 1996.

Vigil, James Diego. *Barrio Gangs: Street Life and Identity in Southern California.* Austin: University of Texas Press, 1988.

Wagner, Jon. "Power and Learning in a Multi-Ethnic High School: Dilemmas of Policy and Practice." In *Ethnic Identity and Power: Cultural Contexts of Political Action in School and Society,* edited by Yali Zou and Enrique T. Trueba. New York: State University of New York Press, 1998.

Wang, Margaret C., Geneva D. Haertel, and Herbert J. Walberg. "Fostering Educational Resilience in Inner-City Schools." In *Children and Youth: Interdisciplinary Perspectives,* edited by Herbert J. Walberg, Olga Reyes, and Roger P. Weissberg. Thousand Oaks, CA: Sage, 1997.

Wells, Amy Stuart. *Hispanic Education in America: Separate and Unequal.* ERIC Digest. Washington, DC: ERIC Clearinghouse on Assessment and Evaluation, 1989. ERIC Document Reproduction Service No. ED 316 616.

"Why Hispanic Women Succeed in Higher Ed." *Hispanic Outlook in Higher Education* 8(11): 12 (1998). First published in *Women in Higher Education* 7(February) (1998).

Williams, Norma. *The Mexican American Family: Tradition and Change.* Dix Hills, NY: General Hall, 1990.

Wilson, William Julius. *The Declining Significance of Race: Blacks and Changing American Institutions.* Chicago: University of Chicago Press, 1980.

———. *The Truly Disadvantaged: The Inner City, the Underclass, and Public Policy.* Chicago: University of Chicago Press, 1987.

———. *When Work Disappears: The World of the New Urban Poor.* New York: Knopf, 1996.

Yáñz-Pérez, A. "IDRA's MIJA Program Expands." *IDRA Newsletter* 23(3): 1, 14 (1996).

Zavella, Patricia. "Reflections on Diversity among Chicanas." In *Challenging Fronteras: Structuring Latina and Latino Lives in the U.S.,* edited by Mary Romero, Pierrette Hondagneu-Sotelo, and Vilma Ortiz. New York: Routledge, 1997.

Zeichner, Kenneth M. *Educating Teachers for Cultural Diversity: NCRTL Special Report.* East Lansing: Michigan State University, National Center for Research on Teacher Learning, 1993.

Zhou, Min. "Growing Up American: The Challenge Confronting Immigrant Children and Children of Immigrants." *Annual Review of Sociology* 23(1997): 61-95.

Zigler, Edward, and Susan Muenchow. *Head Start: The Inside Story of America's Most Successful Educational Experiment.* New York: BasicBooks, 1992.

Index

acculturation, 30, 64, 196n.41
achievement, 8-9, 29-31, 65-66, 85-88, 117, 157-59, 161-62
Achievement for Hispanics through Academic Success (ALAS), 128-31, 179
ACT, 73
Alliance Schools, 133-38
Alvarez, Jeremias, 73-74
American Association of Community Colleges, 179
American Association of University Women Educational Foundation, 189
Annenberg Institute for School Reform, 179-80
ASPIRA Association, 180
AVANCE, 38-41, 180, 193n.24
AVID Center (Advancement Via Individual Determination), 16, 180

bilingual education, 46-48, 50-51, 52-54, 151, 194n.6
birthrates, 4, 77, 165-66, 192n.8

CAMP, 73-74, 182, 187-88, 197n.56
career academies, 70
Center for Law and Education, 181
Chicano/Latino Policy Project, 181
child rearing, 31-34
classroom materials. *See* instructional materials
classroom organization, 26-28
College Assistance Migrant Program. *See* CAMP
college enrollment, 12-15, 13 fig.2, 114
community support, 121-22, 124
Consistency Management and Cooperative Discipline, 181-82
counselors, 66-67, 82
cultural differences
  in child rearing, 31-34
  children's awareness of, 25-26
  recognizing, 34-37
culture
  acculturation, 30, 64, 196n.41

and achievement, 29-31
and classroom organization, 26-28
group and individual, 23-25
home, 64-65
subgroups, 4-7

dropping out, 9-10, 10 table 1, 16, 29-30, 49, 70-71, 79-80, 113

early childhood education, 151-57
Early Head Start, 35-37, 99, 126, 155, 156
EPISO, 136-37
ESL, 49-50, 143, 162-63
ethnic relations, 163-70
Even Start, 126

familism, 76
family, 76-78
family cultures, 59-60, 61-62
family histories, 127-28
family-school programs. *See* parent-school programs
fathers, 35-37, 198n.29
friends. *See* peers
Funds of Knowledge, 41-43, 182

gangs, 88-90
  characteristics of, 88
  female, 88
GED, 10-11, 73, 100, 126, 127
gender
  and achievement, 85-88
  boys, 83-84
  classroom biases, 82-85
  gap, 83, 102-04
  machismo, 86
  school completion, 11-12
  sexual harassment, 92-94
  stereotypes, 75-76, 101-04
Gender Gaps: Where Schools Still Fail Our Children, 102-04
government documents, 191n.1

Handbook of Research on Multicultural Education, 190

Head Start, 60, 108, 126, 154-56
*Hernandez v. Houston Indepen-
dent School District*, 202n.10
Hispanic Dropout Project, 115-16,
117-18, 125
Hispanic Mother-Daughter
Program, 182
home culture, 64-65
home language, 53-54, 64, 67-68,
143
home visits, 42, 43, 118, 161

Idaho College Assistance Migrant
Program (CAMP), 182
immigrants, 1-8, 68-69, 141-51,
191n.1
poverty, 7-8, 106-08, 154
undocumented, 5, 143-49,
202n.10
immigration, 5-7, 142-51
Immigration Act of 1965, 150-51
Immigration Reform Act, 149
*Immigration Reform and Control
Act* (IRCA), 148-49, 203n.19
Industrial Areas Foundation (IAF),
133-39, 176, 188
Institute for Educational Leadership, 183
instructional materials, 82-83
Intercultural Development Research Association (IDRA), 94-
96, 131, 183
intergroup relations. *See* ethnic
relations
International High School, 69

Kyle Family Learning and Career
Center (KFLCC), 126-27, 183

language
assessment, 65-66
differences, 3-4
home, 53-54, 64, 67-68, 143
maintaining Spanish, 52-57
Lau v. Nichols, 142-43, 144
leadership, 66-67, 162-63
limited English proficiency (LEP),
3-4, 19, 67, 143, 151
literacy, 57-63

machismo, 86
Mayan parents, 33
Mexican American Legal Defense
and Educational Fund
(MALDEF), 147, 183-84
Migrant Student Program, 71-73,
197n.55
migrant students, 70-74
MIJA, 94-97
Mobilization for Equity, 131-33, 184
mother-daughter programs, 100-01,
182
mothers, 31-33, 39, 77-78, 100-01
Move It Math, 17, 18
Multicultural Review, 184

National Association for Bilingual
Education, 184
National Center for Education
Statistics, 190
National Clearinghouse for Bilin-
gual Education, 190
National Council of La Raza, 184-85
National Education Longitudinal
Survey (NELS), 30
National Institute for Literacy, 185
National Origins Act, 150
National Research Council, 190
National Task Force on Minority
High Achievement, 185
naturalization, 149-50
Newcomer Program, 185
newcomers' programs, 51-52

origins of Hispanic youth, 8 fig.1
outreach, 67-68

parent involvement in schools, 108-
39, 161
during adolescence, 112-13
barriers to participation, 111-12
knowledge of system, 113-15
monitoring school work, 115-17
philosophies that affect, 109-11
parent-school programs, 34-43,
124-39
ALAS, 128-31, 179
AVANCE, 38-41, 180, 193n.24
family histories, 127-28

Funds of Knowledge, 41,43, 182
Kyle Family Learning and Career Center (KFLCC), 126-27, 183
Mobilization for Equity, 31-33, 184
See also school programs
peers, 85-88, 90-92
PEP programs, 97-100
Plyler v. Doe, 146, 147, 202n.11, 203n.16
poverty, 7-8, 47, 106-08, 154
pregnancy. *See* teen pregnancy
Project GRAD, 16-18, 185-86
Proposition 187, 147, 149, 178, 203nn.14,16
Proposition 227, 46-47, 52, 178, 194n.3

SAT, 12, 73
school attitudes, 117-21, 122-23
school completion, 8 fig.1, 9-12. *See also* dropping out
school enrollment, 2-3
school leadership, 66-67, 162-63
school programs, 16-18, 34-35, 48-52, 64-70, 161-63, 172-76
ALAS, 128-31, 179
AVID, 16, 180
bilingual, 50-51
characteristics of successful, 48-52, 64-70
ESL classes, 49-50
MIJA, 94-97
Move It Math, 17, 18
PEP, 97-100
Project GRAD, 16-18, 185-86
sheltered language content, 50
Success for All, 17, 18, 62-63, 162-63, 186
See also parent-school programs
school success. *See* achievement
school-to-college programs, 69-70
school-to-work programs, 69-70
segregation, 165-70
sexual harassment, 92-94
Sheltered English Approach, 186
sheltered language content programs, 50
SHIPS (Stop Harassment in Public Schools project), 92

Silva v. Levi, 146, 202n.9
stereotypes, 24-25, 75-76, 101-04
success. *See* achievement
Success for All, 17, 18, 62-63, 162-63, 186

TAAS, 97, 135, 138
teachers, 41-43, 61, 66-67, 157-63, 176-78
effective, 159-63
shortage of, 19
training, 157-59
Teaching Tolerance, 186-87
teasing, 33-34, 90
teen pregnancy, 78-81, 97-100
tests and testing, 65-66, 106, 161-62
ACT, 73
GED, 10-11, 73, 100, 126, 127
SAT, 12, 73
TAAS, 97, 135, 138
Texas Adult Literacy Clearinghouse, 187
Texas Civil Rights Project, 92-93, 187
Texas College Assistance Migrant Program (CAMP), 187-88
Texas Education Code 21.031, 144-46, 202nn.9,10
Texas Industrial Areas Foundation (IAF), 133-39, 176, 188
tracking, 15-16, 69, 76, 82, 168-69

undocumented immigrants, 5, 143-49, 202n.10
University of California Linguistic Minority Research Institute, 188
Unz, Ron K., 47
Upward Bound, 69, 188-89
U.S. Department of Education, 189

White House Initiative on Educational Excellence for Hispanic Americans, 189

Ysleta Elementary School, 135-37

Zavala Elementary School, 137-38